It's another great book from CGP...

GCSE Biology is all about **understanding how science works**.
And not only that — understanding it well enough to be able to **question** what you hear on TV and read in the papers.

But don't panic. This book includes all the **science facts** you need to learn, and shows you how they work in the real world. It even includes a **free** Online Edition you can read on your computer or tablet.

How to get your free Online Edition

Just go to **cgpbooks.co.uk/extras** and enter this code...

1376 7015 8855 2813

By the way, this code only works for one person. If somebody else has used this book before you, they might have already claimed the Online Edition.

CGP — still the best! ☺

Our sole aim here at CGP is to produce the highest quality books — carefully written, immaculately presented and dangerously close to being funny.

Then we work our socks off to get them out to you — at the cheapest possible prices.

Contents

Module B4 — It's a Green World

Module B5 — The Living Body

Module B6 — Beyond the Microscope

Published by CGP

From original material by Richard Parsons.

Editors:
Luke Antieul, Joe Brazier, Emma Elder, Edmund Robinson, Hayley Thompson, Karen Wells.

Contributors:
Adrian Schmit, Sophie Watkins.

ISBN: 978 1 84762 609 7

With thanks to Janet Cruse-Sawyer, Sue Hocking and Ann Shires for the proofreading.
With thanks to Laura Jakubowski for the copyright research.

With thanks to Tom D. Thacher, M.D., for permission to reproduce the photograph on page 11.

Data used to draw graph on page 54 developed by the National Center for Health Statistics in collaboration with the National Center for Chronic Disease Prevention and Health Promotion (2000). http://www.cdc.gov/growthcharts

www.cgpbooks.co.uk

Printed by Elanders Ltd, Newcastle upon Tyne.
Clipart from Corel®

The Scientific Process

You need to know a few things about how the world of science works — both for your exams and your controlled assessment. Investigate these next few pages and you'll be laughing all day long on results day.

Scientists Come Up with Hypotheses — Then Test Them

Hundreds of years ago, we thought demons caused illness.

1) Scientists try to explain things. Everything.
2) They start by observing or thinking about something they don't understand — it could be anything, e.g. planets in the sky, a person suffering from an illness, what matter is made of... anything.
3) Then, using what they already know (plus a bit of insight), they come up with a hypothesis — a possible explanation for what they've observed.
4) The next step is to test whether the hypothesis might be right or not — this involves gathering evidence (i.e. data from investigations).
5) To gather evidence the scientist uses the hypothesis to make a prediction — a statement based on the hypothesis that can be tested by carrying out experiments.
6) If the results from the experiments match the prediction, then the scientist can be more confident that the hypothesis is correct. This doesn't mean the hypothesis is true though — other predictions based on the hypothesis might turn out to be wrong.

Scientists Work Together to Test Hypotheses

Then we thought it was caused by 'bad blood' (and treated it with leeches).

1) Different scientists can look at the same evidence and interpret it in different ways. That's why scientists usually work in teams — they can share their different ideas on how to interpret the data they find.
2) Once a team has come up with (and tested) a hypothesis they all agree with, they'll present their work to the scientific community through journals and scientific conferences so it can be judged — this is called the peer review process.
3) Other scientists then check the team's results (by trying to replicate them) and carry out their own experiments to collect more evidence.
4) If all the experiments in the world back up the hypothesis, scientists start to have a lot of confidence in it.
5) However, if another scientist does an experiment and the results don't fit with the hypothesis (and other scientists can replicate these results), then the hypothesis is in trouble. When this happens, scientists have to come up with a new hypothesis (maybe a modification of the old explanation, or maybe a completely new one).

Scientific Ideas Change as New Evidence is Found

Now we know most illnesses are due to microorganisms.

1) Scientific explanations are provisional because they only explain the evidence that's currently available — new evidence may come up that can't be explained.
2) This means that scientific explanations never become hard and fast, totally indisputable fact. As new evidence is found (or new ways of interpreting existing evidence are found), hypotheses can change or be replaced.
3) Sometimes, an unexpected observation or result will suddenly throw a hypothesis into doubt and further experiments will need to be carried out. This can lead to new developments that increase our understanding of science.

You expect me to believe that — then show me the evidence...

If scientists think something is true, they need to produce evidence to convince others — it's all part of testing a hypothesis. One hypothesis might survive these tests, while others won't — it's how things progress. And along the way some hypotheses will be disproved — i.e. shown not to be true.

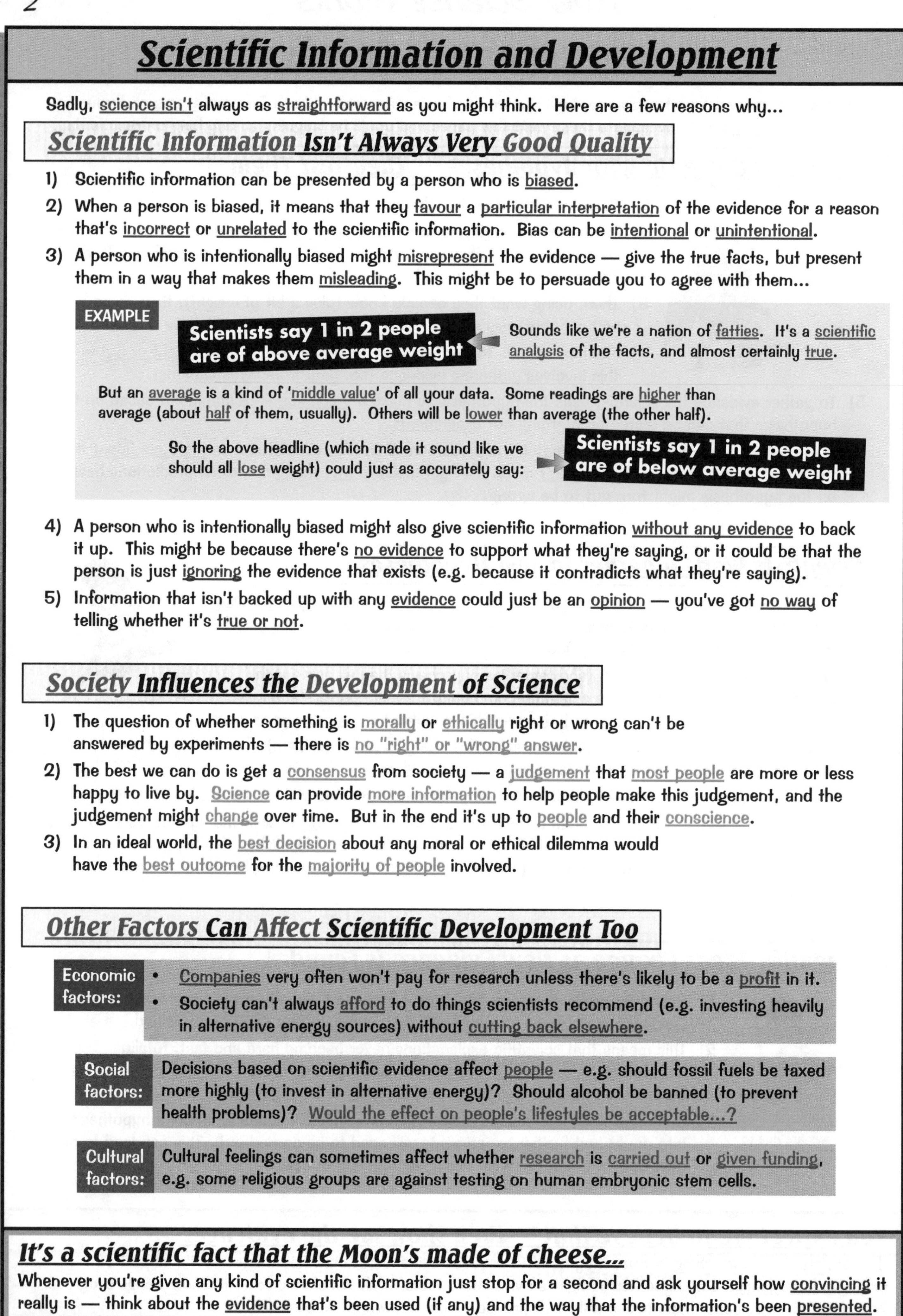

Scientific Information and Development

Sadly, science isn't always as straightforward as you might think. Here are a few reasons why...

Scientific Information Isn't Always Very Good Quality

1) Scientific information can be presented by a person who is biased.
2) When a person is biased, it means that they favour a particular interpretation of the evidence for a reason that's incorrect or unrelated to the scientific information. Bias can be intentional or unintentional.
3) A person who is intentionally biased might misrepresent the evidence — give the true facts, but present them in a way that makes them misleading. This might be to persuade you to agree with them...

EXAMPLE

Scientists say 1 in 2 people are of above average weight

Sounds like we're a nation of fatties. It's a scientific analysis of the facts, and almost certainly true.

But an average is a kind of 'middle value' of all your data. Some readings are higher than average (about half of them, usually). Others will be lower than average (the other half).

So the above headline (which made it sound like we should all lose weight) could just as accurately say:

Scientists say 1 in 2 people are of below average weight

4) A person who is intentionally biased might also give scientific information without any evidence to back it up. This might be because there's no evidence to support what they're saying, or it could be that the person is just ignoring the evidence that exists (e.g. because it contradicts what they're saying).
5) Information that isn't backed up with any evidence could just be an opinion — you've got no way of telling whether it's true or not.

Society Influences the Development of Science

1) The question of whether something is morally or ethically right or wrong can't be answered by experiments — there is no "right" or "wrong" answer.
2) The best we can do is get a consensus from society — a judgement that most people are more or less happy to live by. Science can provide more information to help people make this judgement, and the judgement might change over time. But in the end it's up to people and their conscience.
3) In an ideal world, the best decision about any moral or ethical dilemma would have the best outcome for the majority of people involved.

Other Factors Can Affect Scientific Development Too

Economic factors:

- Companies very often won't pay for research unless there's likely to be a profit in it.
- Society can't always afford to do things scientists recommend (e.g. investing heavily in alternative energy sources) without cutting back elsewhere.

Social factors: Decisions based on scientific evidence affect people — e.g. should fossil fuels be taxed more highly (to invest in alternative energy)? Should alcohol be banned (to prevent health problems)? Would the effect on people's lifestyles be acceptable...?

Cultural factors: Cultural feelings can sometimes affect whether research is carried out or given funding, e.g. some religious groups are against testing on human embryonic stem cells.

It's a scientific fact that the Moon's made of cheese...

Whenever you're given any kind of scientific information just stop for a second and ask yourself how convincing it really is — think about the evidence that's been used (if any) and the way that the information's been presented.

Planning Investigations

That's all the dull stuff about the world of science over — now onto the hands-on part. The next few pages show how practical investigations should be carried out — by both professional scientists and you.

To Make an Investigation a Fair Test You Have to Control the Variables

An important part of planning an investigation is making sure it's a fair test.

1) In a lab experiment you usually change one variable and measure how it affects the other variable.

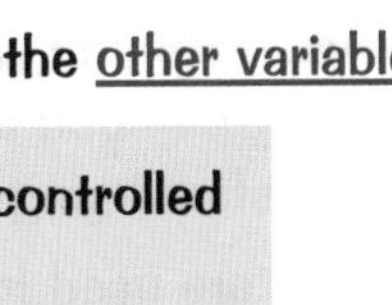

EXAMPLE: you might change only the temperature of an enzyme-controlled reaction and measure how it affects the rate of reaction.

2) To make it a fair test everything else that could affect the results should stay the same (otherwise you can't tell if the thing that's being changed is affecting the results or not — the data won't be reliable).

EXAMPLE continued: you need to keep the pH the same, otherwise you won't know if any change in the rate of reaction is caused by the change in temperature, or the change in pH.

3) The variable that you change is called the independent variable.
4) The variable that's measured is called the dependent variable.
5) The variables that you keep the same are called control variables.
6) Because you can't always control all the variables, you often need to use a control experiment — an experiment that's kept under the same conditions as the rest of the investigation, but doesn't have anything done to it. This is so that you can see what happens when you don't change anything at all.

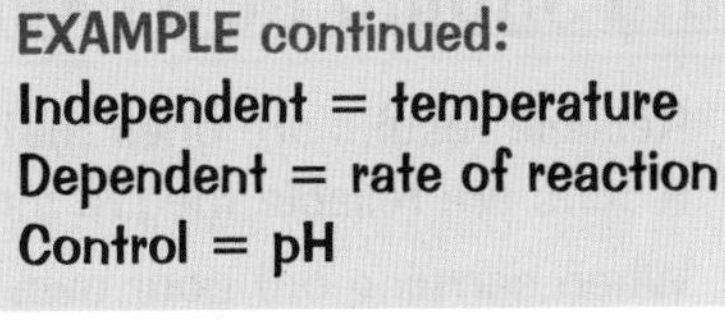

EXAMPLE continued:
Independent = temperature
Dependent = rate of reaction
Control = pH

The Equipment Used has to be Right for the Job

1) The measuring equipment you use has to be sensitive enough to accurately measure the chemicals you're using, e.g. if you need to measure out 11 ml of a liquid, you'll need to use a measuring cylinder that can measure to 1 ml, not 5 or 10 ml.
2) The smallest change a measuring instrument can detect is called its RESOLUTION. E.g. some mass balances have a resolution of 1 g and some have a resolution of 0.1 g.
3) You should also be able to explain why you've chosen each bit of kit.

Experiments Must be Safe

1) Part of planning an investigation is making sure that it's safe.
2) There are lots of hazards you could be faced with during an investigation, e.g. radiation, electricity, gas, chemicals and fire.
3) You should always make sure that you identify all the hazards that you might encounter.
4) You should also come up with ways of reducing the risks from the hazards you've identified.
5) One way of doing this is to carry out a risk assessment:

For an experiment involving a Bunsen burner, the risk assessment might be something like this:

Hazard: Bunsen burner is a fire risk.
Precautions:
- Keep flammable chemicals away from the Bunsen.
- Never leave the Bunsen unattended when lit.
- Always turn on the yellow safety flame when not in use.

Hazard: revision boredom. Precaution: use CGP books

Wow, all this even before you've started the investigation — it really does make them run more smoothly though.

Getting the Data Right

There are a few things that can be done to make sure that you get the best results you possibly can.

Trial Runs Help Figure out the Range and Interval of Variable Values

1) Before you carry out an experiment, it's a good idea to do a trial run first — a quick version of your experiment.
2) Trial runs help you work out whether your plan is right or not — you might decide to make some changes after trying out your method.
3) Trial runs are used to figure out the range of variable values used (the upper and lower limit).
4) And they're used to figure out the interval (gaps) between the values too.

Enzyme-controlled reaction example from previous page continued:

- You might do trial runs at 10, 20, 30, 40 and 50 °C. If there was no reaction at 10 or 50 °C, you might narrow the range to 20-40 °C.
- If using 10 °C intervals gives you a big change in rate of reaction you might decide to use 5 °C intervals, e.g. 20, 25, 30, 35...

Data Should be as Reliable and Accurate as Possible

1) Reliable results are ones that can be consistently reproduced each time you do an experiment. If your results are reliable they're more likely to be true, so you can make valid conclusions from them.
2) When carrying out your own investigation, you can improve the reliability of your results by repeating the readings and calculating the mean (average). You should repeat readings at least twice (so that you have at least three readings to calculate an average result).
3) To make sure your results are reliable you can also take a second set of readings with another instrument, or get a different observer to cross check.
4) Checking your results match with secondary sources, e.g. studies that other people have done, also increases the reliability of your data.
5) You should also always make sure that your results are accurate. Really accurate results are those that are really close to the true answer.
6) You can get accurate results by doing things like making sure the equipment you're using is sensitive enough (see previous page), and by recording your data to a suitable level of accuracy. For example, if you're taking digital readings of something, the results will be more accurate if you include at least a couple of decimal places instead of rounding to whole numbers.

You Can Check For Mistakes Made When Collecting Data

1) When you've collected all the results for an experiment, you should have a look to see if there are any results that don't seem to fit in with the rest.
2) Most results vary a bit, but any that are totally different are called anomalous results.
3) They're caused by human errors, e.g. by a whoopsie when measuring.
4) The only way to stop them happening is by taking all your measurements as carefully as possible.
5) If you ever get any anomalous results, you should investigate them to try to work out what happened. If you can work out what happened (e.g. you measured something wrong) you can ignore them when processing your results.

Reliable data — it won't ever forget your birthday...

All this stuff is really important — without good quality data an investigation will be totally meaningless. So give this page a read through a couple of times and your data will be the envy of the whole scientific community.

Presenting and Interpreting Data

The fun doesn't stop once you've collected your data — it then needs to be presented...

Data Needs to be Organised and Processed

1) Tables are dead useful for organising data.
2) When you draw a table use a ruler and make sure each column has a heading (including the units).
3) Problem is, raw data generally just ain't that useful. You usually have to process it in some way.
4) A couple of the most simple calculations you can perform are the mean (average) and the range (how spread out the data is).

Different Types of Data Should be Presented in Different Ways

1) You'll have to choose the best way to present your data.
2) If the independent variable is categoric (comes in distinct categories, e.g. blood types, metals) you should use a bar chart or a pie chart to display the data.
3) If the independent variable is continuous (numerical data that can have any value within a range, e.g. length, volume, time) you should use a line graph to display the data.

Here are a few useful tips for drawing line graphs:

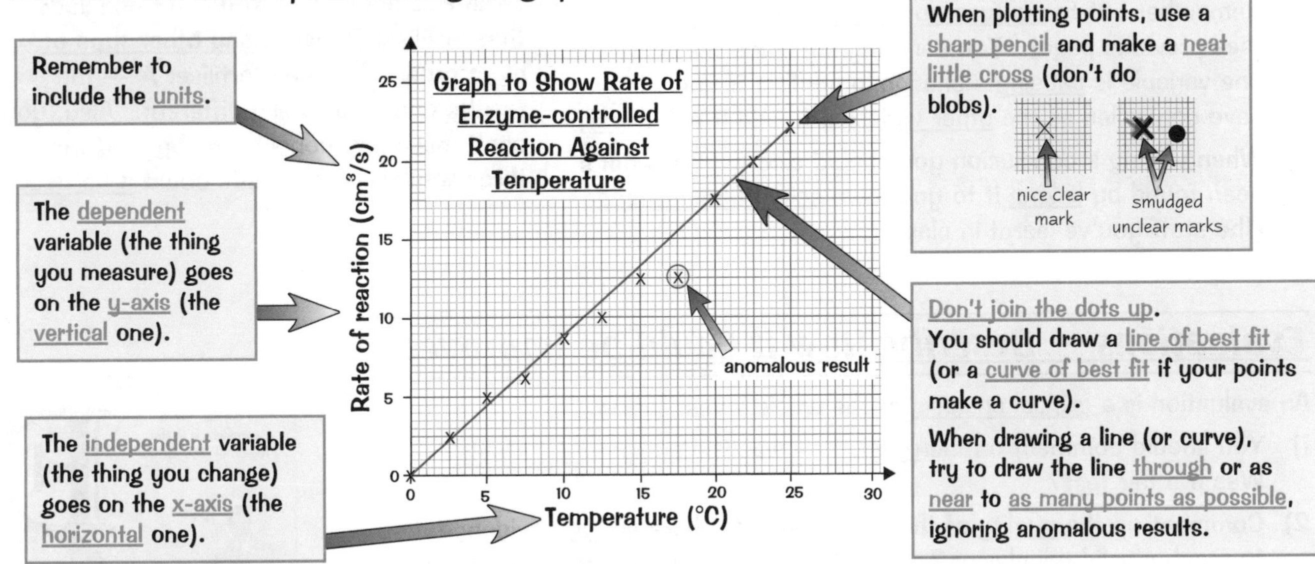

Line Graphs Can Show Relationships in Data

1) Line graphs are great for showing relationships between two variables.
2) Here are the three different types of correlation (relationship) shown on line graphs:

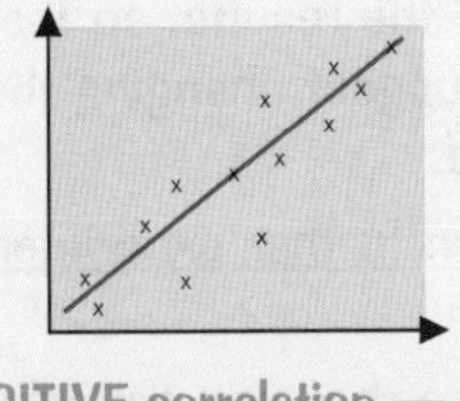

POSITIVE correlation — as one variable increases the other increases.

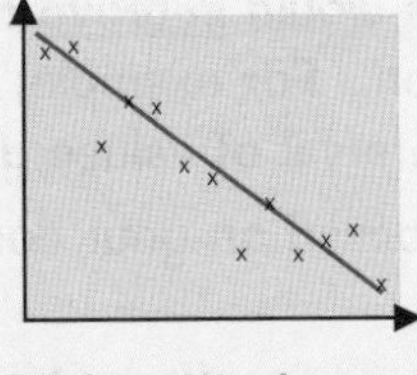

INVERSE (negative) correlation — as one variable increases the other decreases.

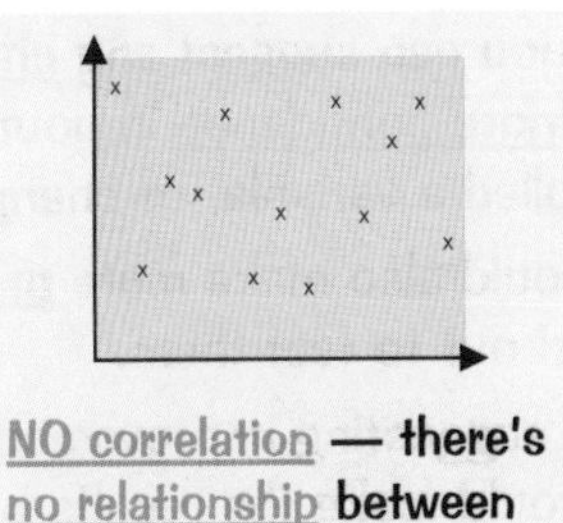

NO correlation — there's no relationship between the two variables.

3) You've got to be careful not to confuse correlation with cause though. A correlation just means that there's a relationship between two variables. It doesn't mean that the change in one variable is causing the change in the other (there might be other factors involved).

Concluding and Evaluating

At the end of an investigation, the conclusion and evaluation are waiting. Don't worry, they won't bite.

A Conclusion is a Summary of What You've Learnt

1) Once all the data's been collected, presented and analysed, an investigation will always involve coming to a conclusion.
2) Drawing a conclusion can be quite straightforward — just look at your data and say what pattern you see.

EXAMPLE: The table on the right shows the heights of pea plant seedlings grown for three weeks with different fertilisers.

Fertiliser	Mean growth (mm)
A	13.5
B	19.5
No fertiliser	5.5

CONCLUSION: Fertiliser B makes pea plant seedlings grow taller over a three week period than fertiliser A.

3) However, you also need to use the data that's been collected to justify the conclusion (back it up).
4) There are some things to watch out for too — it's important that the conclusion matches the data it's based on and doesn't go any further.
5) Remember not to confuse correlation and cause (see previous page). You can only conclude that one variable is causing a change in another if you have controlled all the other variables (made it a fair test).
6) When writing a conclusion you should also explain what's been found by linking it to your own scientific knowledge (the stuff you've learnt in class).

EXAMPLE continued: Fertiliser B made the pea plants grow 6 mm more on average than fertiliser A.

EXAMPLE continued: You can't conclude that fertiliser B makes any other type of plant grow taller than fertiliser A — the results could be totally different. Also, you can't make any conclusions beyond the three weeks — the plants could drop dead.

Evaluations — Describe How it Could be Improved

An evaluation is a critical analysis of the whole investigation.

1) You should comment on the method — was the equipment suitable? Was it a fair test?
2) Comment on the quality of the results — was there enough evidence to reach a valid conclusion? Were the results reliable, accurate and precise?
3) Were there any anomalies in the results — if there were none then say so.
4) If there were any anomalies, try to explain them — were they caused by errors in measurement? Were there any other variables that could have affected the results?
5) When you analyse your investigation like this, you'll be able to say how confident you are that your conclusion is right.
6) Then you can suggest any changes that would improve the quality of the results, so that you could have more confidence in your conclusion. For example, you might suggest changing the way you controlled a variable, or changing the interval of values you measured.
7) You could also make more predictions based on your conclusion, then further experiments could be carried out to test them.
8) When suggesting improvements to the investigation, always make sure that you say why you think this would make the results better.

Evaluation — in my next study I will make sure I don't burn the lab down...

I know it doesn't seem very nice, but writing about where you went wrong is an important skill — it shows you've got a really good understanding of what the investigation was about. It's difficult for me — I'm always right.

Controlled Assessment

At some point you'll have to do the controlled assessment. Here's a bit about it, but make sure you can recite all the stuff we've covered in this section first — it'll really help you out.

There are Three Parts to the Controlled Assessment

1 Research and Collecting Secondary Data

For Part 1 you'll be given some material to introduce the task and a research question. You'll need to read this through and then:

1) Carry out research and collect secondary data (data that other people have collected, rather than data you collect yourself).
2) Show that you considered all the different sources you could have used (e.g. books, the Internet) and chose the ones that were most suitable. You also need to explain why you chose those sources.
3) Write a full list (bibliography) of all the sources you used.
4) Present all the data you collected in an appropriate way, e.g. using tables.

2 Planning and Collecting Primary Data

For Part 2 you'll be given some more information to get your head around. Read this through and then:

1) Come up with a hypothesis based on the information you've been given.
2) Plan an experiment to test your hypothesis. You'll need to think about:
   - What equipment you're going to use (and why that equipment is right for the job).
   - What measurements you're going to take of the dependent variable.
   - How you're going to minimise errors so that your results are accurate and reliable.
   - What range of values you will use for the independent variable.
   - What interval you will use for the independent variable.
   - What variables you're going to control (and how you're going to do it).
   - How many times you're going to repeat the experiment.

There's lots of help on all of these things on pages 3-4.

3) Explain all the choices you made when planning the experiment.
4) Write a risk assessment for the experiment.
5) Carry out the experiment to collect primary data, taking any precautions from the risk assessment.
6) Present all the data you collected in an appropriate way, e.g. using tables.

3 Analysis and Evaluation

For Part 3 you'll have to complete a question paper which will ask you to do things like:

1) Process (e.g. using a bit of maths) and present (e.g. using graphs) both the primary and secondary data you collected in Part 1 and Part 2 in the most appropriate way.
2) Analyse and interpret the data to identify any patterns or relationships.
3) Compare your primary and secondary data to look for similarities and differences.
4) Write a conclusion based on all the data you collected and back it up with your own scientific knowledge. Say whether the secondary data you collected supports the conclusion.
5) Look back to your hypothesis and say whether the data support the hypothesis or not.
6) Evaluate the methods you used to collect the data and the quality of the data that was collected.
7) Say how confident you are in your conclusion and make suggestions for how the investigation could be improved. You'll also need to say why your suggestions would be an improvement.

Read this through and your assessment will be well under control...

You could use this page like a tick list for the controlled assessment — to make sure you don't forget anything.

Fitness and Blood Pressure

If you've ever wondered what the docs on Casualty are on about when they say in excited voices that someone's blood pressure is "92 over 60" or something... well, you're about to find out.

Being Fit is Not the Same as Being Healthy

1) Make sure you know the difference between being fit and being healthy...

HEALTHY means being free of any infections or diseases, whereas being FIT is a measure of how well you can perform physical tasks.

2) Fitness is not a precise term and it can be measured in different ways.
3) Fitness profiles measure strength, speed, agility and flexibility, together with stamina.
4) Stamina is a good indication of cardiovascular efficiency (the ability of the heart to supply the muscles with oxygen). It can be tested by measuring oxygen uptake during exercise, and blood pressure.

Stamina is how long you can keep going.

Blood is Pumped Around Your Body Under Pressure

1) The blood is pumped around the body by the contractions of the heart. These contractions increase the pressure of the blood.
2) The blood leaves the heart and flows through arteries. These split into thousands of tiny capillaries, which take blood to every cell in the body. The blood then flows back to the heart through veins. The pressure gets lower as the blood flows through the system.
3) The blood pressure is at its highest when the heart contracts — this is the systolic pressure. When the heart relaxes, the pressure is at its lowest — this is the diastolic pressure.
4) Blood pressure is measured in mm of mercury (mmHg).
5) In a healthy person it shouldn't be higher than about 135 (systolic pressure) over about 85 (diastolic pressure).
6) There are other factors (apart from your heart contracting) that can increase your blood pressure:

- smoking
- being overweight
- drinking too much alcohol
- being under lots of stress for a long time

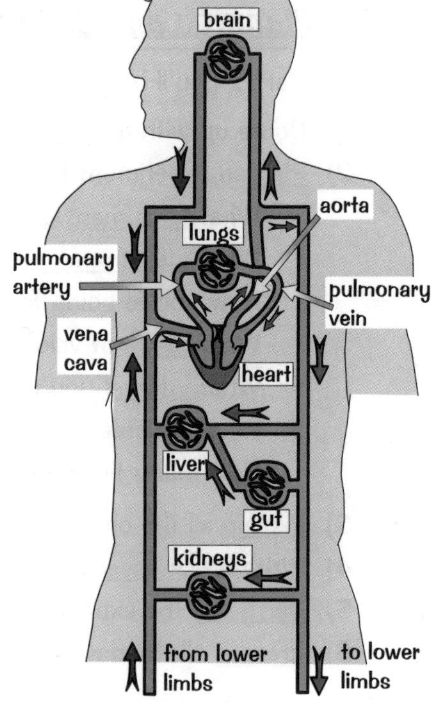

High or Low Blood Pressure Can Cause Health Problems

1) If the pressure of the blood is too high it can cause blood vessels to burst, and this can lead to strokes, brain damage and kidney damage.
2) High blood pressure can be decreased by lifestyle changes, e.g. eating a balanced diet, doing regular exercise, etc. In extreme cases, drugs are used to help correct the problem.
3) Low blood pressure is much less common than high blood pressure, but it can also cause problems. It causes poor circulation and tissues don't get all the food and oxygen they need. If your brain doesn't get enough food and oxygen you'll get dizzy and end up fainting.

My old P.E. teacher was really fit...

The exam might throw you a question asking you to evaluate the different ways of measuring someone's fitness. It might sound tricky, but all you need is a bit of common sense. Basically, the most effective method depends on the activity being carried out. For example, the best measure of fitness for a runner might be speed, whereas for a weight lifter it would be more useful to look at strength. Simple.

High Blood Pressure and Heart Disease

Smoking, in case you hadn't realised by now, is really quite BAD for you. Amongst other things, it's a major cause of high blood pressure — which can lead to all sorts of other health problems (see page 8).

Smoking Can Increase Blood Pressure

Cigarette smoke contains lots of nasty chemicals — some of which can increase blood pressure:

1) CARBON MONOXIDE — this combines with haemoglobin in red blood cells, which reduces the amount of oxygen they can carry. To make up for this (so that the tissues can get enough oxygen) heart rate has to increase. The heart contracts more frequently, which increases blood pressure.

Heart rate is the number of times the heart beats (or contracts) per minute.

2) NICOTINE — this increases heart rate. The heart contracts more often, increasing blood pressure.

A Poor Diet Can Lead to Heart Disease

1) Any disease that affects the heart is known as heart disease (clever). This includes things like heart attacks.
2) If your diet is high in saturated fat or salt, you may be more at risk of developing heart disease.

Saturated Fats Can Cause a Build Up of Cholesterol

1) Cholesterol is a fatty substance. Eating a diet high in saturated fat has been linked to high levels of cholesterol in the blood.
2) You need some cholesterol for things like making cell membranes. But if you get too much cholesterol it starts to build up in your arteries.
3) This forms plaques in the artery wall, which narrow the arteries. The plaques restrict the flow of blood, which can lead to a heart attack (see below).

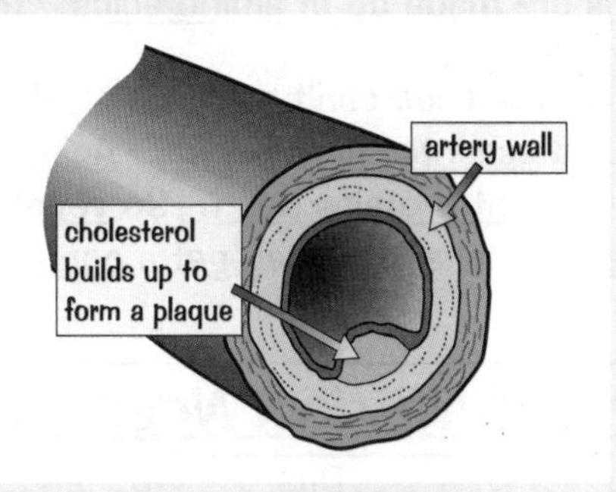

High Salt Levels Can Increase Blood Pressure

1) You need salt as part of a healthy diet. But eating too much salt can cause high blood pressure.
2) High blood pressure increases the risk of damage to the arteries — this damage can encourage the build up of plaques, which can lead to a heart attack.

Narrow Arteries Increase the Risk of a Heart Attack

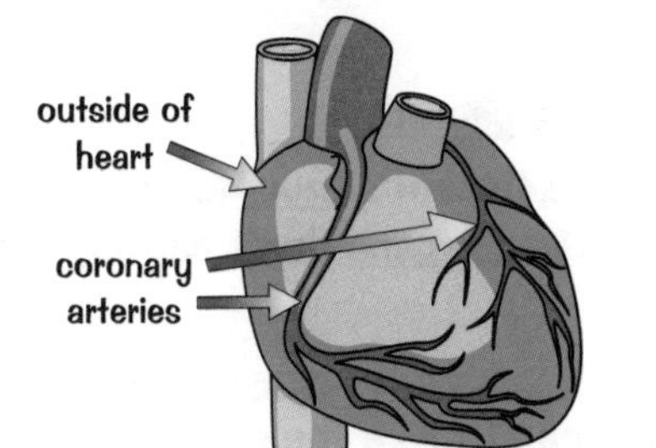

1) The heart muscle is supplied with blood by the coronary arteries.
2) If these become narrowed (e.g. due to plaques in the artery wall) blood flow to the heart is restricted and the heart muscle receives less oxygen.
3) A thrombosis (blood clot) also restricts blood flow.
4) If a thrombosis occurs in an already narrow coronary artery, blood flow to the heart might be blocked completely. If this happens, an area of heart muscle will be cut off from its oxygen supply.
5) This causes a heart attack.

Don't let Exam stress send your blood pressure through the roof...

In your exam you might be given some data to analyse. For example, they might give you a graph showing that as the amount of saturated fat eaten increases, so does the incidence of heart disease. With graphs like this you need to remember that just because both of the variables are increasing, it doesn't mean that one of them is causing the other to increase — there might only be a correlation between them (see page 5 for more on this).

Eating Healthily

As that doctor on the TV said this morning, food isn't just about energy — you need a balanced diet if you want to make sure that everything keeps working as it's supposed to.

A Balanced Diet Supplies All Your Essential Nutrients

A balanced diet gives you all the essential nutrients you need. The six essential nutrients are carbohydrates, proteins, fats, vitamins, minerals and water. You also need fibre (to keep the guts in good working order). Different nutrients are required for different functions in the body:

NUTRIENTS	FUNCTIONS
Carbohydrates	Carbohydrates (e.g. glucose) provide energy.
Fats	Fats provide energy, act as an energy store and provide insulation.
Proteins	Proteins are needed for growth and repair of tissue, and to provide energy in emergencies.
Vitamins and Minerals	Various functions: e.g. vitamin C is needed to prevent scurvy, and iron (a mineral) is needed to make haemoglobin for healthy blood.
Water	To prevent dehydration (where the body doesn't have enough water).

1) Carbohydrates are made up of simple sugars like glucose. They are stored in the liver as glycogen or converted to fats.
2) Fats are made up of fatty acids and glycerol. They can be stored under the skin and around organs as adipose tissue.
3) Proteins are made up of amino acids. They don't get stored.

Some amino acids can't be made by the body, so you have to get them from your diet — these are called essential amino acids. Animal proteins (found in meat) contain all the essential amino acids — plant proteins don't. So vegetarians need to eat proteins from a wide variety of plant sources to make sure they get a complete range of amino acids in their diet.

Animal proteins are called 'first class proteins'. Plant proteins are called 'second class proteins'.

Energy and Nutrient Needs Vary Between People

A balanced diet isn't a set thing — it's different for everyone. The balance of the different nutrients a person needs depends on things like their age, gender and activity level.

- Age → Children and teenagers need more protein for growth. Older people need more calcium to protect against degenerative bone diseases like osteoporosis.
- Gender → Females need more iron to replace the iron lost in menstrual blood.
- Physical activity → Active people need more protein for muscle development, and more carbohydrate for energy.

Some People Choose to Eat a Different Diet

Some people choose not to eat some foods for all sorts of reasons:

1) Religious reasons — e.g. Hindus don't eat cows because they believe they're sacred.
2) Personal reasons — vegetarians don't eat meat for various reasons — some think it's cruel to animals, some don't like the taste, some think it's healthier and some think it's trendy. Vegans don't eat any products from animals, e.g. milk, eggs and cheese.
3) Medical reasons — some people are intolerant to certain foods, e.g. dairy products or wheat. Eating them can make the person feel bloated and ill. This is often because they can't make the enzyme needed to digest that food properly. Some people are allergic to foods (nut allergies are quite common) — they get a severe reaction which can sometimes even be fatal.

I think the problem is that I've got an allergy to sprouts...

Having a food allergy can be a real pain. Just think how many random products have 'May contain nuts' on them. Some people carry a syringe of adrenaline to inject themselves with, just in case.

Diet Problems

You are what you eat, apparently. That makes me baked beans. But at least I'm not toast.

Eating Too Little Protein Can Cause Problems

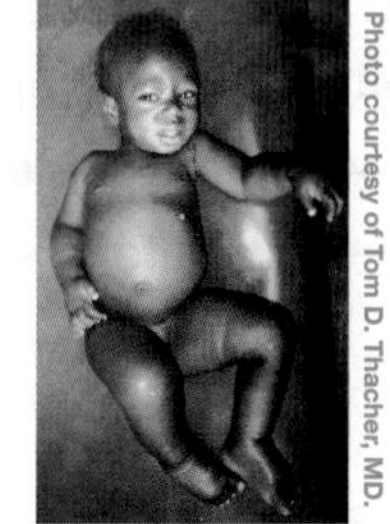
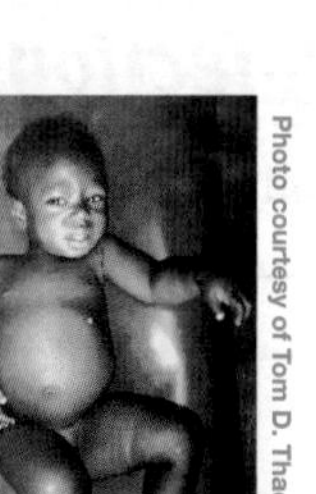

A kwashiorkor sufferer

1) Eating too little protein can cause a condition called kwashiorkor. A common symptom is a swollen stomach.
2) In developing countries lots of people have diets that are too low in protein. There are two main reasons for this:
   - Overpopulation means the demand for protein-rich food is greater than the amount that's available — so not everybody gets enough.
   - There isn't a lot of money to invest in agriculture — without the best farming techniques it's difficult to produce enough protein-rich food for everyone.
3) You can calculate a person's Estimated Average daily Requirement (EAR) of protein using this formula:

4) EAR is just an estimate though. It tells you how much protein the average person of a particular body mass should eat each day.
5) EAR varies with age, e.g. teenagers need to eat more protein than adults because they are still growing.
6) It also changes during and after pregnancy. Pregnant women need extra protein to help their baby grow. A woman who is breast feeding (lactating) needs extra protein in order to produce milk.

Eating Disorders Cause Problems too

1) Some psychological disorders, e.g. anorexia nervosa and bulimia nervosa, can also cause under-nutrition.
2) Anorexia nervosa leads to self-starvation. Bulimia nervosa involves bouts of binge eating, followed by self-induced vomiting. They're both usually caused by low self-esteem and a desire to be 'perfect' — sufferers have a poor self-image.
3) These disorders result in a poor diet, which can cause a host of other illnesses, e.g. liver failure, kidney failure, heart attacks, muscle wastage, low blood pressure and mineral deficiencies. Bulimia can lead to tooth decay (the acid in vomit eats away at the tooth enamel). Both disorders can be fatal.

Body Mass Index Indicates If You're Under- or Overweight

The Body Mass Index (BMI) is used as a guide to help decide whether someone is underweight, normal, overweight or obese. It's calculated from their height and weight:

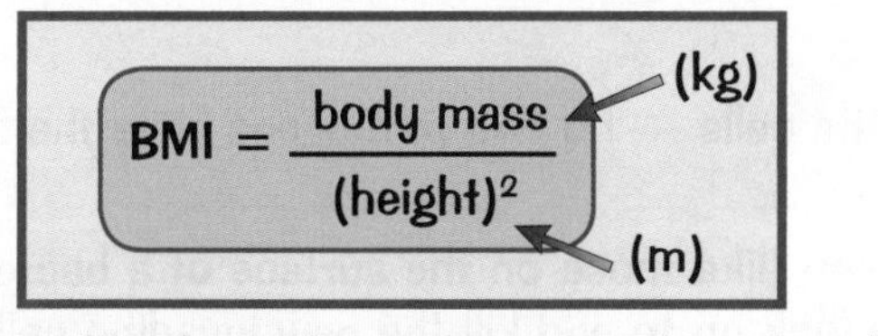

The table shows how BMI is used to classify people's weight.

Body Mass Index	Weight Description
below 18.5	underweight
18.5 - 24.9	normal
25 - 29.9	overweight
30 - 40	moderately obese
above 40	severely obese

BMI isn't always reliable. Athletes have lots of muscle, which weighs more than fat, so they can come out with a high BMI even though they're not overweight. An alternative to BMI is measuring % body fat.

Your EAR for revision = 4.7534 hours...

What a cheery page. Make sure you know exactly how to use those pesky equations. You could end up having to calculate BMI or EAR in the exam. Remember: EAR is an estimate and it varies from person to person.

Infectious Disease

There really are loads of things out to get you, and you really do have to fight attacks off every day.

Infectious Diseases are Caused by Pathogens

Pathogens are microorganisms that cause disease. There are four types:

1) fungi — e.g. athlete's foot is caused by fungi
2) bacteria — e.g. cholera is caused by bacteria
3) viruses — e.g. flu is caused by a virus
4) protozoa (single-celled organisms) — e.g. dysentery can be caused by protozoa.

The symptoms of an infectious disease are caused by cell damage or by toxins produced by the pathogens.

Malaria is an Example of an Infectious Disease

1) Malaria is caused by a protozoan. It's carried by mosquitoes, which are insects that feed on the blood of animals (including humans).
2) The protozoan is a parasite — an organism that lives off another organism (called a host) and often causes it harm (see page 32).
3) The mosquitoes are vectors, meaning they carry the disease without getting it themselves. They pick up the malarial parasite when they feed on an infected animal. Every time the mosquito feeds on another animal it infects it by inserting the parasite into the animal's blood vessels.
4) We know that mozzies carry malaria so we can target them to reduce the spread of infection:
   - The areas of water where mosquitoes lay their eggs can be drained or sprayed with insecticides.
   - Fish can be introduced into the water to eat mosquito larvae.
   - People can be protected from mosquitoes using insecticides and mosquito nets.

Your Immune System Deals with Pathogens

Once pathogens have entered your body they'll reproduce rapidly unless they're destroyed. That's the job of your immune system, and white blood cells are the most important part of it.

White blood cells travel around in your blood and crawl into every part of you, constantly patrolling for pathogens. When they come across an invading microorganism they have three lines of attack:

1) Consuming Them

White blood cells can engulf foreign cells and digest them.

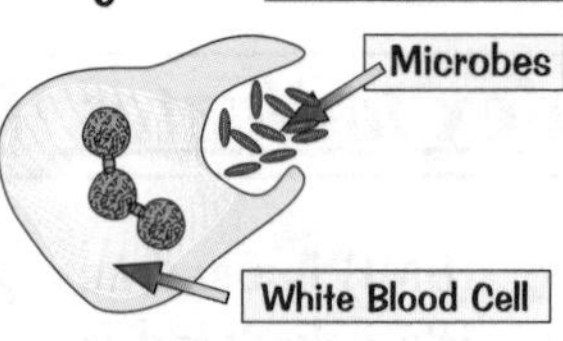

2) Producing Antitoxins

Antitoxins counter the effect of any poisons (toxins) produced by the invading pathogens.

3) Producing Antibodies

1) Every pathogen has unique molecules on the surface of its cells — no two pathogens have the same ones. These molecules are called antigens.
2) When your white blood cells come across a foreign antigen (like those on the surface of a bacterium) they'll start to produce proteins called antibodies, which lock on to and kill the new invading cells. The antibodies produced are specific to that pathogen — they won't lock on to other pathogens.
3) Antibodies are then produced rapidly and flow all round the body to kill all similar bacteria or viruses.
4) Some white blood cells stay around in the blood after the pathogen has been fought off — these are called memory cells. If the person is infected with the same pathogen again these cells will remember it and immediately make antibodies to kill it — the person is naturally immune to that pathogen.

If athletes get athlete's foot — do vicars get dog-cholera...?

White blood cells aren't the body's only defence. Your skin provides a tough layer that stops most pathogens getting in to begin with, and if you get a cut in it, clotting quickly seals it up again. Clever stuff.

Preventing and Treating Infectious Disease

An ounce of prevention is worth a pound of cure. That's what my mum says, anyhow.

Immunisation (Vaccination) Stops You Getting Infections

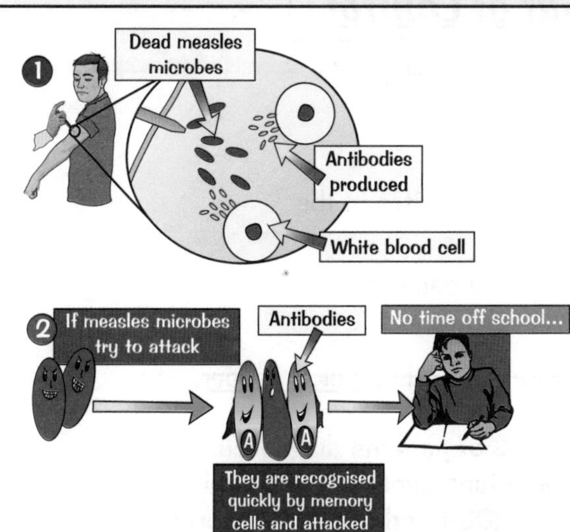

1) When you're infected with a new pathogen it can take your white blood cells a while to produce the antibodies to deal with it. In that time you can get very ill, or maybe even die.
2) To avoid this you can be immunised (vaccinated) against some diseases, e.g. polio or measles.
3) Immunisation involves injecting dead or inactive pathogens into the body. These carry antigens, so even though they're harmless they still trigger an immune response — your white blood cells produce antibodies to attack them.
4) Some of these white blood cells will remain in the blood as memory cells (see previous page) so if live pathogens of the same type ever appear, the antibodies to kill them will be produced immediately.

Immunisation is classed as active immunity:

- Active immunity is where the immune system makes its own antibodies after being stimulated by a pathogen. It includes becoming naturally immune (see previous page) and artificially immune (immunisation). Active immunity is usually permanent.
- Passive immunity is where you use antibodies made by another organism, e.g. antibodies are passed from mother to baby through breast milk. Passive immunity is only temporary.

There are Benefits and Risks Associated with Immunisation

1) Immunisation stops you from getting ill... a pretty obvious benefit.
2) And if most people are immunised the disease won't be able to spread as easily.
3) But there can be short-term side effects, e.g. swelling and redness at the site of injection and feeling a bit under the weather for a week or two afterwards.
4) You can't have some vaccines if you're already ill, especially if your immune system is weakened.
5) Some people think that immunisation can cause other disorders, e.g. one study suggested a link between the MMR (measles, mumps and rubella) vaccine and autism. Scientists now know it's perfectly safe, but for a few years many parents weren't willing to take the risk.

You Can Take Antibiotics to Get Rid of Some Infections

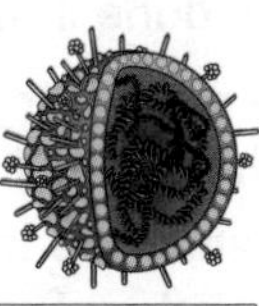
A horrid Flu Virus

1) Antibiotics are drugs that kill bacteria without killing your own body cells.
2) They're very useful for clearing up bacterial infections that your body is having trouble with, however they don't kill viruses.
3) Antivirals can be used to treat viral infections. Antivirals are drugs that stop viruses from reproducing.
4) Some bacteria are naturally resistant to (not killed by) certain antibiotics. Misuse of antibiotics (e.g. doctors overprescribing them or patients not finishing a course) has increased the rate of development of resistant strains. So nowadays you won't get antibiotics for a mild infection, only for something more serious. MRSA (the hospital 'superbug') is the best-known example of an antibiotic-resistant strain.

GCSEs are like antibiotics — you have to finish the course...

Science isn't just about doing an experiment, finding the answer and telling everyone about it — scientists often disagree. Not that long ago different scientists had different opinions on the MMR vaccine — and argued about its safety. Many different studies were done before scientists concluded it was safe.

Cancer and Drug Development

If you've ever thought you might be a hypochondriac, this page may not do you any favours. Still, at least you'll learn all about how drugs are developed.

Cancer is Caused by Body Cells Dividing Out of Control

This forms a tumour (a mass of cells). Tumours can either be benign or malignant:

1) **Benign** — This is where the tumour grows until there's no more room. The cells stay where they are. This type isn't normally dangerous.
2) **Malignant** — This is where the tumour grows and can spread to other sites in the body. Malignant tumours are dangerous and can be fatal.

Having a healthy lifestyle and diet can reduce your risk of getting some cancers:

1) Not smoking reduces your chances of getting lung cancer.
2) Eating less processed meat and more fibre may reduce your risk of getting colon cancer.

Different types of cancer have different survival rates, e.g. 77% of patients diagnosed with breast cancer survive for at least 5 years, whereas only 6% of lung cancer patients do. They also have different mortality (death) rates, e.g. between 2004 and 2006 the mortality rate for men with lung cancer was 53 per 100,000 of the male population, whereas the mortality rate for men with prostate cancer was only 29 per 100,000.

Drugs Developed to Treat Disease Need to be Tested

New drugs developed to treat any kind of disease need to be thoroughly tested before they can be used to make sure they're safe and that they work. This is the usual way that drugs are developed and tested:

Computer models are often used first of all — these simulate a human's response to a drug, so you don't need to test on live animals at this stage. They can identify promising drugs to be tested in the next stage, but it's not as accurate as actually seeing the effect on a live organism.

The drugs are then developed further by testing on human tissues. However, you can't use human tissue to test drugs that affect whole/multiple body systems, e.g. testing a drug for blood pressure must be done on a whole animal, i.e. one that has an intact circulatory system.

The last step is to develop and test the drug using animals. The law in Britain states that any new drug must be tested on two different live mammals. Some people think it's cruel to test on animals, but others believe this is the safest way to make sure a drug isn't dangerous before it's given to humans.

After the drug has been tested on animals it's tested on humans:

1) This is done in a study called a clinical trial.
2) There are two groups of patients. One is given the new drug, the other is given a placebo (a 'sugar pill' that looks like the real drug but doesn't do anything). This is done so scientists can see the actual difference the drug makes — it allows for the placebo effect (when the patient expects the treatment to work and so feels better, even though the treatment isn't doing anything).
3) Scientists sometimes test new drugs against the best existing treatment rather than a placebo. This tells them how well the new drug compares to what we already have.
4) Clinical trials are blind — the patient in the study doesn't know whether they're getting the drug or the placebo. In fact, they're often double blind — neither the patient nor the scientist knows until all the results have been gathered.

Double Blindman's Buff — now that's got to be fun...

In the exam they might give you data relating to the survival or mortality (death) rates of different types of cancer and ask you to interpret it. Shouldn't be a problem if you can read a graph.

Drugs: Use and Harm

Drugs (both the legal kind and the illegal kind) might be in the exam. So get reading.

Drugs Can be Beneficial or Harmful

1) Drugs are substances which alter the way the body works. Some drugs are medically useful, such as antibiotics (e.g. penicillin). But many drugs are dangerous if misused.
2) This is why you can buy some drugs over the counter at a pharmacy, but others are restricted so you can only get them on prescription — your doctor decides if you should have them.
3) Some people get addicted to drugs — this means they have a physical need for the drug, and if they don't get it they get withdrawal symptoms. It's not just illegal drugs that are addictive — many legal ones are as well, e.g. caffeine in coffee. Caffeine withdrawal symptoms include irritability and shaky hands.
4) Tolerance develops with some drugs — the body gets used to having it and so you need a higher dose to give the same effect. This can happen with both legal drugs (e.g. alcohol), and illegal drugs (e.g. heroin).
5) If someone's addicted to a drug but wants to get off it, rehabilitation can help — this is where you get help and support to try and overcome an addiction.

You need to know all about these drugs...

1) Depressants — e.g. alcohol, solvents and temazepam. These decrease the activity of the brain, which slows down the responses of the nervous system, causing slow reactions and poor judgement of speed and distances (which is why drink driving is dangerous).
2) Stimulants — e.g. nicotine, ecstasy, caffeine. These do the opposite of depressants — they increase the activity of the brain. This makes you feel more alert and awake. Stimulant drugs are often used to treat depression.

See page 18 for more detail on how stimulants and depressants work.

3) Painkillers — e.g. aspirin and paracetamol. Mild painkillers like aspirin work by reducing the number of 'painful' stimuli at the nerve endings near an injury.
4) Performance enhancers — e.g. anabolic steroids (testosterone, for example). These are sometimes taken by athletes. They help build muscle and allow the athletes to train harder. But they're banned by most sports organisations.
5) Hallucinogens — e.g. LSD. They distort what's seen and heard by altering the pathways that the brain sends messages along.

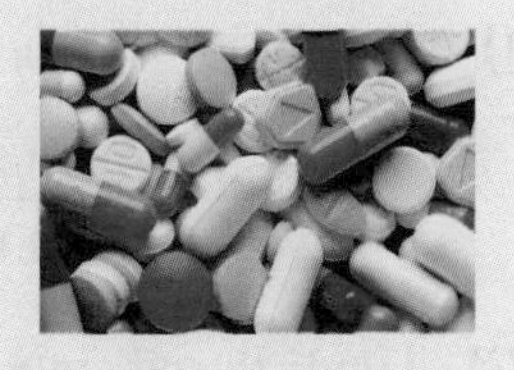

Some Drugs are Illegal

1) In the UK, illegal drugs are classified into three main categories — Classes A, B and C. Which class a drug is in depends on how dangerous it is — Class A drugs are the most dangerous.

- CLASS A drugs include heroin, LSD, ecstasy and cocaine.
- CLASS B drugs include cannabis and amphetamines (speed).
- CLASS C drugs include anabolic steroids and tranquillisers.

2) Using or dealing Class A drugs is most serious — you could get a lengthy prison sentence. Being caught with Class C drugs will probably only get you a warning, although prison's still a possibility.
3) In all cases, supplying a drug to others usually results in a greater punishment than just using it yourself.

Drugs — they can cure you or kill you...

Many people take drugs of some kind, e.g. caffeine in coffee, headache tablets, alcohol, hay fever medicine or an inhaler for asthma. Most of these are okay if you're careful with them and don't go overboard. It's misuse that can get you into trouble (e.g. a paracetamol overdose can kill you). Read the packet.

Smoking and Alcohol

Everyone knows that drinking a lot and smoking don't do you much good. Sadly, it's unlikely that your exam question will ask you to say whether they're good or bad — it's the fiddly little details they'll want you to know.

Alcohol is a Depressant Drug

1) Alcohol's main effect is to reduce the activity of the nervous system — it's a depressant (see page 15).
2) The positive side of this is that it makes people feel less inhibited. (Many people think that alcohol in moderation helps people to socialise and relax with each other.)
3) However, alcohol is poisonous. Alcohol is broken down by enzymes in the liver and some of the products are toxic. If you drink too much alcohol over a long period of time these toxic products can cause the death of liver cells, forming scar tissue that stops blood reaching the liver — this is called cirrhosis. If the liver can't do its normal job of cleaning the blood, dangerous substances start to build up and damage the rest of the body.
4) Alcohol also causes dehydration, which can damage other cells in the body (including in the brain).
5) Being drunk leads to impaired judgement, poor balance, poor coordination, slurred speech, blurred vision and sleepiness. This is why you're not allowed to drive, fly a plane or operate heavy machinery when you're drunk.

There are legal alcohol limits...
For driving in the UK it's 80 milligrams of alcohol in 100 millilitres of blood.
For pilots it's 20 milligrams of alcohol per 100 millilitres of blood.

And there are also 'lifestyle guidelines'...
Doctors recommend drinking no more each week than 21 'units' of alcohol for a man, and 14 for a woman, where 1 unit is:
(i) half a pint of average strength beer,
(ii) 1 small glass of wine,
(iii) 1 standard pub measure of spirits, etc.

Smoking Causes All Sorts of Illnesses

Burning cigarettes produce nicotine, which is what makes smoking addictive. They also produce carbon monoxide, tar, and particulates — which can all cause illness and other problems. E.g.

1) Heart disease:

   Carbon monoxide reduces the oxygen carrying capacity of the blood. If the heart muscle doesn't receive enough oxygen it can lead to a heart attack (see page 9).

2) Lung, throat, mouth and oesophageal cancer:

   Tar from cigarette smoke collects in the lungs. It's full of toxic chemicals, some of which are carcinogens (cause cancer). Carcinogens make mutations in the DNA more likely. If this happens, cell division can go out of control and malignant tumours (see page 14) can form.

3) A smoker's cough and severe loss of lung function, which can lead to diseases like emphysema:

   Smoking damages the cilia on the epithelial tissue lining the trachea, bronchi and bronchioles (tubes in the lungs), which encourages mucus to be produced. But excess mucus can't be cleared because the cilia are damaged, so it sticks to air passages causing smoker's cough. The lungs also lose their elasticity, causing emphysema.

4) Low birth weight babies:

   Low oxygen in the blood of pregnant women (caused by carbon monoxide) can deprive the foetus of oxygen, leading to a small baby at birth.

The tar in cigarettes makes cilia black...

In the exam you might be asked to interpret data on the effects of smoking or alcohol, e.g. birth weights of babies born to mothers who smoke compared to those who don't, or the link between reaction time and alcohol level, etc. Don't panic — they'll give you any information you need to answer the question.

Receptors — The Eye

Your body has sense organs containing receptors that gather information about the world around you. My own personal favourite is the eye, which is sensitive to light and responsible for sight.

Learn the Eye with All Its Labels:

1) The cornea refracts (bends) light into the eye.
2) The iris controls how much light enters the pupil (the hole in the middle).
3) The lens also refracts light, focusing it onto the retina.
4) The retina is the light sensitive part and it's covered in receptors called rods and cones, which detect light.
5) Rods are more sensitive in dim light but can't sense colour.
6) Cones are sensitive to different colours but are not so good in dim light (red-green colour blindness is due to a lack of certain specialised cone cells).
7) The optic nerve carries impulses from the receptors to the brain.

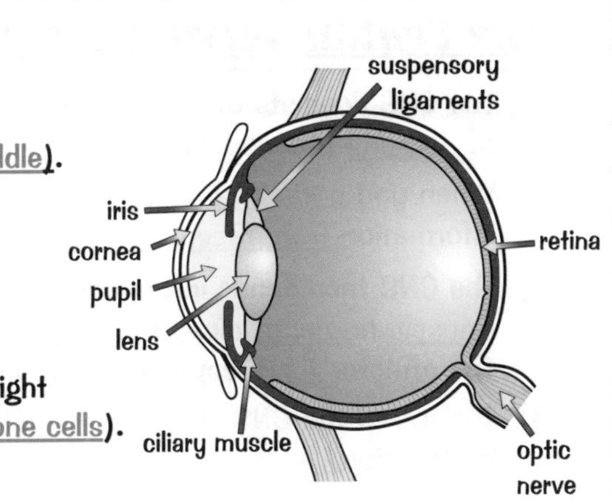

Focusing on Near and Distant Objects

The lens is elastic, so the eye can focus light by changing the shape of the lens — this is known as accommodation.

To look at distant objects:

1) The ciliary muscle relaxes, which allows the suspensory ligaments to pull tight.
2) This pulls the lens into a less rounded shape so light is refracted less.

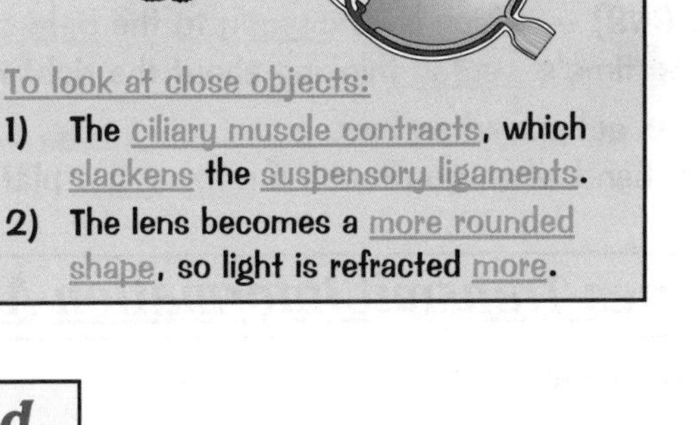

To look at close objects:

1) The ciliary muscle contracts, which slackens the suspensory ligaments.
2) The lens becomes a more rounded shape, so light is refracted more.

Some People are Long- or Short-sighted

Long-sighted people are unable to focus on near objects:

1) This occurs when the lens is the wrong shape and doesn't bend the light enough or the eyeball is too short.
2) The images of near objects are brought into focus behind the retina.
3) You can use glasses or contact lenses with a convex lens to correct it.

Short-sighted people are unable to focus on distant objects:

1) This occurs when the lens is the wrong shape and bends the light too much or the eyeball is too long.
2) The images of distant objects are brought into focus in front of the retina.
3) You can use glasses or contact lenses with a concave lens to correct it.

An alternative to glasses or contact lenses is to have corneal laser surgery.

Binocular Vision Lets You Judge Depth

1) Some animals, including humans, have two eyes which work together — this is binocular vision.
2) When you look at an object, your brain compares the images seen by each eye.
3) The more similarities between the images, the further away the object.
4) This allows us to judge distances well, but gives us a narrow field of vision.

I think I'm a little long-sighted...

If you can read this you've got better eyesight than me!

To see how important binocular vision is, cover one eye and try pouring water into a glass at arm's length.

Neurones and Reflexes

Ever wondered how you can pull your hand away from a hot pan faster than you can say "Yowzers, that hurt"? It's all to do with reflex actions, so read on to find out more. Go on, you know you want to.

The Central Nervous System (CNS) Coordinates Information

1) The CNS consists of the brain and spinal cord. The nervous system is made up of the three types of neurone (nerve cell) — sensory neurones, relay neurones and motor neurones.
2) When you detect a change in your environment (a stimulus) your sensory neurones carry the information from receptors (e.g. light receptors in the back of the eye) to the CNS.
3) The CNS then sends information to an effector (muscle or gland) along a motor neurone. The effector then responds accordingly.
4) The job of the CNS is to COORDINATE the information.

Reflex Actions Stop You Injuring Yourself

1) The nervous system uses electrical impulses to allow very quick responses. Reflex actions are automatic (done without thinking) so they're even quicker.
2) The conscious brain isn't involved in a reflex arc. The sensory neurone connects to a relay neurone in the spinal cord (part of the CNS) — which links directly to the right motor neurone, so no time's wasted thinking about the right response.
3) Reflex actions often have a protective role, e.g. snatching back your hand when you touch a burning hot plate happens almost before you realise you've done it.

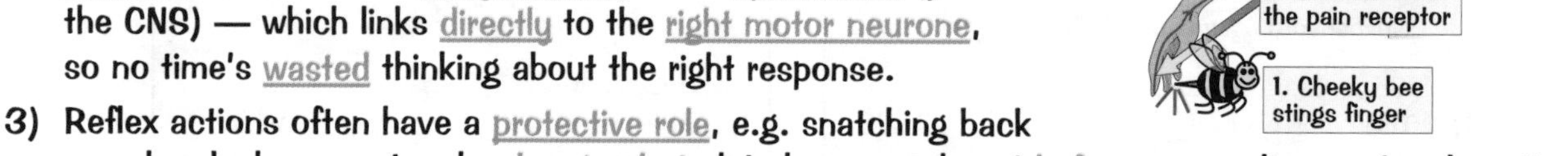

Neurones Transmit Information Around the Body as Electrical Impulses

1) The electrical impulse is passed along the axon of the cell.
2) Neurones have branched endings (dendrites) so they can connect with lots of other neurones.
3) They have a sheath along the axon that acts as an electrical insulator, which speeds up the electrical impulse.
4) They're long, which also speeds up the impulse (connecting with another neurone slows the impulse down, so one long neurone is much quicker than lots of short ones joined together).
5) The connection between two neurones is called a synapse. It's basically just a very tiny gap:

Here's a typical motor neurone:

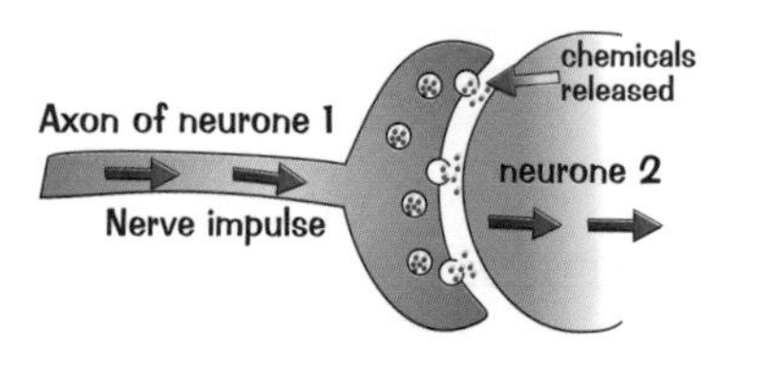

- The electrical impulse triggers the release of transmitter chemicals, which diffuse across the gap.
- These chemicals bind to receptor molecules in the membrane of the next neurone. This sets off a new electrical impulse.
- Stimulant drugs increase the amount of transmitter chemical at some synapses, which increases the frequency of impulses along neurone 2.
- Depressants bind with receptor molecules on the membrane of neurone 2, blocking the electrical impulse. This decreases brain activity.

Don't let the thought of exams play on your nerves...

Another example of a reflex is when the pupil in your eye constricts in bright light — it stops your eye getting damaged. Control of your posture happens automatically too — thanks to reflex arcs.

Homeostasis

Homeostasis involves balancing body functions to maintain a 'constant internal environment'. Smashing.

Homeostasis is Maintaining a Constant Internal Environment

Conditions in your body need to be kept steady so that cells can function properly. This involves balancing inputs (stuff going into your body) with outputs (stuff leaving). For example...

1) Levels of CO_2 — respiration constantly produces CO_2, which you need to get rid of.
2) Water content — you need to keep a balance between the water you gain (in drink, food, and from respiration) and the water you pee, sweat and breathe out.
3) Body temperature — you need to get rid of excess body heat when you're hot, but retain heat when the environment is cold.

A mechanism called negative feedback works automatically to help you keep all these things steady:

NEGATIVE FEEDBACK

Changes in the environment trigger a response that counteracts the changes — e.g. a rise in body temperature causes a response that lowers body temperature.

This means that the internal environment tends to stay around a norm, the level at which the cells work best.

This only works within certain limits — if the environment changes too much then it might not be possible to counteract it.

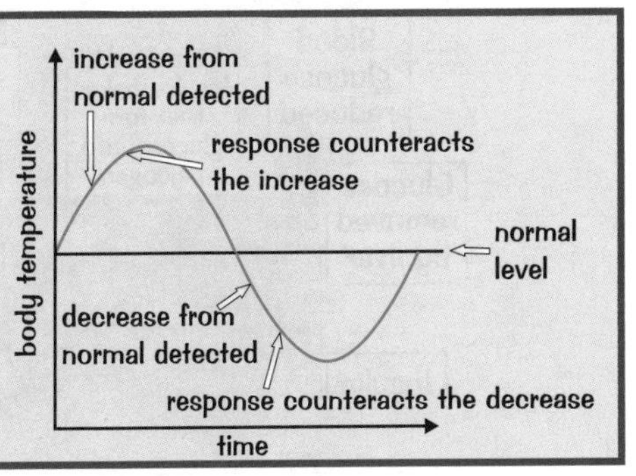

Body Temperature is Controlled by the Brain

All enzymes have an optimum temperature they work best at.
For enzymes in the human body it's about 37 °C.

1) There's a thermoregulatory centre in the brain which acts as your own personal thermostat.
2) It contains receptors that are sensitive to the blood temperature in the brain. It also receives impulses from the skin that provide information about skin temperature. The brain can respond to this information and bring about changes in the body's temperature using the nervous and hormonal systems to initiate temperature control mechanisms. For example:

When You're TOO HOT:

1) Hairs lie flat.
2) Lots of sweat is produced — when sweat evaporates it uses heat from the skin. This transfers heat from your skin to the environment, which cools you down.
3) Blood vessels close to the surface of the skin widen. This allows more blood to flow near the surface, so it can radiate more heat into the surroundings. This is called vasodilation.

If you're exposed to high temperatures you can get dehydrated and you could get heat stroke. This can kill you (see below).

When You're TOO COLD:

1) Hairs stand on end to trap an insulating layer of air which helps keep you warm.
2) Very little sweat is produced.
3) Blood vessels near the surface constrict (vasoconstriction) so that less heat can be transferred from the blood to the surroundings.
4) You shiver, and the movement generates heat in the muscles.

Your body temperature can drop to dangerous levels if you're exposed to very low temperatures for a long time — this is called hypothermia. If you don't get help quickly you can die.

If you do enough revision, you can avoid negative feedback...

If you're in really high temperatures for a long time you can get heat stroke — sweating stops because you're so dehydrated and there's a big rise in your body temperature. Your enzymes can't work properly and important reactions get disrupted — if you don't cool down you could collapse and die. Fortunately, good old British drizzle means that heat stroke needn't worry the majority of us. Lucky old us.

Controlling Blood Sugar Level

Blood sugar level is controlled as part of homeostasis, using the hormone insulin. Learn how it works.

Insulin Controls Blood Sugar Level

1) Eating foods containing carbohydrate puts glucose into the blood from the gut.
2) Normal respiration in cells removes glucose from the blood.
3) Vigorous exercise also removes a lot of glucose from the blood.
4) The level of glucose in the blood must be kept steady. Changes in blood glucose are monitored and controlled by the pancreas, using insulin...

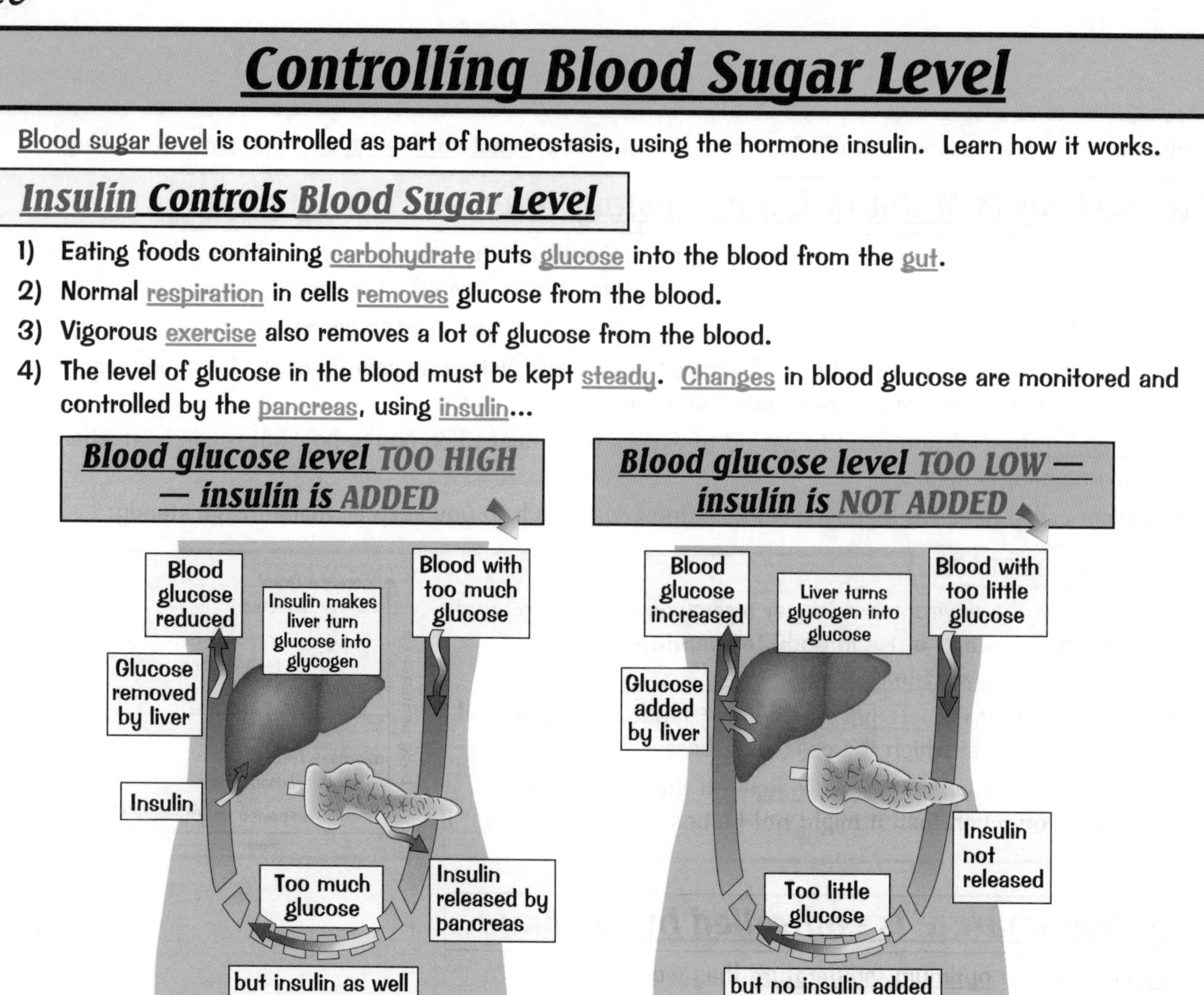

Glycogen can be stored in the liver until the blood sugar level is low again.

Insulin is a hormone. Hormones travel in the blood, so it can take quite a while for them to get to where they're needed in the body, i.e. their target organ. Electrical impulses sent along the nerves travel much faster. This means it takes the body longer to respond to a hormone than to a nervous impulse.

Having Diabetes Means You Can't Control Your Blood Sugar Level

Diabetes is a condition that affects your ability to control your blood sugar level. There are two types:

1) Type 1 diabetes is where the pancreas produces little or no insulin.
The result is that a person's blood glucose level can rise to a level that can kill them.

People with type 1 diabetes can partly control the condition by having a carefully controlled diet, but they also need insulin therapy. This usually involves injecting insulin into the blood several times a day (often at mealtimes). This makes sure that glucose is removed from the blood quickly once food has been digested. This stops the level of glucose in the blood from getting too high and is a very effective treatment. The amount of insulin needed depends on the person's diet and how active they are.

2) Type 2 diabetes is where a person becomes resistant to insulin (their body's cells don't respond properly to the hormone). This can also cause blood sugar level to rise to a dangerous level.

Type 2 diabetes is usually just controlled by limiting the intake of foods rich in simple carbohydrates, i.e. sugars (which cause glucose levels to rise rapidly).

My blood sugar feels low after all that — pass the biscuits...

This stuff can seem a bit confusing at first, but if you learn those two diagrams, it'll all start to get a lot easier. Don't forget that there are two types of diabetes — and different ways of controlling them.

Plant Hormones and Growth

Plants don't just grow randomly. Plant hormones make sure they grow in the right direction.

Auxins are Plant Growth Hormones

1) Auxins are plant hormones which control growth at the tips of shoots and roots. They move through the plant in solution (dissolved in water).
2) Auxin is produced in the tips and diffuses backwards to stimulate the cell elongation process which occurs in the cells just behind the tips.
3) Auxin promotes growth in the shoot, but actually inhibits growth in the root.
4) Auxins are involved in the growth responses of plants to light (phototropism) and gravity (geotropism).

Auxins Change the Direction of Root and Shoot Growth

SHOOTS ARE POSITIVELY PHOTOTROPIC (grow towards light)

1) When a shoot tip is exposed to light, it accumulates more auxin on the side that's in the shade than the side that's in the light.
2) This makes the cells grow (elongate) faster on the shaded side, so the shoot bends towards the light.

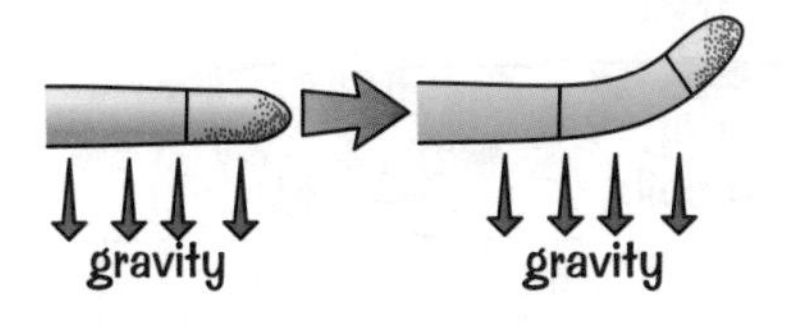

SHOOTS ARE NEGATIVELY GEOTROPIC (grow away from gravity)

1) When a shoot is growing sideways, gravity produces an unequal distribution of auxin in the tip, with more auxin on the lower side.
2) This causes the lower side to grow faster, bending the shoot upwards.

ROOTS ARE POSITIVELY GEOTROPIC (grow towards gravity)

1) A root growing sideways will also have more auxin on its lower side.
2) But in a root the extra auxin inhibits growth. This means the cells on top elongate faster, and the root bends downwards.

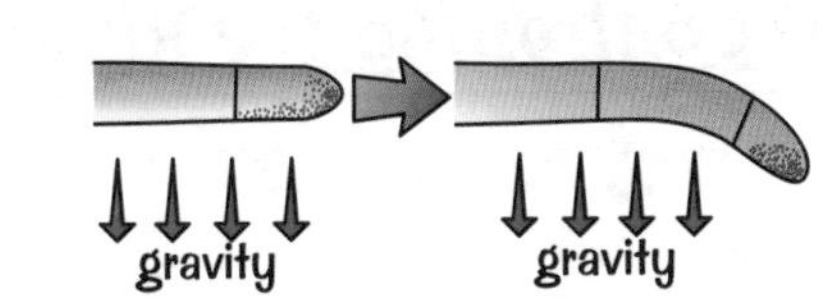

ROOTS ARE NEGATIVELY PHOTOTROPIC (grow away from light)

1) If a root starts being exposed to some light, more auxin accumulates on the more shaded side.
2) The auxin inhibits cell elongation on the shaded side, so the root bends downwards, back into the ground.

Experiments Have Shown How Auxins Work

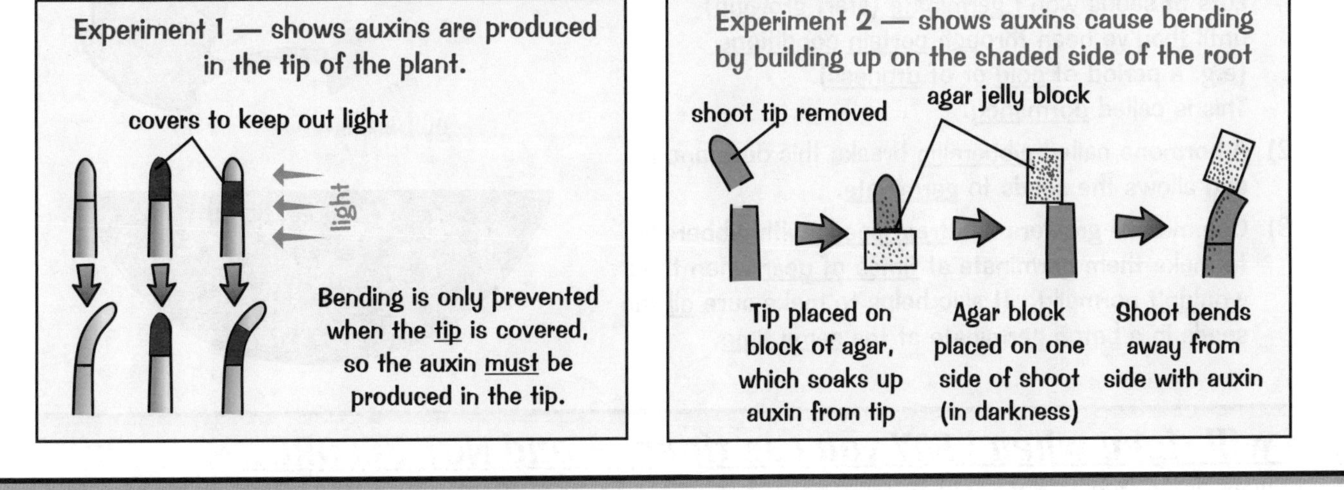

A plant auxin to a bar — 'ouch'...

Shoots grow towards light and roots grow towards gravity — that's not too hard to remember, now, is it.

Commercial Use of Plant Hormones

Plant hormones can be extracted, or artificial copies can be made. They can then be used to do all kinds of useful things, including killing weeds, growing cuttings and ripening fruit.

1) As Selective Weedkillers

1) Most weeds growing in fields of crops or in a lawn are broad-leaved, in contrast to grasses and cereals which have very narrow leaves.
2) Selective weedkillers have been developed from plant growth hormones which only affect the broad-leaved plants.
3) They totally disrupt their normal growth patterns, which soon kills them, whilst leaving the grass and crops untouched.

2) Growing from Cuttings with Rooting Powder

1) A cutting is part of a plant that has been cut off it, like the end of a branch with a few leaves on it.
2) Normally, if you stick cuttings in the soil they won't grow, but if you add rooting powder, which contains a plant growth hormone, they will produce roots rapidly and start growing as new plants.
3) This enables growers to produce lots of clones (exact copies) of a really good plant very quickly.

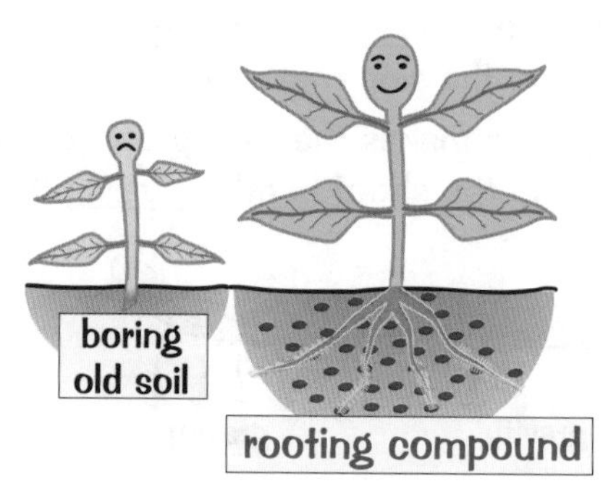

3) Controlling the Ripening of Fruit

1) Plant hormones can be used to delay the ripening of fruits — either while they are still on the plant, or during transport to the shops.
2) This allows the fruit to be picked while it's still unripe (and therefore firmer and less easily damaged).
3) Ripening hormone is then added and the fruit will ripen on the way to the supermarket and be perfect just as it reaches the shelves.

4) Controlling Dormancy

1) Lots of seeds won't germinate (start growing) until they've been through certain conditions (e.g. a period of cold or of dryness). This is called dormancy.
2) A hormone called gibberellin breaks this dormancy and allows the seeds to germinate.
3) Commercial growers can treat seeds with gibberellin to make them germinate at times of year when they wouldn't normally. It also helps to make sure all the seeds in a batch germinate at the same time.

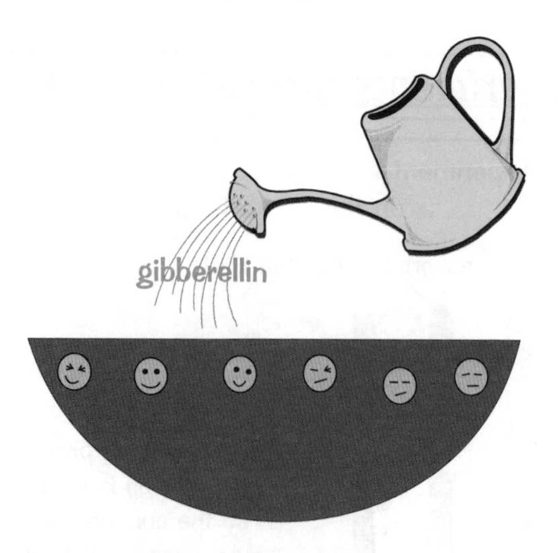

You will ripen when I SAY you can ripen — and NOT BEFORE...

If you want some fruit to ripen, put it into a paper bag with a banana. The banana releases a ripening hormone called ethene which causes the fruit to ripen. Bad apples also release lots of ethene. Unfortunately this means if you've got one bad apple in a barrel, you'll soon have lots of bad apples.

Genes and Chromosomes

This page is a bit tricky, but it's dead important that you get to grips with all the stuff on it — because you're going to hear a lot more about it over the next few pages...

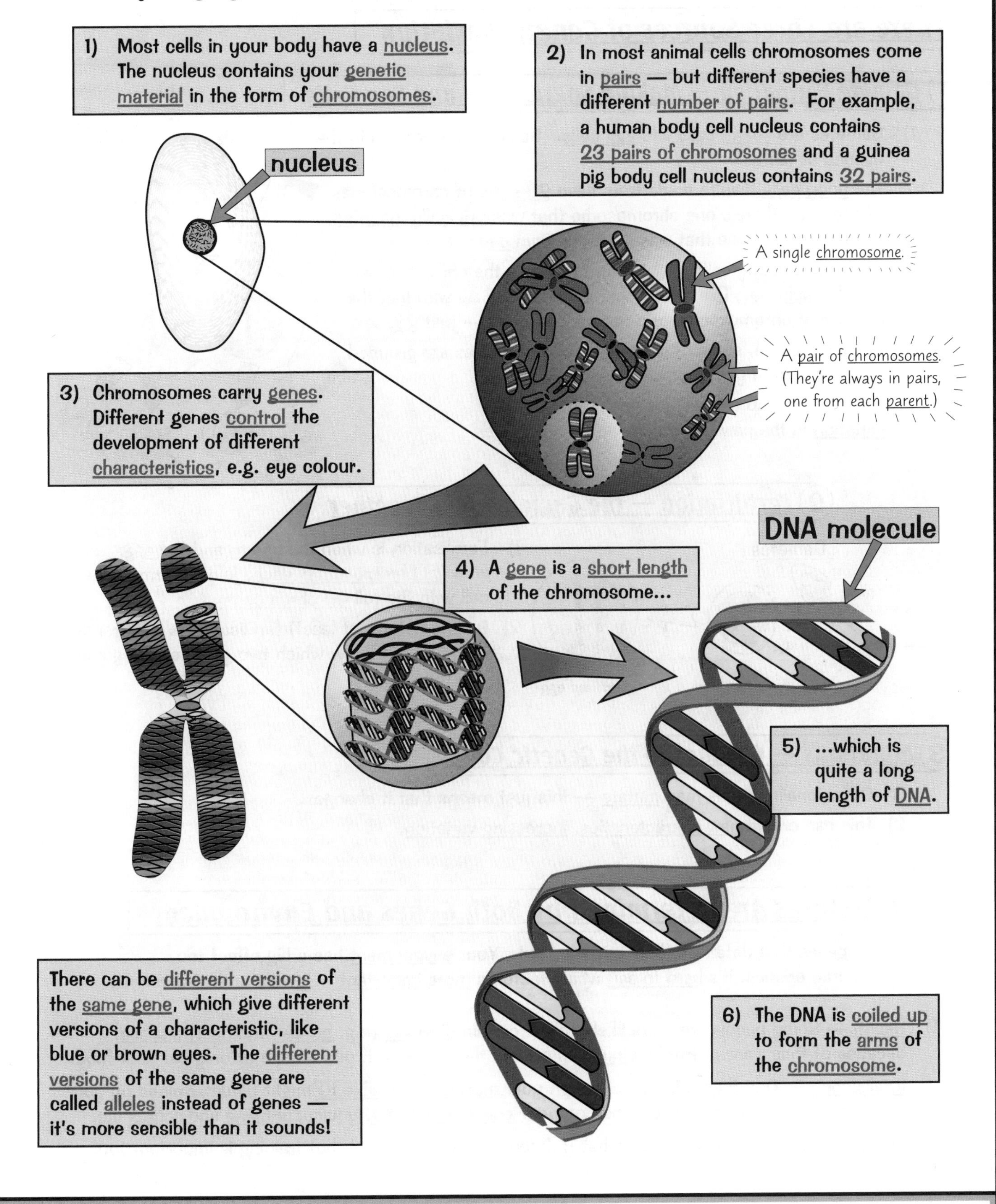

It's hard being a DNA molecule, there's so much to remember...

This is the bare bones of genetics, so you definitely need to understand everything on this page or you'll find the rest of this topic dead hard. The best way to get all of these important facts engraved in your mind is to cover the page, scribble down the main points and sketch out the diagrams...

Genetic Variation

Everyone (except identical twins) has different genes to everyone else. There are a few reasons why, so stick with me. If that wasn't enough, the environment also affects how we turn out. Sheesh.

There are Three Sources of Genetic Variation

1) Gamete Formation — Making Sperm Cells and Egg Cells

1) Gametes are sperm cells and egg cells. Gametes are formed in the ovaries or testes.
2) The body cells they're made from have 23 pairs of chromosomes. In each pair there's one chromosome that was originally inherited from mum, and one that was inherited from dad.
3) When these body cells split to form gametes the chromosomes are also split up. This means that gametes end up with half the number of chromosomes of a normal body cell — just 23.
4) In each gamete, some of your dad's chromosomes are grouped with some from your mum.
5) This shuffling up of chromosomes leads to variation in the new generation.

Body cell with its pairs of chromosomes.

(Blue chromosomes are from mum.)
(Red chromosomes are from dad.)

These are the gametes.

2) Fertilisation — the Gametes Join Together

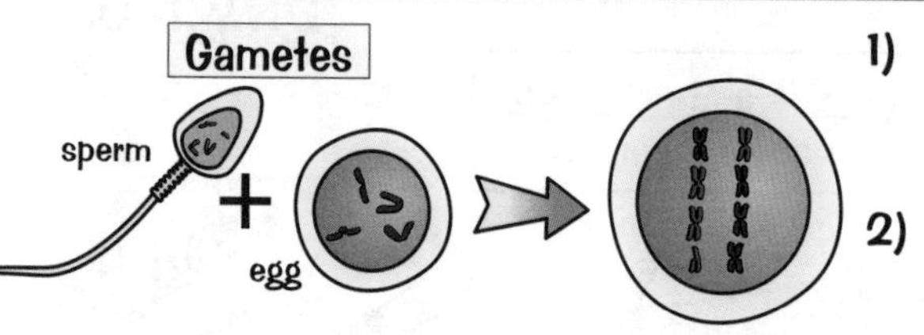

1) Fertilisation is when the sperm and the egg, with 23 chromosomes each, join to form a new cell with the full 46 chromosomes.
2) But (in nature, at least) fertilisation is a bit random — you don't know which two gametes are going to join together.

3) Mutations — Changes to the Genetic Code

1) Occasionally a gene may mutate — this just means that it changes.
2) This can create new characteristics, increasing variation.

Most Features Are Determined by Both Genes and Environment

It's not just genes that determine how you turn out. Your environment has a big effect too.
For some characteristics, it's hard to say which factor is more important — genes or environment...

1) Health — Some people are more likely to get certain diseases (e.g. cancer and heart disease) because of their genes. But lifestyle also affects the risk, e.g. if you smoke or only eat junk food.
2) Intelligence — One theory is that although your maximum possible IQ might be determined by your genes, whether you get to it depends on your environment, e.g. your upbringing and school life.
3) Sporting ability — Again, genes probably determine your potential, but training is important too.

So if you weren't picked for netball — blame your parents...

So in sexual reproduction a mixture of chromosomes is randomly shuffled into gametes.
Then a random gamete fuses with another random gamete at fertilisation (oh, the romance of it all).

Genetic Diagrams

In the exam they could ask about the inheritance of any kind of characteristic that's controlled by a single gene. Luckily, the basic idea's always the same, whatever the gene...

Genetic Diagrams Show the Possible Genes of Offspring

1) Alleles are different versions of the same gene.
2) Most of the time you have two of each gene (i.e. two alleles) — one from each parent.
3) If the alleles are different you have instructions for two different versions of a characteristic (e.g. blue eyes or brown eyes), but you only show one version of the two (e.g. brown eyes). The version of the characteristic that appears is caused by the dominant allele. The other allele is said to be recessive. The recessive allele is only expressed if there's no dominant allele present.
4) In genetic diagrams letters are used to represent genes. Dominant alleles are always shown with a capital letter, and recessive alleles with a small letter.
5) If you're homozygous for a trait you have two alleles the same for that particular gene, e.g. CC or cc. If you're heterozygous for a trait you have two different alleles for that particular gene, e.g. Cc.
6) Your genetic makeup (i.e. the alleles you have for a particular gene) is known as your genotype. The characteristics that these alleles produce (e.g. brown eyes) is known as your phenotype.

You Need to be Able to Interpret, Explain and Construct Them

Imagine you're cross-breeding hamsters, and that some have a normal, boring disposition while others have a leaning towards crazy acrobatics. And suppose you know the behaviour is due to one gene...

Let's say that the allele which causes the crazy nature is recessive — so use a 'b'.
And normal (boring) behaviour is due to a dominant allele — call it 'B'.

1) For an organism to display a recessive characteristic, both its alleles must be recessive — so a crazy hamster must have the alleles 'bb' (i.e. it must be homozygous for this trait).
2) However, a normal hamster could be BB (homozygous) or Bb (heterozygous), because the dominant allele (B) overrules the recessive one (b).
3) Here's what happens if you breed from two heterozygous hamsters:

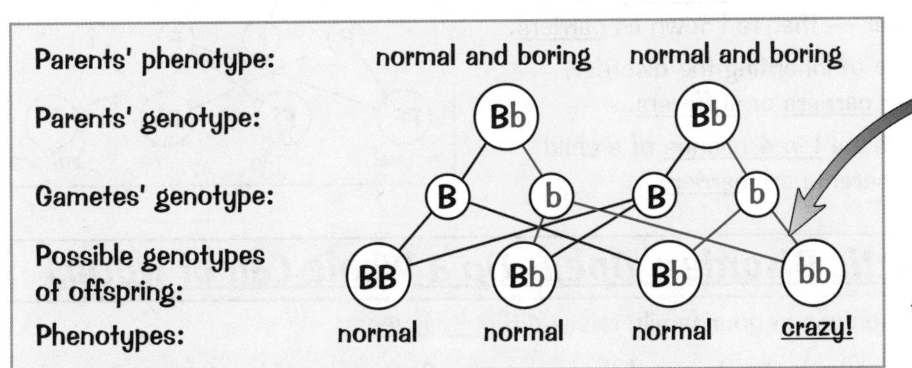

The lines show all the possible ways the parents' alleles could combine. Remember, only one of these possibilities would actually happen for any one offspring.

When you breed two organisms together to look at a characteristic that's controlled by one gene, it's called a MONOHYBRID CROSS.

There's a 75% chance of having a normal, boring hamster, and a 25% chance of a crazy one. (To put that another way... you'd expect a 3:1 ratio of normal:crazy hamsters.)

4) This is a genetic diagram too — it shows exactly the same thing as the one above. Diagrams like these are called Punnett squares.

Parent's genotype: Bb (columns); Parent's genotype: Bb (rows); Possible offspring:

	B	b
B	BB	Bb
b	Bb	bb

It's not just hamsters that have the wild and scratty allele...

...my sister definitely has it too. Remember, 'results' like this are only probabilities. It doesn't mean it'll actually happen. (If you have my luck, you'll end up trying to contain a mini-riot of nine lunatic baby hamsters.)

Sex Inheritance and Genetic Disorders

There's a lot to learn about genes and inheritance. This is the last page though, I promise.

Your Chromosomes Control Whether You're Male or Female

There are 23 matched pairs of chromosomes in every human body cell. The 23rd pair are labelled XY. They're the two chromosomes that decide whether you turn out male or female.

All men have an X and a Y chromosome: XY
The Y chromosome causes male characteristics.

All women have two X chromosomes: XX
The XX combination causes female characteristics.

This is true for all mammals, but not for some other organisms, e.g. plants.

There's an Equal Chance of Having a Boy or a Girl...

...and there's a genetic diagram to prove it.

Even though we're talking about inheriting chromosomes here and not single genes, the genetic diagram still works the same way.

When you plug all the letters into the diagram, it shows that there are two XX results and two XY results, so there's the same probability of getting a boy or a girl.

Don't forget that this 50:50 ratio is only a probability. If you had four kids they could all be boys.

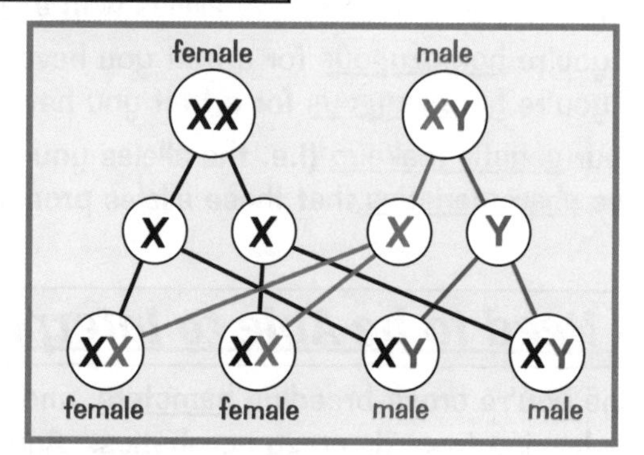

Genetic (Inherited) Disorders are Caused by Faulty Genes

Here's an example: cystic fibrosis is a genetic disorder that causes the body to produce a lot of thick, sticky mucus in the air passages and in the pancreas.

1) The allele which causes cystic fibrosis is a recessive allele, 'f', carried by about 1 person in 25.
2) Because it's recessive, people with only one copy of the allele won't have the disorder — they're known as carriers.
3) For a child to have a chance of inheriting the disorder, both parents must be either carriers or sufferers.
4) As the diagram shows, there's a 1 in 4 chance of a child having the disorder if both parents are carriers.

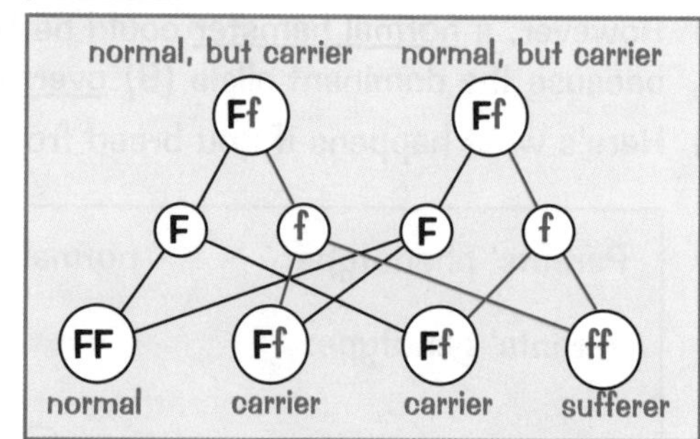

Knowing About Genetic Disorders Opens Up a Whole Can of Worms

Knowing there are inherited conditions in your family raises difficult issues:

- Should all family members be tested to see if they're carriers? Some people might prefer not to know, but is this fair on any partners or future children they might have?
- Is it right for someone who's at risk of passing on a genetic condition to have children? Is it fair to put them under pressure not to, if they decide they want children?
- It's possible to test a foetus for some genetic conditions while it's still in the womb. But if the test is positive, is it right to terminate the pregnancy? The family might not be able to cope with a sick or disabled child, but why should that child have a lesser right to life than a healthy child? Some people think abortion is always wrong under any circumstances.

What do you get when you cross a snowman with a vampire?

...frostbite. There are lots of other genetic disorders — e.g. red-green colour blindness and sickle cell anaemia. To work out the chance of any inherited disorders being passed on, follow the same method.

Revision Summary for Module B1

That was a long section, but kind of interesting, I reckon. These questions will show what you know and what you don't... if you get stuck, have a look back to remind yourself. But before the exam, make sure you can do all of them without any help — that's the only way you'll know you're ready.

1) What's the difference between 'fit' and 'healthy'? Can you be one without being the other?
2)* Below are the blood pressure measurements of a group of smokers and a group of non-smokers.

Group A	Person 1	Person 2	Person 3	Person 4	Person 5	Person 6
Systolic pressure (mm Hg)	126	100	110	110	114	112
Diastolic pressure (mm Hg)	84	72	60	78	66	68

Group B	Person 1	Person 2	Person 3	Person 4	Person 5	Person 6
Systolic pressure (mm Hg)	138	150	122	118	120	116
Diastolic pressure (mm Hg)	100	100	80	78	84	68

a) Is Group A likely to be smokers or non-smokers? Explain your answer.
b) How many of the smokers would be considered to have high blood pressure?
c) What would you advise these smokers to do to help reduce their blood pressure?

3) Explain one way that smoking can increase blood pressure.
4) How do narrow arteries increase the risk of a heart attack?
5) Explain why plant proteins are called 'second class proteins'.
6) Explain what causes the condition called kwashiorkor.
Why is this condition more common in developing countries?
7) Explain how psychological disorders can cause under-nutrition.
8) What is the meaning of the term 'parasite'?
9) Explain how antibodies destroy pathogens.
10) Explain how immunisation stops you getting infections.
11) Explain the difference between benign and malignant tumours.
12) What is a double blind clinical trial?
13) What effect does a stimulant have on brain activity? Give two examples of stimulants.
14) Describe how drinking too much alcohol can damage your liver.
15) Explain why smoking can give you a 'smoker's cough'.
16) Describe the path of light through the eye.
17) Describe the path taken by a reflex arc.
18) Draw a diagram of a typical motor neurone, labelling all its parts.
19) Explain how negative feedback helps to maintain a constant internal environment.
20) Describe how body temperature is reduced when you're too hot.
21) Explain how insulin controls blood sugar levels.
22) What is the difference between how type 1 and type 2 diabetes are usually controlled?
23) What are auxins?
24) Shoots are negatively geotropic. How are auxins responsible for this?
25) Give three ways that plant growth hormones are used commercially.
26) How many pairs of chromosomes are there in most human body cells?
27) What is an allele?
28) Name three sources of genetic variation.
29) Why is your ability at sport determined by both your genes and your environment?
30)* Draw a genetic diagram for a cross between a man with blue eyes (bb) and a woman who has green eyes (Bb). The gene for blue eyes (b) is recessive.
31) Which chromosomes determine your gender? Draw a genetic diagram showing that there's an equal chance of a baby being a boy or a girl.

* Answers on p.124

Classification

It seems to be a basic human urge to want to classify things — that's the case in biology anyway...

Classification is Organising Living Organisms into Groups

1) Classification systems are important in science because they help us to understand how organisms are related (evolutionary relationships) and how they interact with each other (ecological relationships).
2) Classification systems can be natural or artificial:

   Natural classification systems are based on the evolutionary relationships and genetic similarities between organisms.

   Artificial classification systems are based on appearance rather than genes. They're used to identify organisms.

3) Living things are divided into kingdoms (e.g. the plant kingdom).
4) The kingdoms are then subdivided into smaller and smaller groups — phylum, class, order, family, genus, species.

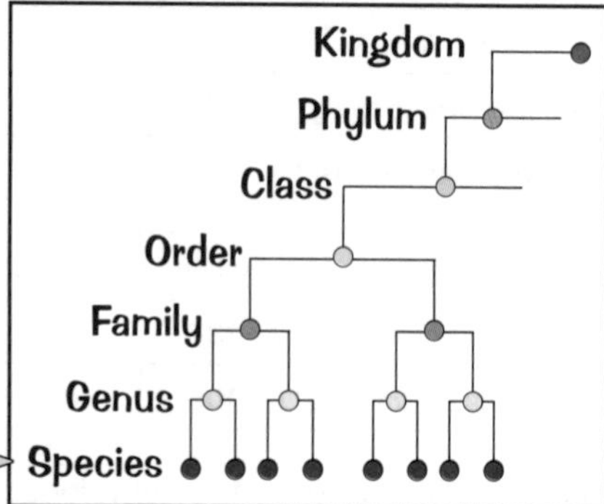

5) A genus is a group of closely-related species — and a species is a group of organisms that can interbreed to produce fertile offspring (see the next page).
6) It can be difficult to classify organisms into these distinct groups though because many organisms share characteristics of multiple groups.

Classification Systems Change Over Time

1) When a classification system is created it fits everything we know so far about different groups of organisms.
2) But as scientists discover new species (and learn more about the species that they've already discovered) they might have to adapt classification systems to fit their new findings:

- Newly discovered species might not really fit into any of the categories. These could be living species or newly discovered fossils, e.g. the archaeopteryx fossil has features of two different classes (birds and reptiles), so it's hard to know where to place it.
- DNA sequencing allows us to see genetic differences between different groups. As this data is collected, we might find out that two groups aren't actually as closely related as we'd thought — or two groups that we thought were very different might turn out to be close relatives.

Evolutionary Relationships can be Shown with Evolutionary Trees

1) You can draw evolutionary trees to show how closely related different species are to each other. It's just like drawing a family tree.
2) Evolutionary trees show common ancestors and relationships between species. The more recent the common ancestor, the more closely related the two species — and the more characteristics they're likely to share.
3) To find out about the evolutionary relationships between organisms, scientists analyse lots of different genes responsible for lots of different characteristics.
4) Studying lots of characteristics for a large group of organisms involves analysing huge amounts of DNA data and is only really possible thanks to advances in ICT.

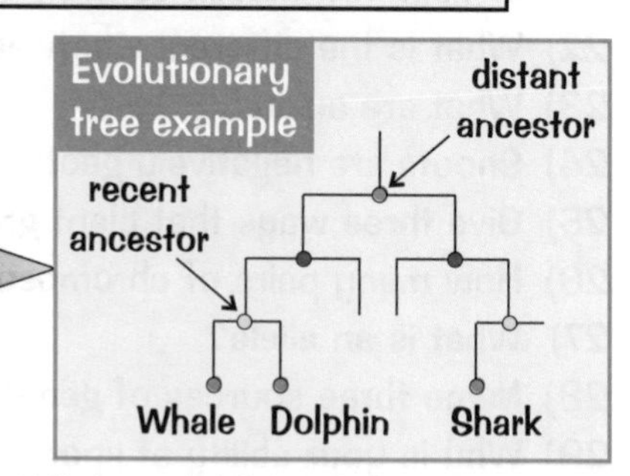

Whales and dolphins have a recent common ancestor so are closely related. They're both more distantly related to sharks.

Every evolutionary tree has a few bad apples...

There are loads of different types of organisms out there — so no wonder classification systems can get a bit unwieldy. This makes life no easier for you, I'm afraid — you've got to know about classification for your exam.

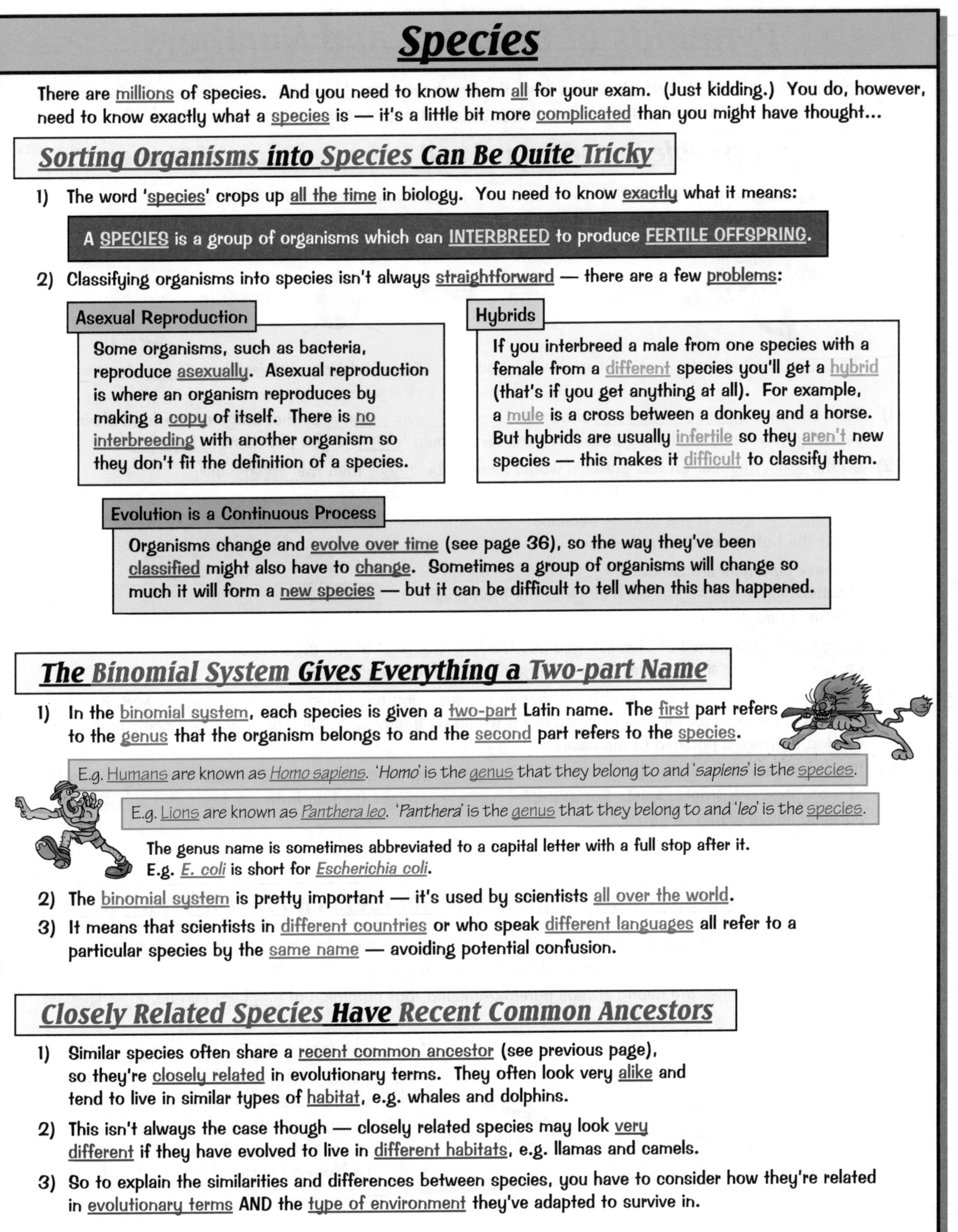

Species

There are millions of species. And you need to know them all for your exam. (Just kidding.) You do, however, need to know exactly what a species is — it's a little bit more complicated than you might have thought...

Sorting Organisms into Species Can Be Quite Tricky

1) The word 'species' crops up all the time in biology. You need to know exactly what it means:

A SPECIES is a group of organisms which can INTERBREED to produce FERTILE OFFSPRING.

2) Classifying organisms into species isn't always straightforward — there are a few problems:

Asexual Reproduction

Some organisms, such as bacteria, reproduce asexually. Asexual reproduction is where an organism reproduces by making a copy of itself. There is no interbreeding with another organism so they don't fit the definition of a species.

Hybrids

If you interbreed a male from one species with a female from a different species you'll get a hybrid (that's if you get anything at all). For example, a mule is a cross between a donkey and a horse. But hybrids are usually infertile so they aren't new species — this makes it difficult to classify them.

Evolution is a Continuous Process

Organisms change and evolve over time (see page 36), so the way they've been classified might also have to change. Sometimes a group of organisms will change so much it will form a new species — but it can be difficult to tell when this has happened.

The Binomial System Gives Everything a Two-part Name

1) In the binomial system, each species is given a two-part Latin name. The first part refers to the genus that the organism belongs to and the second part refers to the species.

E.g. Humans are known as *Homo sapiens*. '*Homo*' is the genus that they belong to and '*sapiens*' is the species.

E.g. Lions are known as *Panthera leo*. '*Panthera*' is the genus that they belong to and '*leo*' is the species.

The genus name is sometimes abbreviated to a capital letter with a full stop after it. E.g. *E. coli* is short for *Escherichia coli*.

2) The binomial system is pretty important — it's used by scientists all over the world.
3) It means that scientists in different countries or who speak different languages all refer to a particular species by the same name — avoiding potential confusion.

Closely Related Species Have Recent Common Ancestors

1) Similar species often share a recent common ancestor (see previous page), so they're closely related in evolutionary terms. They often look very alike and tend to live in similar types of habitat, e.g. whales and dolphins.
2) This isn't always the case though — closely related species may look very different if they have evolved to live in different habitats, e.g. llamas and camels.
3) So to explain the similarities and differences between species, you have to consider how they're related in evolutionary terms AND the type of environment they've adapted to survive in.

Binomial system — uh oh, sounds like maths...

It's possible to breed lions and tigers together — it's true — they produce hybrids called tigons and ligers. They look a bit like lions and a bit like tigers... as you'd expect. In the same way, a bat is (probably) just a hybrid of a bird and a cat. And a donkey is the result of breeding a dog and a monkey. Really, I swear.

Pyramids of Biomass and Numbers

A trophic level is a feeding level. It comes from the Greek word trophe meaning 'nourishment'. The amount of energy, biomass and usually the number of organisms all decrease as you move up a trophic level.

You Need to be able to Understand and Draw Pyramids of Biomass

Luckily it's pretty easy — they'll give you all the information you need to do it in the exam.
Here's an example of a food chain you might be given:

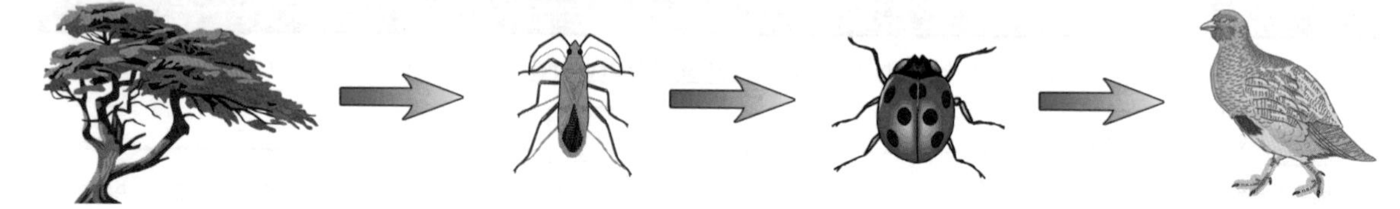

1000 kg of pear tree feeds... 5 kg of aphids which feeds... 1.5 kg of ladybirds which feeds... 0.5 kg of partridge.

These figures are the 'dry biomass' for each organism — see below.

1) Each bar on a pyramid of biomass shows the mass of living material at that stage of the food chain — basically how much all the organisms at each level would 'weigh' if you put them all together.
2) So the 'pear tree' bar on this pyramid would need to be longer than the 'aphids' bar, which in turn should be longer than the 'ladybirds' bar... and so on.
3) The pear tree goes at the bottom because it's at the bottom of the food chain.
4) Biomass pyramids are almost always pyramid-shaped because biomass is lost at each stage in the food chain (see next page).

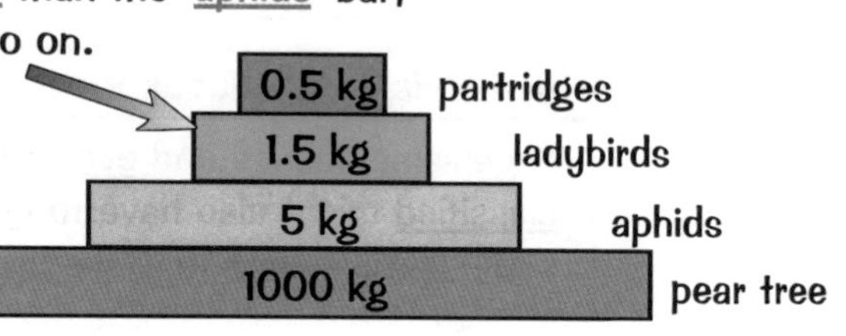

5) To construct a pyramid of biomass you use the 'dry biomass' of the organisms, i.e. you'd dry out all the water from the organisms before weighing them.
6) Measuring dry biomass can be difficult though because you have to kill the organisms to work it out. This might be okay for an area of grass but it would be unethical to kill lots of animals every time you wanted to make a pyramid of biomass.
7) It can sometimes be difficult to construct an accurate pyramid of biomass because some organisms feed at more than one trophic level. For example, partridges might feed on both ladybirds and aphids so the pyramid above would be wrong.

Pyramids of Biomass and Pyramids of Numbers can be Different Shapes

1) Pyramids of numbers are similar to pyramids of biomass, but each bar on a pyramid of numbers shows the number of organisms at that stage of the food chain — not their mass.
2) Pyramids of biomass are nearly always pyramid-shaped, but pyramids of numbers can be other shapes:

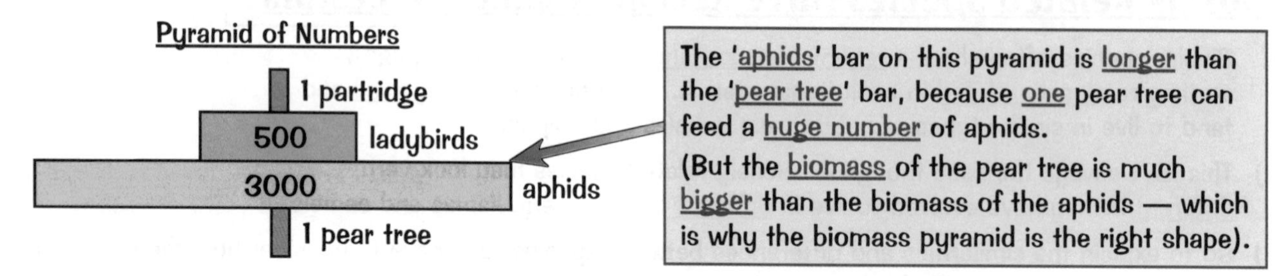

Constructing pyramids is a breeze — just ask the Egyptians...

If you're drawing a pyramid to scale, make sure you know exactly how much room you're going to need before you start. Trust me — there's nothing worse than drawing a lovely bar representing 1000 kg of apple tree, then realising you haven't got enough space to fit the earwigs in. Just thinking about it's making me feel uneasy...

Energy Transfer and Energy Flow

Organisms need to get their energy from somewhere. Producers can capture their own (by photosynthesis) but everything else has to eat to get it. You need to know about how it's passed on.

All That Energy Just Disappears Somehow...

1) Energy from the Sun is the source of energy for nearly all life on Earth.
2) Plants use a small percentage of the light energy from the Sun to make food during photosynthesis. This energy then works its way through the food chain as animals eat the plants and each other.
3) The energy lost at each stage is used for staying alive, i.e. in respiration, which powers all life processes.
4) Most of this energy is eventually lost to the surroundings as heat. This is especially true for mammals and birds, whose bodies must be kept at a constant temperature which is normally higher than their surroundings.
5) Material and energy are also lost from the food chain as waste products. Egestion is when food that can't be digested passes out as faeces. Excretion is when the waste products of bodily processes are released e.g. urine.
6) Waste products and uneaten parts (e.g. bones) can become starting points for other food chains. For example, houseflies just love to eat faeces. Yum.

Material and energy are both lost at each stage of the food chain. This explains why you get biomass pyramids. Most of the biomass is lost and so does not become biomass in the next level up. It also explains why you hardly ever get food chains with more than about five trophic levels. So much energy is lost at each stage that there's not enough left to support more organisms after four or five stages.

You Need to be Able to Interpret Data on Energy Flow

rosebush: 80 000 kJ greenfly: 10 000 kJ ladybird: 900 kJ bird: 40 kJ

1) The numbers show the amount of energy available to the next level. So 80 000 kJ is the amount of energy available to the greenfly, and 10 000 kJ is the amount available to the ladybird.
2) You can work out how much energy has been lost at each level by taking away the energy that is available to the next level from the energy that was available from the previous level. Like this:

   Energy lost at 1st trophic level as heat and waste products = 80 000 kJ – 10 000 kJ = 70 000 kJ.
3) You can also calculate the efficiency of energy transfer — this just means how good it is at passing on energy from one level to the next.

$$\text{efficiency} = \frac{\text{energy available to the next level}}{\text{energy that was available to the previous level}} \times 100$$

So at the 1st trophic level, efficiency of energy transfer = 10 000 kJ ÷ 80 000 kJ × 100 = 12.5% efficient.

Ah ah ah ah stayin' alive, stayin' alive...

The Bee Gees were definitely on to something — staying alive is important, but it does require a lot of energy. Remember — hardly any of this energy makes it to the next level in the food chain and most of it's lost as heat.

Interactions Between Organisms

Organisms interact in tons of different ways...

Organisms Compete to Survive

1) In order to survive and reproduce, organisms must COMPETE against each other for the resources that they need to live (e.g. food and shelter).
2) Similar organisms in the same habitat will be in the closest competition because they'll be competing for similar ecological niches.

A species' ecological 'niche' is how it fits in to its ecosystem. It depends on things like where the individuals live and what they feed on.

3) There are two types of competition between organisms:

INTERSPECIFIC COMPETITION is where organisms compete for resources against individuals of another species.

INTRASPECIFIC COMPETITION is where organisms compete for resources against individuals of the same species.

4) Intraspecific competition often has a bigger impact on organisms than interspecific competition.
5) This is because individuals of the same species have exactly the same needs, so they'll compete for lots of resources. E.g. a blue tit might compete with another blue tit for food, shelter and a mate, but a blue tit and a great tit might only compete for the same food source.

Populations of Prey and Predators Go in Cycles

In a community containing prey and predators (as most of them do of course):

1) The population of any species is usually limited by the amount of food available.
2) If the population of the prey increases, then so will the population of the predators.
3) However as the population of predators increases, the number of prey will decrease.

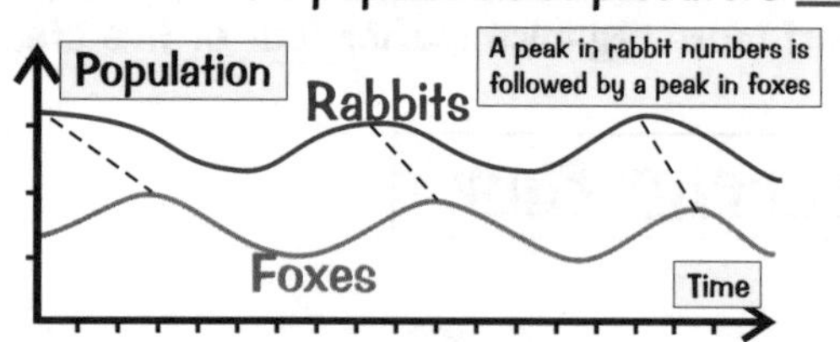

E.g. More grass means more rabbits.
More rabbits means more foxes.
But more foxes means fewer rabbits.
Eventually fewer rabbits will mean fewer foxes again.
This up and down pattern continues...

4) Predator-prey cycles are always out of phase with each other. This is because it takes a while for one population to respond to changes in the other population. E.g. when the number of rabbits goes up, the number of foxes doesn't increase immediately because it takes time for them to reproduce.

Parasitic and Mutualistic Relationships are Other Types of Interactions

Some organisms depend entirely on other species to survive. So where an organism lives and its abundance (population size) is often influenced by the distribution and abundance of these species.

1) PARASITES live off a host. They take what they need to survive, without giving anything back. This often harms the host — which makes it a win-lose situation.

- Tapeworms absorb lots of nutrients from the host, causing them to suffer from malnutrition.
- Fleas are parasites. Dogs gain nothing from having fleas (unless you count hundreds of bites).

2) MUTUALISM is a relationship where both organisms benefit — so it's a win-win relationship.

- 'Cleaner species' e.g. oxpeckers live on the backs of buffalo. Not only do they eat pests on the buffalo, like ticks, flies and maggots (providing the oxpeckers with a source of food), but they also alert the animal to any predators that are near, by hissing.
- Lots of plants are pollinated by insects, allowing them to reproduce. In return, the insects get a sip of sweet, sugary nectar.

Adaptations

If that stuff about parasites and fleas left you scratching your head (groan), then you'll be pleased to read about something a bit different. The next few pages are about adaptation. Oh boy...

Adaptations Help Organisms to Survive

1) Adaptations are the features that organisms have that make them better suited to their environment.
2) Organisms that are adapted to their environment are better able to compete for resources.
3) This means that they're more likely to survive, reproduce and pass on their adaptations to their offspring.

Organisms can be Specialists or Generalists

SPECIALISTS are organisms which are highly-adapted to survive in a SPECIFIC HABITAT. For example giant pandas are adapted to eat just bamboo.

GENERALISTS are organisms that are adapted to survive in a RANGE OF DIFFERENT HABITATS. For example black rats are able to survive in forests, cities and in areas of farmland.

1) In a habitat where the conditions are stable (i.e. they're not changing), specialists will out-compete generalists as they're better adapted to the specific conditions.
2) But if the conditions in the habitat change (e.g. a species of prey becomes extinct), specialists will be out-competed by generalists. Specialists won't be adapted to the new conditions, but generalists are adapted to a range of conditions so will be more likely to survive.

Some Organisms Have Biochemical Adaptations to Extreme Conditions

1) Some organisms can tolerate extreme conditions, e.g. a very high or low pH or temperature.
2) Organisms that are adapted to live in seriously extreme conditions (like super hot volcanic vents or at high pressure on the sea bed) are called extremophiles.
3) In order to survive these sorts of harsh conditions, organisms have some pretty nifty adaptations:

Example 1

- Extremophile bacteria that live in very hot environments have enzymes that work best at a much higher optimum temperature than enzymes from other organisms.
- These enzymes are able to function normally at temperatures that would denature (destroy) enzymes from other organisms. For example, the bacteria *Thermus thermophilus* grows best in environments where the temperature is about 65°C.

Example 2

- Organisms that live in very cold environments sometimes have special antifreeze proteins.
- These proteins interfere with the formation and growth of ice crystals in the cells, stopping the cells from being damaged by ice.

Doctor doctor, I only eat bamboo...

I think you need to talk to a specialist about that...

The wolf in Little Red Riding Hood had some great adaptations for eating children — big eyes for seeing, big ears for hearing and big sharp teeth for biting. The one adaptation it was missing was an axe-proof exoskeleton.

Adaptations to Cold Environments

Different organisms are adapted to cope with different temperatures. They need to make sure they're not too hot or too cold, otherwise the enzymes controlling the reactions in their cells will go haywire.

Some Organisms Have Adapted to Living in Cold Environments

1) Organisms that live in cold environments have a whole host of adaptations to help them survive.
2) Most adaptations to cold environments are based on reducing heat loss to the environment.

Anatomical Adaptations Can Reduce Heat Loss

Anatomical adaptations are features of an organism's anatomy (body structure) that help it to survive. Anatomical adaptations to the cold include:

1) Having a thick coat or a layer of blubber to insulate the body and trap heat in.
2) Having a large size and compact body shape to give a small surface area to volume ratio. This reduces heat loss as less body heat can be lost through the surface of the skin.

SURFACE AREA TO VOLUME RATIOS

- A surface area to volume ratio is just a way of comparing how much surface area something has compared to it's size.
- Small objects have larger surface area to volume ratios than large objects.
- In cold environments, large organisms lose less heat to their surroundings than small organisms — because of their smaller surface area to volume ratio.

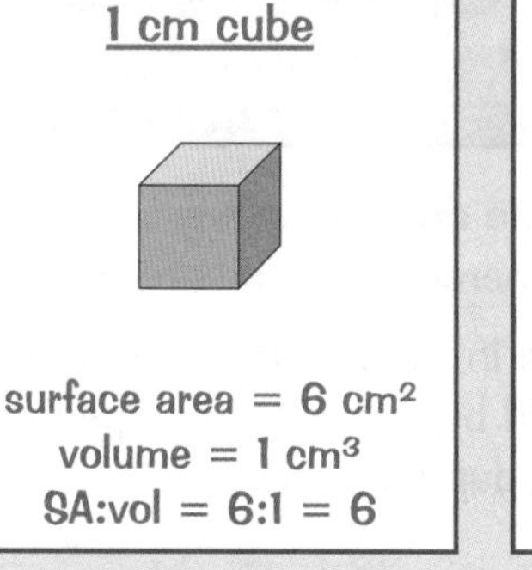

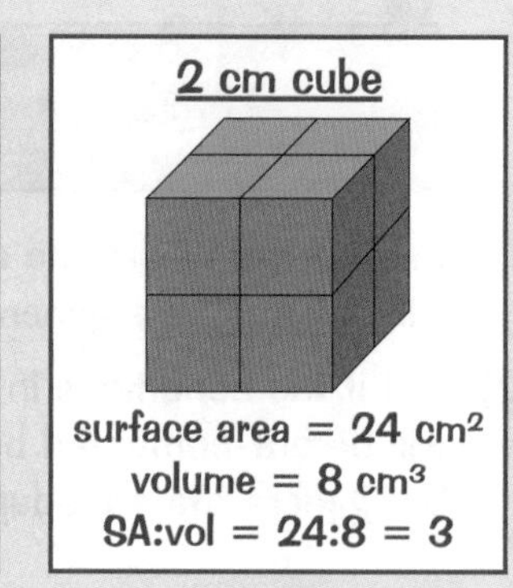

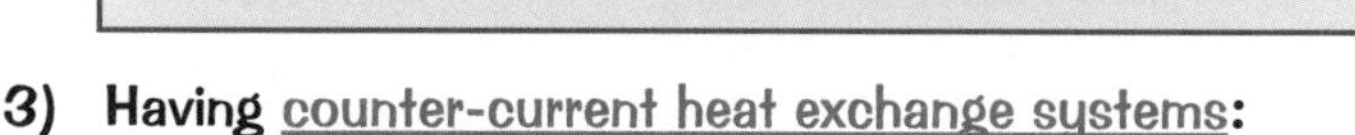

3) Having counter-current heat exchange systems:
   - Animals like penguins have to stand on cold ice all day.
   - Blood vessels going to and from the feet carry blood that flows in opposite directions.
   - The vessels pass close to each other, allowing heat to transfer between them.
   - Warm blood flowing in arteries to the feet heats cold blood returning to the heart in the veins.
   - This means that the feet stay cold, but it stops cold blood from cooling down the rest of the body.

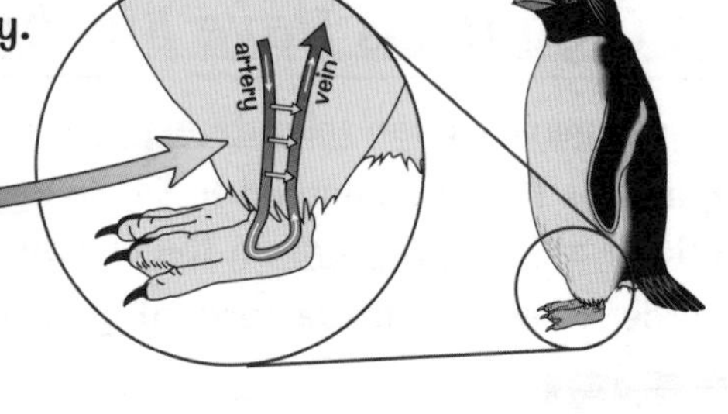

Some Organisms Also Have Behavioural Adaptations to the Cold

1) Many species migrate to warmer climates during the winter months to avoid having to cope with the cold conditions.
2) Other species hibernate during the winter months. This saves energy as the animal doesn't have to find food or keep itself as warm as if it was active.
3) Some species (like penguins) huddle together to keep warm.

I'm boiling.

Now I know why Dad refuses to put the heating on...

It's not his fault he's got a smaller surface area to volume ratio than me. He's just lucky to be so well adapted to the cold — what with his thick layer of blubber and hairy shoulders to keep him warm. It's just not fair. Make sure you've got surface area to volume ratios sussed — you'll need them on the next page too.

Adaptations to Hot and Dry Environments

Brrrrr. Trying to survive in freezing conditions isn't easy, but keeping your cool when it's hot and stuffy is no walk in the park either...

Some Organisms Have Adapted to Living in Hot Environments

Keeping cool in hot environments is all about increasing heat loss and reducing heat gain.

Behavioural Adaptations Can Increase Heat Loss and Reduce Heat Gain

1) Animals that live in very hot climates often spend the day in the shade or underground to minimise the amount of heat their bodies gain from their surroundings.
2) Animals can also reduce their heat gain by being active at night, when it is much cooler.
3) Animals can increase heat loss by bathing in water. As the water evaporates it transfers heat from the skin to the surroundings, cooling the animal down.

Anatomical Adaptations Can Also Increase Heat Loss

1) Animals that are adapted to survive in hot environments are often small. This gives them a large surface area to volume ratio (see previous page), which allows them to lose more body heat to their surroundings.
2) Other adaptations, like having large ears, can also increase an animal's surface area to volume ratio and help them to lose heat. Large thin ears allow more blood to flow near the surface of the skin — so more heat from the blood can be radiated to the surroundings.
3) Some animals (e.g. camels) store fat in just one part of the body (e.g. the camel's hump) — this stops the rest of the body from being too well insulated and allows heat to be lost more easily.

Some Organisms Have Adapted to Living in Dry Environments

Organisms that live in dry environments have to be adapted to minimise the amount of water that they lose to the environment.

Some desert plants...

1) ... have a rounded shape, giving them a small surface area to volume ratio to minimise water loss from the surface.
2) ... have a thick waxy layer (called a cuticle) and spines instead of leaves to further reduce water loss.
3) ... store water in their stems to allow them to survive in times of extreme drought.
4) ... have shallow, but very extensive, roots to ensure water is absorbed quickly over a large area.

Some desert animals...

1) ... have specialised kidneys that allow them to produce very concentrated urine, with a very low water content.
2) ... have no sweat glands, preventing them from losing water through sweating.
3) ... spend lots of time in underground burrows, where the air contains more moisture than on the surface.

That's a lovely cravat — no it's not, it's a cacti...

Remember, a large surface area compared to volume increases heat loss — which is great for organisms living in hot environments. But it also means water is lost more easily — not so great in dry environments.

Evolution and Speciation

Evolution is where species change slowly over time. It's the genetic variation between the individuals of a species that makes evolution possible.

Only the Fittest Survive

Charles Darwin came up with a really important theory about evolution.
It's called the theory of natural selection:

Charles Darwin

1) Darwin knew that organisms in a species show wide variation. He also knew that organisms have to compete for limited resources in an ecosystem.
2) Darwin concluded that the organisms that are the best adapted (the fittest) would be more successful competitors and would be more likely to survive. This idea is called the 'survival of the fittest'.
3) The successful organisms that survive are more likely to reproduce and pass on the adaptations that made them successful to their offspring.
4) The organisms that are less well adapted would be less likely to survive and reproduce, so they are less likely to pass on their characteristics to the next generation.
5) Over time, successful adaptations become more common in the population and the species changes — it evolves.

New Discoveries Have Helped to Develop the Theory of Natural Selection

1) Darwin's theory wasn't perfect — he couldn't give a good explanation for why new characteristics appeared or exactly how individual organisms passed on beneficial adaptations to their offspring.
2) That's because DNA wasn't discovered until 50 years after his theory was published.
3) We now know that adaptations are controlled by genes. New adaptations arise because of mutations (changes in DNA). Successful adaptations are passed on to future generations in the genes that parents contribute to their offspring.

The Development of a New Species is Called Speciation

1) Over a long period of time, organisms may change so much because of natural selection that a completely new species is formed. This is called speciation.
2) Speciation happens when populations of the same species change enough to become reproductively isolated — this means that they can't interbreed to produce fertile offspring.
3) Reproductive isolation can be caused by geographic isolation. Here's how:

- A physical barrier divides a population of a species, e.g. a river changes its course. The two new populations are unable to mix.
- Different mutations create different new features in the two groups of organisms.
- Natural selection works on the new features so that, if they are of benefit, they spread through each of the populations.
- Since conditions on each side of the barrier will be slightly different, the features that are beneficial will be different for each population.
- Eventually, individuals from the two populations will have such different features that they won't be able to breed together to produce fertile offspring. They'll have become reproductively isolated and the two groups will be separate species.

"Natural selection" — sounds like vegan chocolates...

Natural selection's all about the organisms with the best characteristics surviving to pass on their genes so that the whole species ends up adapted to its environment. It doesn't happen overnight though.

Theories of Evolution

There's no doubt about it — Darwin was a very intelligent guy. Lots of people didn't agree with his theory though, in fact it made some people downright angry. It's a hard life being a scientist.

Not Everyone Agreed with Darwin...

Darwin's theory of evolution by natural selection was very controversial at the time — for various reasons...

1. The theory went against common religious beliefs about how life on Earth developed — it was the first plausible explanation for our own existence without the need for a "Creator" (God). This was very bad news for the religious authorities of the time, who ridiculed his ideas.

2. Darwin couldn't explain why new, useful characteristics appeared or how they were inherited (see previous page).

3. There wasn't enough evidence to convince many scientists, because not many other studies had been done into how organisms change over time.

Lamarck Had a Conflicting Theory of Evolution

Darwin's theory of evolution, which he published in a book called 'On the Origin of Species', wasn't the only one. A French chap called Lamarck had a different idea:

1) Lamarck argued that if a characteristic was used a lot by an animal then it would become more developed. Lamarck reckoned that these acquired characteristics could be passed on to the animal's offspring. For example, if a rabbit did a lot of running and developed big leg muscles, Lamarck believed that the rabbit's offspring would also have big leg muscles.
2) But people eventually concluded that acquired characteristics don't have a genetic basis — so they're unable to be passed on to the next generation. This is why Lamarck's theory was rejected.

Nowadays, Most People Accept Darwin's Theory

The theory of evolution by natural selection is now widely accepted.
Here are a couple of reasons why:

1) The theory has been debated and tested independently by a wide range of scientists, and no-one has managed to conclusively prove that the theory is wrong.
2) The theory offers a plausible explanation for so many observations of plants and animals, e.g. their physical characteristics and behavioural patterns.

For a bit more on how scientists develop theories, see the 'How Science Works' section, page 1.

This stuff's not too tricky — you should find it a walk in Lamarck...

Because his theory turned out to be flawed, it's all too easy to poke fun at Lamarck. Remember though that he was a very smart guy and just happened to get the wrong end of the stick. When he first published it, his work was praised by many other successful scientists. Poor old Lamarck — it wasn't that bad a theory.

The Carbon Cycle and Decomposition

Carbon is constantly moving between the atmosphere, the soil and living things in the carbon cycle.

The Carbon Cycle Shows How Carbon is Recycled

Carbon is an important element in the materials that living things are made from.
It's constantly being recycled in nature:

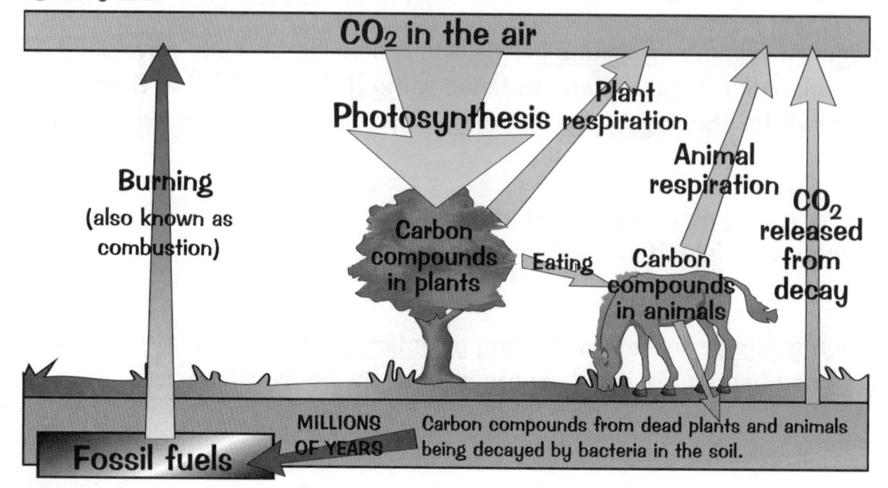

This diagram isn't half as bad as it looks. Learn these important points:

1) There's only one arrow going down. The whole thing is 'powered' by photosynthesis.
2) In photosynthesis plants convert the carbon from CO_2 in the air into sugars. Plants can then incorporate this carbon into other carbohydrates, as well as fats and proteins.
3) Eating passes the carbon compounds in the plant along to animals in a food chain or web.
4) Both plant and animal respiration while the organisms are alive releases CO_2 back into the air.
5) Plants and animals eventually die and decay. They're then broken down by bacteria and fungi in the soil. These decomposers release CO_2 back into the air by respiration as they break down the material.
6) Over millions of years, material from dead plants and animals can also form fossil fuels like coal and oil. When these fossil fuels are burned CO_2 is released back into the air.

Decomposition is Slower in Waterlogged and Acidic Soils

1) Recycling of carbon and other nutrients takes longer in waterlogged soils than in well-drained soils.
2) This is because the bacteria and fungi that decompose organic material usually need oxygen to respire and produce energy. Waterlogged soils don't have much oxygen — so the decomposers have less energy and work more slowly.
3) Nutrient recycling also takes longer in highly acidic soils than in neutral soils. This is because extremes of pH slow down the reproduction of decomposers or kill them outright.

Carbon is Also Recycled in The Sea

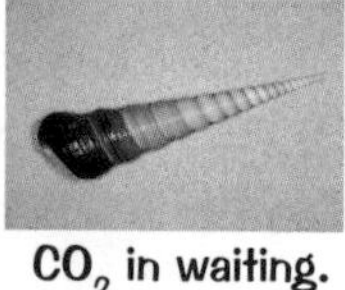

CO_2 in waiting.

1) There's another major recycling pathway for carbon in the sea.
2) Millions of species of marine organisms make shells made of carbonates.
3) When these organisms die the shells fall to the ocean floor and eventually form limestone rocks.
4) The carbon in these rocks returns to the atmosphere as CO_2 during volcanic eruptions or when the rocks are weathered down.
5) The oceans can also absorb large amounts of CO_2, acting as huge stores of carbon called 'carbon sinks'.

Come on out, it's only a little carbon cycle, it can't hurt you...

Much. But if you revise this page you'll be able to beat the carbon questions into submission in the exam. Yay.

The Nitrogen Cycle

Nitrogen, just like carbon, is constantly being recycled. So the nitrogen in your proteins might once have been in the air. And before that it might have been in a plant. Or even in some horse wee. Nice.

Nitrogen is Recycled in the Nitrogen Cycle

1) The atmosphere contains 78% nitrogen gas, N_2. This is very unreactive and so it can't be used directly by plants or animals.
2) Nitrogen is needed for making proteins for growth, so living organisms have to get it somehow.
3) Plants get their nitrogen from the soil, so nitrogen in the air has to be turned into nitrates before plants can use it. Nitrogen compounds are then passed along food chains and webs as animals eat plants (and each other).
4) Decomposers (bacteria and fungi in the soil) break down proteins in rotting plants and animals, and urea in animal waste, into ammonia. This returns the nitrogen compounds to the soil — so the nitrogen in these organisms is recycled.

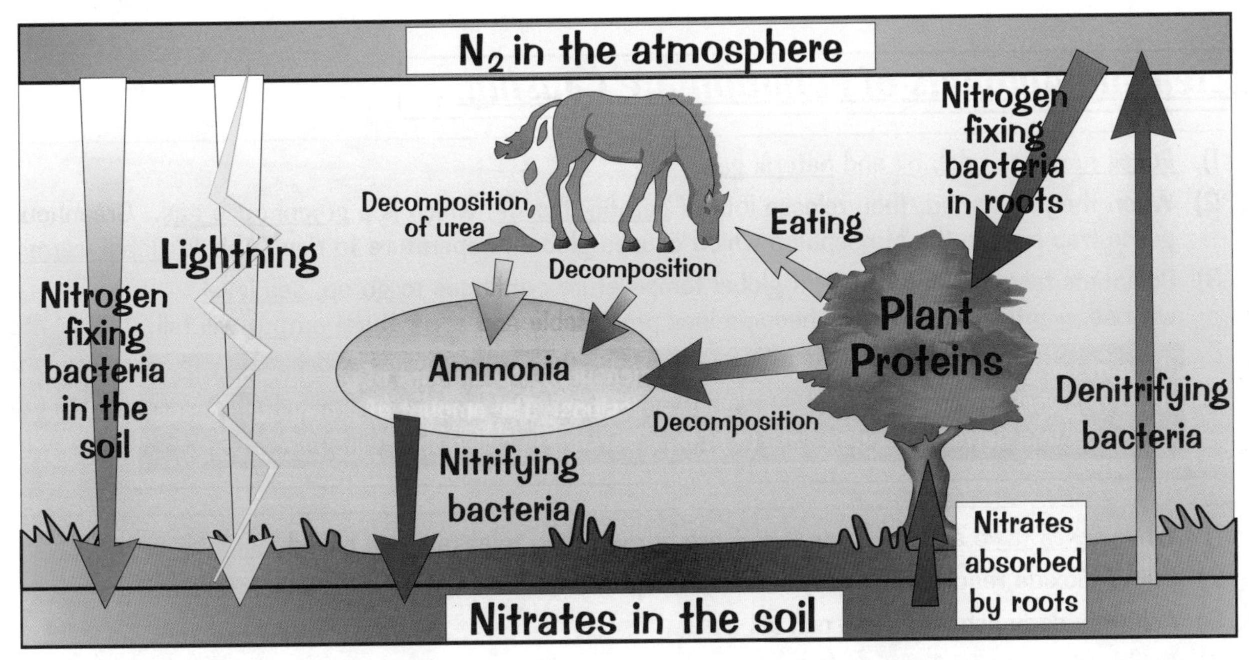

5) Nitrogen fixation isn't an obsession with nitrogen — it's the process of turning N_2 from the air into nitrogen compounds in the soil which plants can use. There are two main ways that this happens:
   a) Lightning — there's so much energy in a bolt of lightning that it's enough to make nitrogen react with oxygen in the air to give nitrates.
   b) Nitrogen-fixing bacteria in roots and soil (see below).
6) There are four different types of bacteria involved in the nitrogen cycle:
   a) DECOMPOSERS — decompose proteins and urea and turn them into ammonia.
   b) NITRIFYING BACTERIA — turn ammonia in decaying matter into nitrates.
   c) NITROGEN-FIXING BACTERIA — turn atmospheric N_2 into nitrogen compounds that plants can use.
   d) DENITRIFYING BACTERIA — turn nitrates back into N_2 gas. This is of no benefit to living organisms.
7) Some nitrogen-fixing bacteria live in the soil. Others live in nodules on the roots of legume plants (e.g. peas and beans). This is why legume plants are so good at putting nitrogen back into the soil. The plants have a mutualistic relationship (see page 32) with the bacteria — the bacteria get food (sugars) from the plant, and the plant gets nitrogen compounds from the bacteria to make into proteins. So the relationship benefits both of them.

It's the cyyyycle of liiiiife...

People sometimes forget that when we breathe in, we're breathing in mainly nitrogen. It's a pretty boring gas, colourless and with no taste or smell. But nitrogen is vital to living things, because the amino acids that join together to make proteins (like enzymes) all contain nitrogen.

Human Impact on the Environment

Pollution is one of the hot topics in the news at the moment (literally, if you're talking global warming).

Human Population is Increasing

1) The world's human population is rising exponentially — which means it's increasing very quickly.
2) Populations increase when the birth rate (the number of people who are born each year) is higher than the death rate (the number of people who die each year).
3) The rapidly increasing population is putting pressure on the environment — more resources are being used up and more pollution's being produced.
4) The higher standard of living amongst more developed countries demands even more resources, and although these developed countries have only a small proportion of the world's population, they cause a large proportion of the pollution.

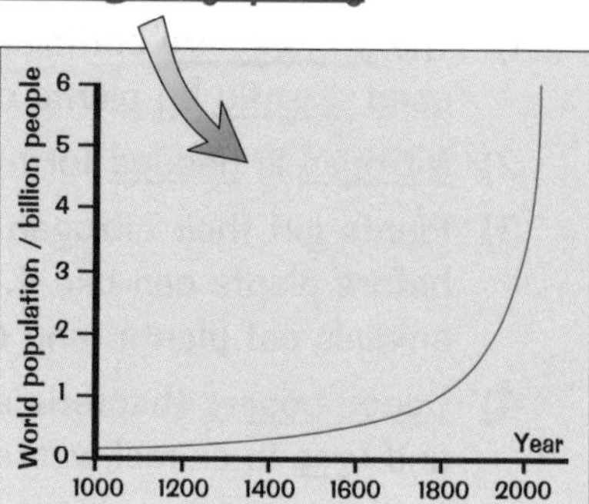

Increasing Amounts of Pollution are Causing...

1) GLOBAL WARMING

1) Fossil fuels are coal, oil and natural gas.
2) When they're burned, they release lots of carbon dioxide, which is a greenhouse gas. Greenhouse gases trap heat in the atmosphere which causes global temperature to rise. This is global warming.
3) Scientists have predicted that, if global temperature continues to go up, sea level will rise, weather systems will become less predictable and agricultural output will fall.

Lots of people, companies and countries are measuring the amount of greenhouse gases they're giving off, so they can reduce their emissions. The amount of greenhouse gases given off in a certain period of time (e.g. by a person) is called their carbon footprint.

2) ACID RAIN

1) When fossil fuels and waste materials are burned they release a gas called sulfur dioxide.
2) Sulfur dioxide reacts with water in the atmosphere to form sulfuric acid which falls as acid rain.
3) Acid rain damages soils, and can kill trees.
4) Acid rain can cause lakes to become more acidic. This has a severe effect on the lake's ecosystem. Many organisms are sensitive to changes in pH and can't survive in more acidic conditions. Many plants and animals die.
5) Acid rain damages limestone, ruining buildings and stone statues.

3) OZONE DEPLETION

1) CFCs (chlorofluorocarbons) used to be used in aerosols, fridges, air-conditioning units, and polystyrene foam.
2) They break down ozone in the upper atmosphere.
3) This allows more harmful UV rays to reach the Earth's surface.
4) Being exposed to more UV rays will increase the risk of skin cancer (although this can be reduced with suncream). Australia has high levels of skin cancer because it is under an ozone hole.
5) The increase in UV rays might also kill plankton in the sea — this could have a massive effect on the sea ecosystem because plankton are at the bottom of the food chain. Scientists predict that fish levels will drop (meaning, among other things, less food for us to eat).

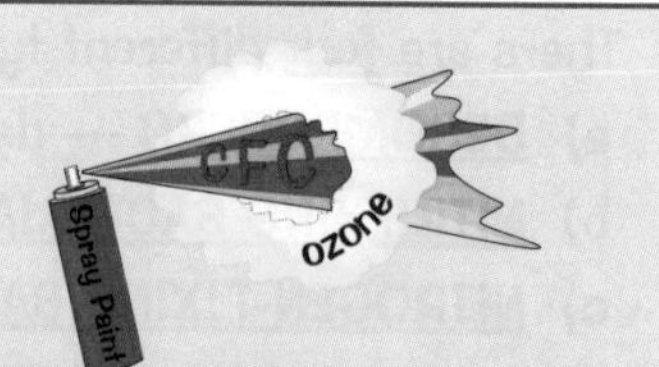

Global warming — you might need to invest in a new pair of shorts...

More people means more demand for food, energy, land and raw materials — and more waste and pollution. The worst culprits are people like us in developed countries who want energy for their comfortable lifestyles.

Human Impact on the Environment

There are a few different ways to gauge just how badly we are polluting the planet — here are two of 'em.

Indicator Species Can Be Used to Show Pollution

By looking for indicator species, you can tell if an area is polluted or not.

1) Some species can only survive in unpolluted conditions, so if you find lots of them, you know it's a clean area.

   Lichens are used to monitor air quality — they're damaged by pollution. The cleaner the air, the greater the diversity of lichens that survive.

   Mayfly larvae are used to monitor water quality — they can't survive in polluted water. The cleaner the water, the more mayfly larvae survive.

2) Other species have adapted to live in polluted conditions — so if you see a lot of them you know there's a problem.

   Water lice, rat-tailed maggots and sludgeworms all indicate polluted water. But out of these, rat-tailed maggots and sludgeworms indicate a very high level of pollution.

Pollution Level Can Be Measured

There are a couple of ways of using indicator species to measure pollution:

1) You could do a simple survey to see if a species is present or absent from an area. This is a quick way of telling whether an area is polluted or not, but it's no good for telling how polluted an area is.
2) Counting the number of times an indicator species occurs in an area will give you a numerical value, allowing measurements from different areas to be compared so you can see how polluted an area is.

You can also measure pollution directly, for example:

1) Sensitive instruments can measure the concentrations of chemical pollutants, e.g. carbon dioxide or sulfur dioxide, in samples of air or water.
2) Satellite data can also be used to indicate pollutant level, e.g. satellites can show where the ozone layer is thin or absent, which is linked to the CFC level (see previous page).

Both Ways of Looking at Pollution Level Have Their Weaknesses

	Advantages	Disadvantages
Living methods (indicator species)	• Using living methods is a relatively quick, cheap and easy way of saying whether an area is polluted or not. No expensive equipment or highly trained workers are needed.	• Factors other than pollution (e.g. temperature) can influence the survival of indicator species so living methods aren't always reliable.
Non-living methods	• Directly measuring the pollutants gives reliable, numerical data that's easy to compare between different sites. • The exact pollutants can be identified too.	• Non-living methods often require more expensive equipment and trained workers than methods that use indicator species.

These are just a few examples — you may be able to think of other advantages and disadvantages of the two methods.

Sludgeworms and rat-tailed maggots — harbingers of doom...

I don't envy the person that has to trudge through the polluted water looking for rat-tailed maggots. Monitoring pollution is important though — it can have some pretty big impacts — so someone's gotta do it.

Endangered Species

Loads of species are endangered these days. But we can do things to help...

Many Factors Can Cause a Species to Become Extinct

1) ENDANGERED species, like tigers, have very low numbers left in the wild. They're in danger of becoming EXTINCT, where there's none of them at all — like the dodo and woolly mammoth.
2) Species are at risk of extinction if the following factors fall below a critical level:
   - The number of habitats — it's hard for organisms to find resources like food and shelter if there aren't enough suitable habitats to support them.
   - The number of individuals — if there are only a few individual members of a species left, it'll be hard to find mates. It also means there won't be much genetic variation in the population.
   - Genetic variation — this is the number of different alleles (forms of a gene) in a population. If genetic variation is low, then a species is less likely to be able to adapt to changes in the environment or survive the appearance of a new disease.

You Need to be Able to Evaluate Conservation Programmes

Conservation programmes are designed to help save endangered plants and animals. They involve things like protecting habitats, creating artificial environments and captive breeding.
You can EVALUATE how successful a conservation programme is likely to be by looking at:

1) GENETIC VARIATION — the species being conserved should have enough genetic variation to survive the appearance of new diseases and to cope with environmental change (see above).
2) VIABILITY OF POPULATIONS — populations should be able to reproduce — so they must contain both males and females of reproductive age. They should also be large enough to prevent related individuals having to breed together — this is called inbreeding and it reduces genetic variation.
3) AVAILABLE HABITATS — there should be plenty of suitable habitats to live in. The right type of habitat is especially important if the organisms being conserved are specialists (see p. 33).
4) INTERACTION BETWEEN SPECIES — it's important that species interact with each other as they would in their natural environment, e.g. predator species should be allowed to hunt prey.

Conservation Programmes Benefit Wildlife and Humans

Conservation programmes do more than just benefit endangered species — they often help humans too:

1) PROTECTING THE HUMAN FOOD SUPPLY — over-fishing has greatly reduced fish stocks in the world's oceans. Conservation programmes can ensure that future generations will have fish to eat.
2) ENSURING MINIMAL DAMAGE TO FOOD CHAINS — if one species becomes extinct it will affect all the organisms that feed on and are eaten by that species, so the whole food chain is affected. This means conserving one species may help others to survive.
3) PROVIDING FUTURE MEDICINES — many of the medicines we use today come from plants. Undiscovered plant species may contain new medicinal chemicals. If these plants are allowed to become extinct, perhaps through rainforest destruction, we could miss out on valuable medicines.
4) CULTURAL ASPECTS — individual species may be important in a nation's or an area's cultural heritage, e.g. the bald eagle is being conserved in the USA as it is regarded as a national symbol.

It's a shame exams aren't an endangered species...

Even if you're someone who hates all plants and animals and much prefers concrete, remember that there are human benefits to protecting wildlife — and you need to know what they are.

Sustainable Development

It's not all doom and gloom... if we do things sustainably we'll be OK.

Development Has to be Sustainable

As the human population gets bigger...

1) We need to produce more food — so we'll need more land for farming.
2) We use up more energy. At the moment the vast majority of energy comes from burning fossil fuels. But these are rapidly running out — we need to find an alternative energy source.
3) We're producing more waste — it all needs to be put somewhere and a lot of it's polluting the Earth.

We need to find a way to exist where we don't damage the environment. This is 'sustainable development':

SUSTAINABLE DEVELOPMENT means providing for the needs of today's increasing population without harming the environment.

Sustainable development needs to be carefully planned and it needs to be carried out all over the Earth. This means there needs to be cooperation locally, nationally and internationally.

EXAMPLES OF WHAT'S BEING DONE TO PROMOTE SUSTAINABLE DEVELOPMENT:

1) Fishing quotas have been introduced to prevent some types of fish, such as cod, from becoming extinct in certain areas. This means they'll still be around in years to come.
2) To make the production of wood and paper sustainable there are laws insisting that logging companies plant new trees to replace those that they've felled.

Education is important. If people are aware of the problems, they may be more likely to help — e.g. by not buying certain types of fish and only buying wood products from sustainably managed forests. Sustainable development also helps endangered species by considering the impacts on their habitats.

Case Study: Whales — Some Species are Endangered

1) Whales have commercial value (they can be used to make money) when they're alive and dead.
2) They're a tourist attraction — people go to some areas especially to see the whales.
3) Whale meat and oil can be used, and cosmetics can be made from a waxy substance in their intestines. However, this has led to some species of whale becoming endangered.
4) The International Whaling Commission (IWC) has struggled to get nations to agree to restrict whaling. In 1982 the member nations declared a stop to whaling, the only exception being Norway, which still catches whales. Taking a small number of whales ('culling') for scientific research is allowed and is carried out by Japan, Iceland and the Faroe Islands.
5) But it's hard to check that countries are sticking to the agreement, and even when anyone is caught, the IWC doesn't have the authority to enforce any kind of punishment. So a lot of illegal whaling goes on.
6) Some whales are kept in captivity — there are different views about this:
   - Whales don't have much space in captivity and they are sometimes used for entertaining people. Some people think it's wrong that the whales lose their freedom and that they would be much happier in the wild, but captive whales do increase awareness of the animals and their problems.
   - Captive breeding programmes allow whales to be bred in numbers and released back into the wild.
   - Research on captive whales can help us understand their needs better to help conservation. There is still a lot we don't fully understand about whales, e.g. whale communication, their migration patterns and how they survive in very deep water.

Fishermen are just too effishent...

(groan...)

Whales are amazing animals — it'd be a huge pity if they were wiped out and weren't around for future generations. It's not just deliberate hunting that's a problem for them — they often get tangled up in fishing nets or collide with ships. And pollution doesn't do them much good either. It's a tough life.

Revision Summary for Module B2

Believe it or not, it's already time for another round of questions. Do as many as you can and if there are some that you're finding really fiddly, don't panic. Have a quick flick over the relevant topics and give the questions another go once you've had another chance to read the pages. Good luck — not that you need it.

1) What group comes between 'family' and 'species' when classifying organisms?
2) Give two reasons why classification systems change over time.
3) What is a species?
4) What is the binomial system? Explain why it is important.
5) Why might two unrelated species look very similar?
6) What does each bar on a pyramid of biomass represent?
7) Below are two pyramid diagrams. One is a pyramid of biomass and one is a pyramid of numbers. Which diagram is which? Explain your answer.

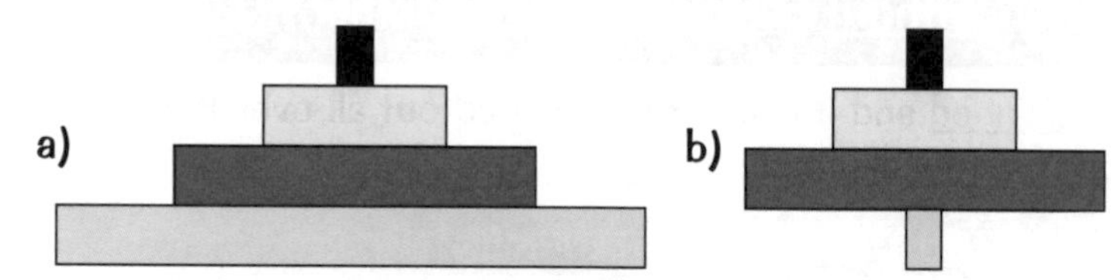

8) Give two ways that energy is lost at each stage in the food chain.
9) Why is it unusual to find a food chain with more than five trophic levels?
10) What is intraspecific competition?
11) Sketch a graph of prey and predator populations and explain the pattern shown.
12) What is the difference between a parasitic and a mutualistic relationship? Give an example of each.
13) 'In a habitat with stable conditions, specialists will out-compete generalists.' True or false?
14) Describe how extremophile bacteria are able to survive very high temperatures.
15) What are antifreeze proteins?
16) How does having a small surface area to volume ratio help organisms to keep warm in cold climates?
17) Explain how counter-current heat exchange systems keep penguins from getting too cold.
18) Describe one anatomical adaptation that increases heat loss for an animal that lives in a hot environment.
19) Describe two ways that desert plants are adapted to survive in dry conditions.
20) Describe Darwin's theory of evolution by natural selection.
21) Describe how speciation can happen through geographical isolation.
22) How did Lamarck's theory of evolution contrast with Darwin's?
23) Give two reasons why the theory of evolution by natural selection is now widely accepted.
24) Explain how carbon is removed from the air in the carbon cycle.
25) Describe two processes that release carbon dioxide into the atmosphere.
26) Explain the role that decomposers play in the nitrogen cycle.
27) What role do nitrogen-fixing bacteria play in the nitrogen cycle?
28) What does the term 'carbon footprint' mean?
29) Name a gas that causes acid rain. Where does this gas come from?
30) Give one effect of ozone depletion from pollution by CFCs.
31) What are indicator species? Give examples.
32) Give one disadvantage of using indicator species to measure pollution.
33) Give four factors you'd look at to evaluate a conservation programme.
34) Give four ways in which conservation programmes benefit humans.
35) What are the commercial values of whales?
36) Name two aspects of whale biology that we don't fully understand.

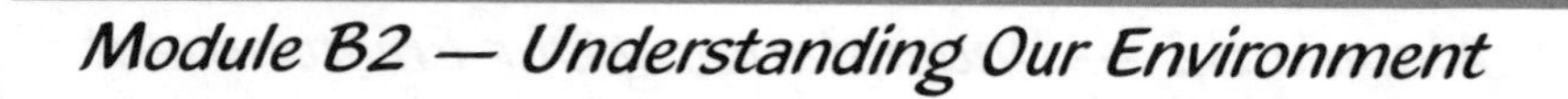

Cells

Biology's all about living stuff. And all living stuff contains cells. So let's make a start with cells...

Learn These Animal Cell Structures...

The following cell structures are found in most animal cells:

Nucleus — contains DNA in the form of chromosomes (see next page).

Cell membrane — holds the cell together and controls what goes in and out.

Ribosome — where proteins are synthesised (see page 47).

Cytoplasm — gel-like substance where most of the cell's chemical reactions happen.

Mitochondria — where most of the reactions involved in respiration take place. Respiration provides energy for cell processes (see page 55). Cells that need lots of energy contain many mitochondria, e.g.

- liver cells — which carry out lots of energy-demanding metabolic reactions,
- muscle cells — which need energy to contract (and cause movement).

Cell structures are tiny — some are even too small to be seen with a light microscope, e.g. ribosomes.

...And These Plant Cell Structures Too

Plant cells usually have all the structures that animal cells have, plus a few extra:

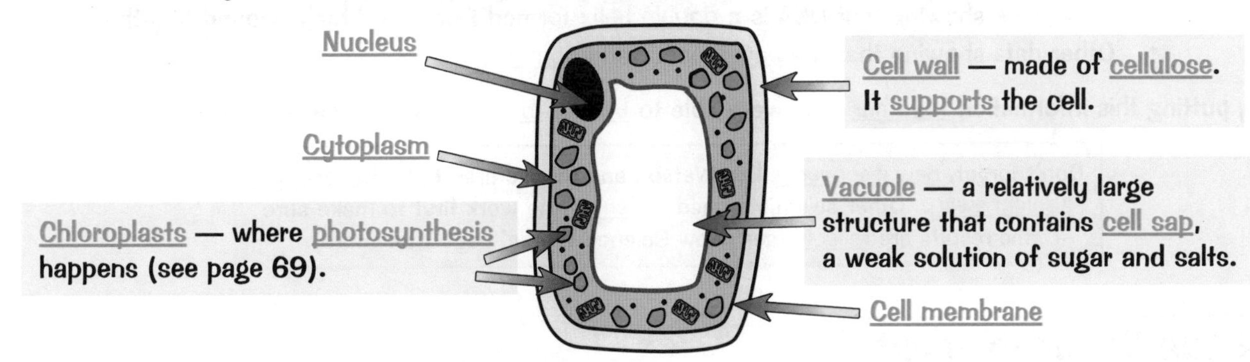

Bacterial Cells Are A Bit Different

Bacterial cells are smaller and simpler than plant and animal cells...

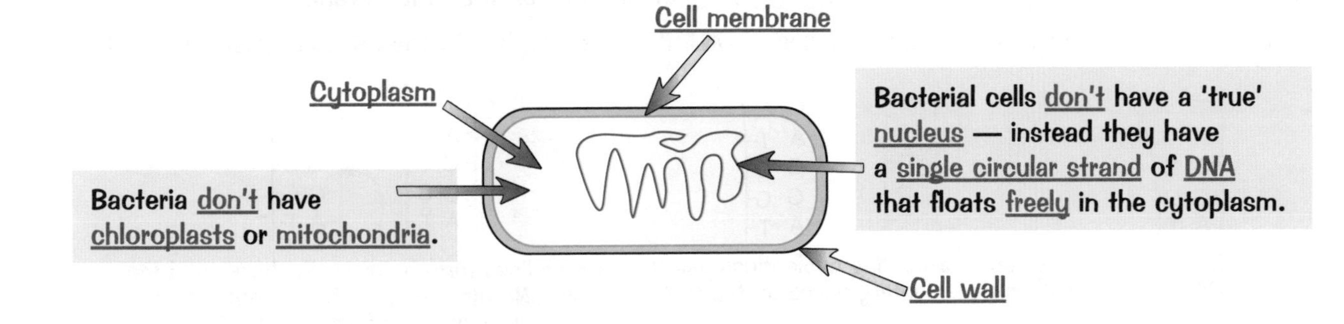

Cell structures — become a property developer...

This page needs learning from top to bottom. These cell structures crop up everywhere in biology — so make sure you know them all. You also need to know what makes bacterial cells that bit different from plant and animal cells — it's mainly the lack of anything interesting like a nucleus, chloroplasts or mitochondria.

DNA is a big, big deal in Biology, but the mystery of its structure was only solved relatively recently.

Chromosomes Are Made of DNA

1) Chromosomes are long molecules of coiled up DNA. The DNA is divided up into short sections called genes (see next page).
2) DNA is a double helix (a double-stranded spiral). Each of the two DNA strands is made up of lots of small groups called "nucleotides".
3) Each nucleotide contains a small molecule called a "base". DNA has just four different bases.
4) You only need to know the four bases by their first initials — A, C, G and T.
5) Each base forms cross links to a base on the other strand. This keeps the two DNA strands tightly wound together.
6) A always pairs up with T, and C always pairs up with G. This is called complementary base-pairing.

A DNA Double Helix

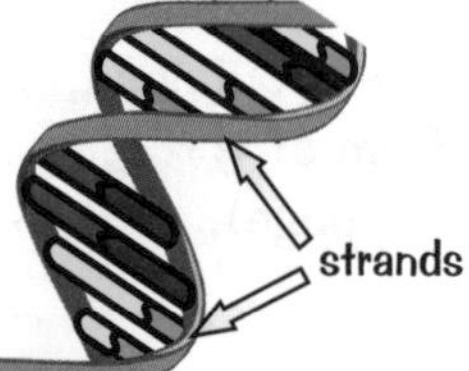

Watson and Crick Were The First to Model DNA

1) Scientists struggled for decades to work out the structure of DNA.
2) Francis Crick and James Watson were the first scientists to build a model of DNA — they did it in 1953.
3) They used data from other scientists to help them understand the structure of the molecule. This included:
   - X-ray data showing that DNA is a double helix formed from two chains wound together.
   - Other data showing that the bases occurred in pairs.
4) By putting this information together they were able to build a model showing what DNA looks like.

Don't forget, new discoveries like Watson and Crick's aren't widely accepted straight away. Other scientists need to repeat the work first to make sure the results are reliable (see 'How Science Works' page 1 for more).

DNA Can Replicate Itself

1) DNA copies itself every time a cell divides, so that each new cell still has the full amount of DNA.
2) In order to copy itself, the DNA double helix first 'unzips' — to form two single strands.
3) New nucleotides (floating freely in the nucleus) then join on using complementary base-pairing (A with T and C with G). This makes an exact copy of the DNA on the other strand.
4) The result is two double-stranded molecules of DNA that are identical to the original molecule of DNA.

Molecule of DNA unzips.

Bases on free-floating nucleotides pair up with complementary bases on the DNA.

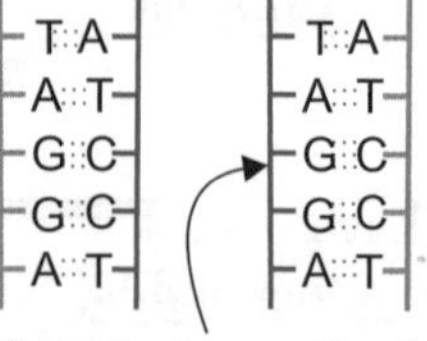

Cross links form between the bases and the old DNA strands, and the nucleotides are joined together to form double strands.

Q: What do DNA and a game of rounders have in common...?

Answer: four bases, and don't you forget it. Scientists spent years and years trying to work out the structure of DNA. When Watson and Crick finally cracked it, it became the scientific discovery of the twentieth century.

Protein Synthesis

So here's how life works — DNA molecules contain a genetic code that determines which proteins are built. The proteins determine how all the cells in the body function. Simple, eh.

Proteins are Made by Reading the Code in DNA

1) DNA controls the production of proteins (protein synthesis) in a cell.
2) A section of DNA that codes for a particular protein is called a gene.
3) Proteins are made up of chains of molecules called amino acids. Each different protein has its own particular number and order of amino acids.
4) This gives each protein a different shape, which means each protein can have a different function.
5) It's the order of the bases in a gene that decides the order of amino acids in a protein.
6) Each amino acid is coded for by a sequence of three bases in the gene.
7) The amino acids are joined together to make proteins, following the order of the bases in the gene.

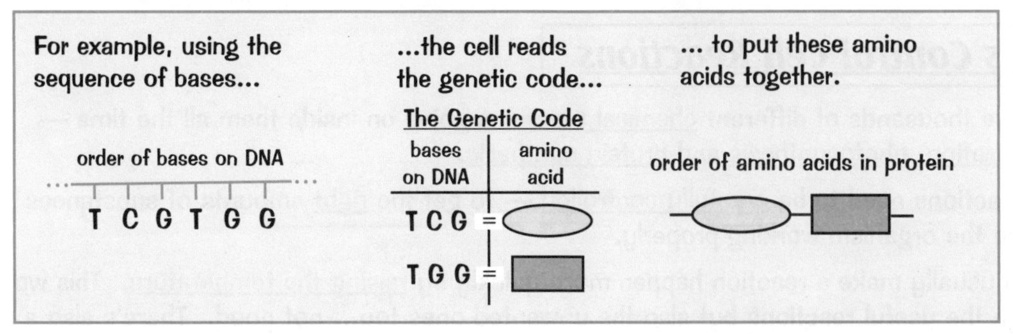

8) Each gene contains a different sequence of bases — which is what allows it to code for a unique protein.

mRNA Carries The Code to The Ribosomes

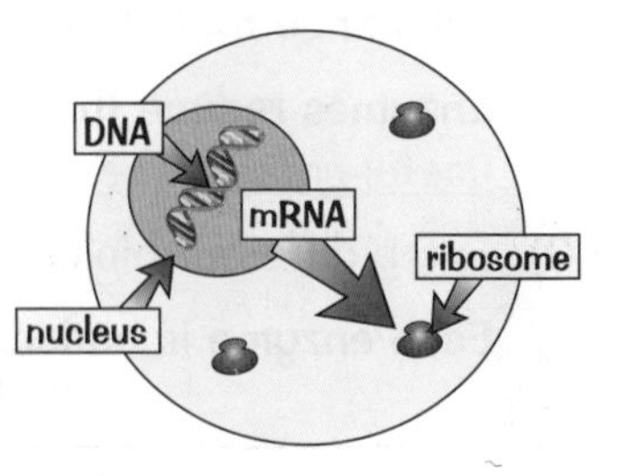

1) Proteins are made in the cell cytoplasm by tiny structures called ribosomes.
2) To make proteins, ribosomes use the code in the DNA. DNA is found in the cell nucleus and can't move out of it because it's really big. So the cell needs to get the code from the DNA to the ribosome.
3) This is done using a molecule called mRNA — which is made by copying the code from DNA.
4) The mRNA acts as a messenger between the DNA and the ribosome — it carries the code between the two.

DNA Controls A Cell By Controlling Protein Production

1) The proteins produced in a cell affect how it functions. Some of them determine cell structure, others (like enzymes) control cell reactions — see next page.
2) Different types of cell have different functions because they make different proteins.
3) They only make certain proteins because only some of the full set of genes is used in any one cell. Some genes are "switched off", which means the proteins they code for aren't produced.
4) The genes that are switched on determine the function of the cell. E.g. in a muscle cell only the genes that code for muscle cell proteins are switched on. Genes that code for proteins specific to bone, nerve or skin cells are all switched off. This allows the muscle cell to function as... well, a muscle cell.

And I thought the aliens were in control...

... but it turns out that DNA is really where it's at. Or maybe aliens are controlling my DNA that's controlling my proteins that are controlling my... Anyway. Make sure you know all the details on this page — it's a tricky one.

Functions of Proteins

Proteins are handy little things. They carry messages around the body, and even control chemical reactions.

Proteins Have Many Different Functions

There are hundreds of different proteins and they all have different functions.
Thankfully, you don't need to know about all of them — just these four examples:

See page 56 for more on haemoglobin.

1) ENZYMES — see below.
2) CARRIER MOLECULES — used to transport smaller molecules. E.g. haemoglobin (found in red blood cells) binds to oxygen molecules and transports them around the body.
3) HORMONES — used to carry messages around the body. E.g. insulin is a hormone released into the blood by the pancreas to regulate the blood sugar level.
4) STRUCTURAL PROTEINS — are physically strong. E.g. collagen is a structural protein that strengthens connective tissues (like ligaments and cartilage).

Enzymes Control Cell Reactions

1) Cells have thousands of different chemical reactions going on inside them all the time — like respiration, photosynthesis and protein synthesis.
2) These reactions need to be carefully controlled — to get the right amounts of substances and keep the organism working properly.
3) You can usually make a reaction happen more quickly by raising the temperature. This would speed up the useful reactions but also the unwanted ones too... not good. There's also a limit to how far you can raise the temperature inside a living creature before its cells start getting damaged.
4) So living things produce ENZYMES, which act as BIOLOGICAL CATALYSTS. A catalyst is a substance that speeds up a reaction, without being changed or used up in the reaction itself.
5) Enzymes reduce the need for high temperatures and we only have enzymes to speed up the useful chemical reactions in the body.
6) Every different biological reaction has its own enzyme designed especially for it.
7) Each enzyme is coded for by a different gene, and has a unique shape which it needs to do its job.

Enzymes are Very Specific

1) Chemical reactions usually involve things either being split apart or joined together.
2) The substrate is the molecule changed in the reaction.
3) Every enzyme has an active site — the part where it joins on to its substrate to catalyse the reaction.
4) Enzymes are really picky — they usually only work with one substrate. The posh way of saying this is that enzymes have a high specificity for their substrate.
5) This is because, for the enzyme to work, the substrate has to fit into the active site. If the substrate's shape doesn't match the active site's shape, then the reaction won't be catalysed. This is called the 'lock and key' mechanism, because the substrate fits into the enzyme just like a key fits into a lock.

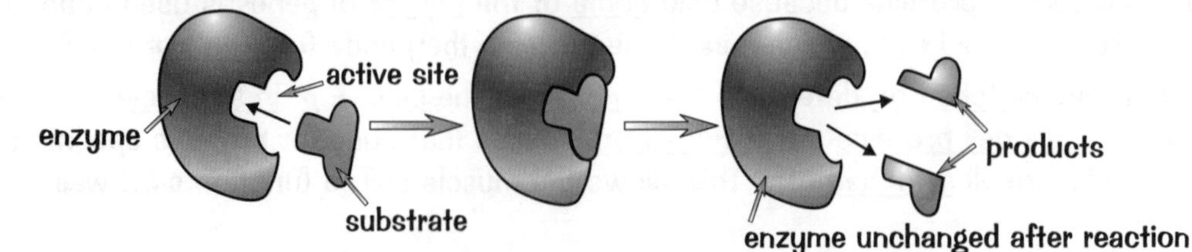

If the lock & key mechanism fails, you get in through a window...

Enzymes aren't just useful for controlling chemical reactions in the body — we even put them in things like biological washing powders to catalyse the breakdown of nasty stains (like tomato ketchup).

More On Enzymes

Enzymes are fussy blighters — they want the right temperature and the right pH, too...

Enzymes Like it Warm but Not Too Hot

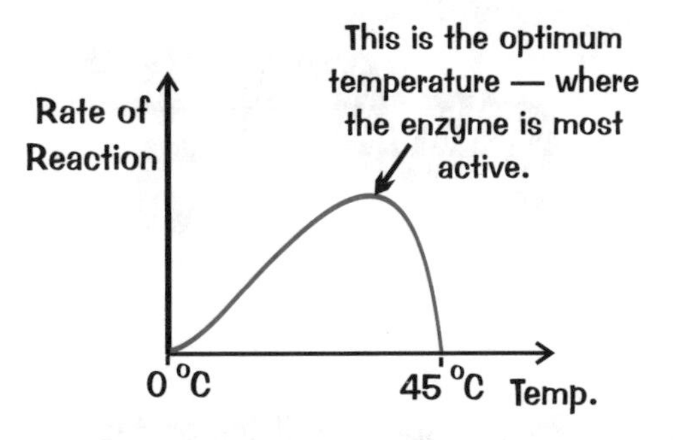

1) Changing the temperature changes the rate of an enzyme-catalysed reaction.
2) Like with any reaction, a higher temperature increases the rate at first. This is because more heat means the enzymes and the substrate particles have more energy. This makes the enzymes and the substrate particles move about more, so they're more likely to meet up and react — they have a higher collision rate.
3) Low temperatures have the opposite effect — there's a lower collision rate and so a slower reaction.
4) If it gets too hot, some of the bonds holding the enzyme together will break.
5) This makes the enzyme lose its shape — its active site doesn't fit the shape of the substrate any more. This means it can't catalyse the reaction and the reaction stops — the enzyme can't function.
6) The enzyme is now said to be denatured. Its change in shape is irreversible (permanent).
7) Each enzyme has its own optimum temperature when the reaction goes fastest. This is the temperature just before it gets too hot and starts to denature. The optimum temperature for the most important human enzymes is about 37 °C — the same temperature as our bodies. Lucky for us.

Enzymes Like The Right pH Too

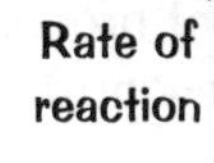

1) The pH also has an effect on enzymes.
2) If the pH is too high or too low, it interferes with the bonds holding the enzyme together. This changes the shape of the active site and denatures the enzyme.

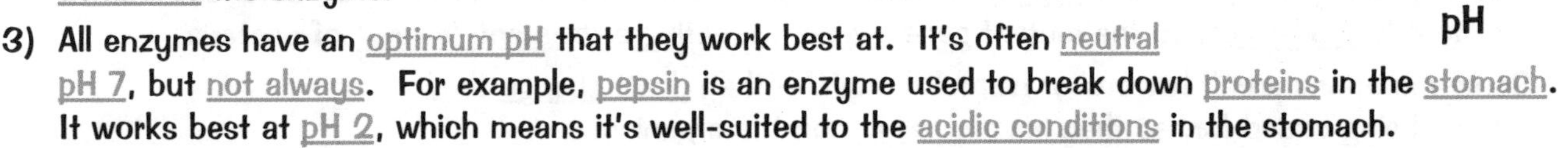

3) All enzymes have an optimum pH that they work best at. It's often neutral pH 7, but not always. For example, pepsin is an enzyme used to break down proteins in the stomach. It works best at pH 2, which means it's well-suited to the acidic conditions in the stomach.

Q_{10} Values Show How Rate of Reaction Changes with Temperature

1) The Q_{10} value for a reaction shows how much the rate changes when the temperature is raised by 10 °C.
2) You can calculate it using this equation:

$$Q_{10} = \frac{\text{rate at higher temperature}}{\text{rate at lower temperature}}$$

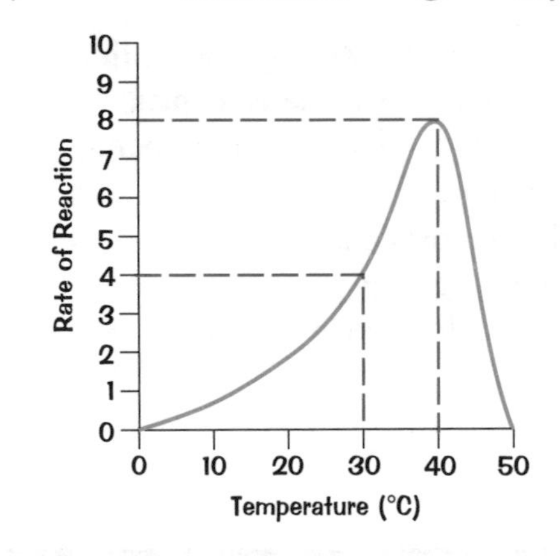

3) The graph on the left shows the rate of a reaction between 0 °C and 50 °C. Here's how to calculate the Q_{10} value of the reaction using the rate at 30 °C and at 40 °C:

$$Q_{10} = \frac{\text{rate at 40 °C}}{\text{rate at 30 °C}} = \frac{8}{4} = 2$$

The reaction data you get in the exam could be in a graph like this or in a table.

4) A Q_{10} value of 2 means that the rate doubles when the temperature is raised by 10 °C. A Q_{10} value of 3 would mean that the rate trebles.

If only enzymes could speed up revision...

Make sure you understand this denaturing malarkey — and learn how to calculate and interpret a Q_{10} value.

Mutations

Mutations are really common — but sadly, they hardly ever give any of us superpowers.

Gene Mutations are Changes to Genes

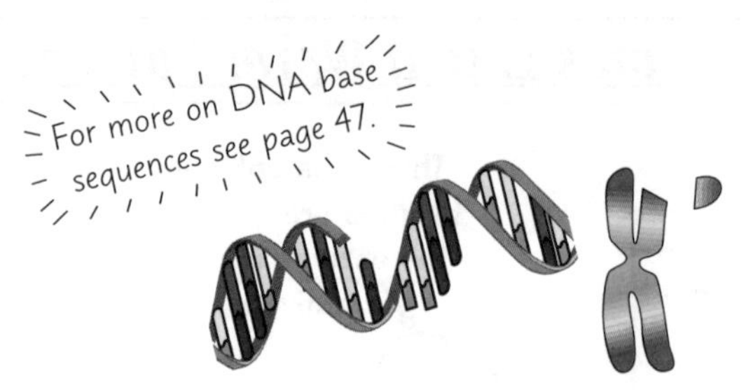

1) A mutation is a change in the DNA base sequence.
2) If a mutation occurs within a gene, it could stop the production of the protein the gene normally codes for — or it might mean a different protein is produced instead.

Most Mutations are Harmful

1) Producing the wrong protein or no protein at all can be a bit of a disaster — especially if the protein is an important enzyme or something.
2) If a mutation occurs in reproductive cells, then the offspring might develop abnormally or die at an early stage of their development.
3) If a mutation occurs in body cells, the mutant cells can sometimes start to multiply in an uncontrolled way and invade other parts of the body. This is cancer.

Some Mutations are Beneficial, Some Have No Effect

1) Occasionally, a different protein might be produced after a mutation that actually benefits the organism — the new protein is an improvement on the one it was supposed to be.
2) This gives the organism a survival advantage over the rest of the population. It passes on the mutated DNA to its offspring, and they survive better too, so soon the mutation becomes common in the population.
3) This is natural selection and evolution at work. A good example is a mutation in a bacterium that makes it resistant to antibiotics, so the mutant gene lives on, creating a resistant "strain" of bacteria.
4) Some mutations aren't harmful or helpful though — they don't change the protein being coded for, so they have no effect on the organism.

Radiation and Certain Chemicals Cause Mutations

Mutations can happen spontaneously — when a chromosome doesn't quite copy itself properly. However, the chance of a mutation is increased if you're exposed to:

1) Ionising radiation, including X-rays and ultraviolet light, together with radiation from radioactive substances. For each of these examples, the greater the dose of radiation, the greater the chance of mutation.
2) Certain chemicals which are known to cause mutations. Such chemicals are called mutagens. If the mutations produce cancer then the chemicals are often called carcinogens. Cigarette smoke contains chemical mutagens (or carcinogens).

My mutant fish army will take over the world — I call it evilution...

All living organisms have experienced mutation at some point in their evolutionary history. That's why we don't all look the same. Make sure you know what can cause a mutation — it might well turn up in the exam.

Multiplying Cells

Cell division — pretty important if you're planning on being bigger than an amoeba. Which I am, one day.

Being Multicellular Has Some Important Advantages

There's nothing wrong with single-celled organisms — they're pretty successful. Bacteria, for example, aren't in danger of extinction any time soon. But there are some big advantages in being multicellular, and so some organisms have evolved that way. Here are some advantages you should know:

1) Being multicellular means you can be bigger. This is great because it means you can travel further, get your nutrients in a variety of different ways, fewer things can eat or squash you, etc.
2) Being multicellular allows for cell differentiation. Instead of being just one cell that has to do everything, you can have different types of cells that do different jobs. Your cells can be specially adapted for their particular jobs, e.g. carrying oxygen in the blood, reacting to light in the eyes.
3) This means multicellular organisms can be more complex — they can have specialised organs, different shapes and behaviour — and so can be adapted specifically to their particular environment.

However, being multicellular means that an organism also has to have specialised organ systems, including:

- A system to communicate between different cells, e.g. a nervous system.
- A system to supply cells with the nutrients they need, e.g. a circulatory system.
- A system that controls the exchange of substances with the environment, e.g. a respiratory system.

Mitosis Makes New Cells for Growth and Repair

"Mitosis is when a cell reproduces itself by splitting to form two identical offspring."

This happens in the body when you want identical cells — e.g. when you want to grow and you need lots of the same type of cell or when you need to replace worn-out cells and repair tissues. The important thing to understand in mitosis is what happens to the DNA.

1) Before mitosis starts, the DNA in the cell is replicated (see page 46).
2) Then at the beginning of mitosis, the DNA coils into double-armed chromosomes. These arms are exact copies of each other — they contain exactly the same DNA.

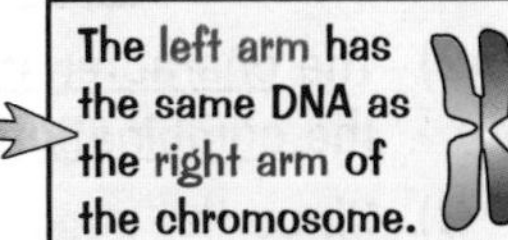

3) The chromosomes line up at the centre of the cell, and then divide as cell fibres pull them apart. The two arms of each chromosome go to opposite poles (ends) of one cell. Membranes form around each of these two different sets of chromosomes.
4) The cytoplasm divides, and you get two new cells containing exactly the same genetic material.
5) And that's mitosis. You've ended up with two new cells that are genetically identical to each other. Before these can divide again, the DNA has to replicate itself to give each chromosome two arms again.

Right — now that I have your undivided attention...

There's no denying that mitosis can seem tricky at first. But don't worry — just go through it slowly, one step at a time. Even if the exam's tomorrow. Panicking and rushing through it won't help at all.

Meiosis, Gametes and Fertilisation

People can look very similar to their mum and dad, often a good mix of the two. Here's why.

Meiosis is Another Type of Cell Division — It Creates Gametes

1) Gametes are formed by meiosis in the ovaries and testes. Gametes are the sex cells — eggs and sperm.
2) The body cells of mammals are diploid. This means that each of the organism's body cells has two copies of each chromosome in its nucleus — one from the organism's mum, and one from its dad.
3) But gametes are haploid — they only have one copy of each chromosome. This is so that when the egg and the sperm combine, they'll form a cell with the diploid number of chromosomes (see below).

Meiosis Involves Two Divisions

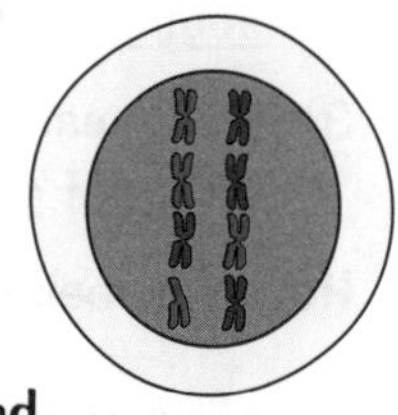

1) Meiosis starts in exactly the same way as mitosis — the DNA replicates and curls up to form double-armed chromosomes (see previous page).
2) After replication the chromosomes arrange themselves into pairs. Humans have 23 pairs of chromosomes, that's 46 altogether. Both chromosomes in a pair contain information about the same features. One chromosome comes from your mum and one from your dad.

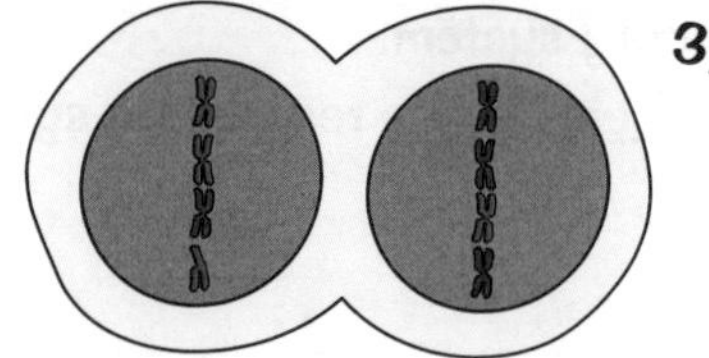

3) In the first division these pairs split up — the chromosomes in each pair move to opposite poles of the cell. In each of the two new cells, there are no pairs at all — just one of each of the 23 different types. Each new cell ends up with a mixture of your mum's and dad's chromosomes, but only half the usual number of chromosomes.
4) The second division of meiosis is like mitosis on the last page — each chromosome splits in half and one arm ends up in each new cell.
5) And that's meiosis. You've ended up with four new cells — two after the first division, and then each of those splits again. The cells are genetically different from each other because the chromosomes all get shuffled up during meiosis and each gamete only gets half of them, at random.

Fertilisation Creates Genetic Variation

Gametes

haploid sperm

haploid egg

diploid zygote — fertilised egg

1) At fertilisation male and female gametes combine to form a diploid cell. This cell is called a zygote.
2) The characteristics of the zygote are controlled by the combination of genes on its chromosomes.
3) Since the zygote will have inherited chromosomes from two parents, it will show features of both parents, but won't be exactly like either of them.

Sperm Cells are Adapted for Their Function

Sperm cell

acrosome

A sperm's function is to transport the male's DNA to the female's egg.

1) Sperm are small and have long tails so they can swim to the egg.
2) Sperm have lots of mitochondria (see page 45) to provide the energy needed to swim this distance.
3) Sperm also have an acrosome at the front of the 'head', which can release the enzymes they need to digest their way through the membrane of the egg cell.

No sniggering in the back, please...

For many kids in year seven, the mere sight of a sperm is enough to convulse them in giggles. Those of them that don't think it's an innocent tadpole, anyway. But that's not the case for you lot. We hope.

Stem Cells, Differentiation and Growth

Plants and animals have different tactics for growth, but they both have stem cells.

Animals Stop Growing, Plants Can Grow Continuously

Plants and animals grow differently:

1) Animals tend to grow until they reach a finite size (full growth) and then stop growing. Plants often grow continuously — even really old trees will keep putting out new branches.
2) In animals, growth happens by cell division. In plants, growth in height is mainly due to cell enlargement (elongation). Growth by cell division usually just happens in areas of the plant called meristems (at the tips of the roots and shoots).

Stem Cells Can Turn into Different Types of Cells

1) Differentiation is the process by which a cell changes to become specialised for its job. In most animal cells, the ability to differentiate is lost at an early stage, but lots of plant cells don't ever lose this ability.
2) Most cells in your body are specialised for a particular job. E.g. white blood cells are brilliant at fighting invaders but can't carry oxygen, like red blood cells.
3) Some cells are undifferentiated. They can develop into different types of cells, tissues and organs depending on what instructions they're given. These cells are called STEM CELLS.
4) Stem cells are found in early human embryos. They have the potential to turn into any kind of cell at all. This makes sense if you think about it — all the different types of cell found in a human being have to come from those few cells in the early embryo.
5) Adults also have stem cells, but they're only found in certain places, like bone marrow. These aren't as versatile as embryonic stem cells — they can't turn into any cell type at all, only certain ones.

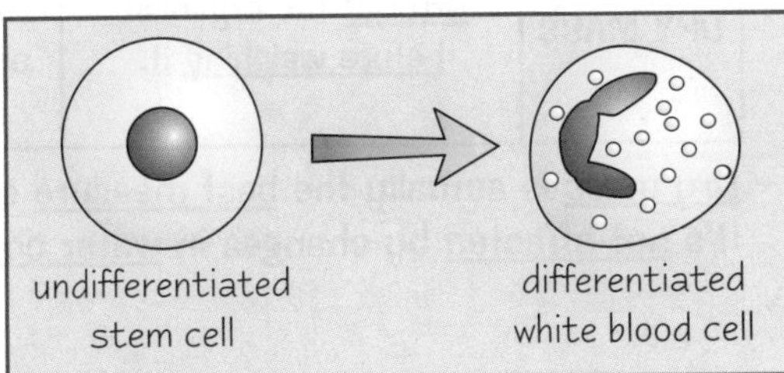

Stem Cells May be Able to Cure Many Disorders

1) Medicine already uses stem cells to cure disease. For example, people with blood disorders (e.g. leukaemia and sickle cell anaemia) can be cured by bone marrow transplants. Bone marrow contains adult stem cells that turn into new blood cells (but nothing else) to replace faulty old ones.
2) Very early human embryos contain a lot of stem cells. Scientists can extract these cells and grow them. They think they may eventually be able to grow tissues to treat medical conditions, e.g. nerve cells to cure brain damage and spinal injuries, skin cells for skin grafts, etc. This is known as stem cell therapy.

Some People Are Against Stem Cell Research

1) Some people are against stem cell research because they feel that human embryos shouldn't be used for experiments since each one is a potential human life. Others think that curing patients who already exist and who are suffering is more important than the rights of embryos.
2) One fairly convincing argument in favour of this point of view is that the embryos used in the research are usually unwanted ones from fertility clinics which, if they weren't used for research, would probably just be destroyed. But of course, campaigners for the rights of embryos usually want this banned too.
3) Around the world, there are now 'stocks' of stem cells that scientists can use for their research. Some countries (e.g. the USA) won't fund research to make new stem cell stocks, but in the UK it's allowed as long as it follows strict guidelines.

But florists cell stems — and nobody complains about that...

Research has recently been done into getting stem cells from alternative sources. E.g. some researchers think it might be possible to get cells from umbilical cords to behave like embryonic stem cells.

Growth

Growth is an increase in size or mass. But you need to know a lot more than that...

There are Different Methods for Measuring Growth

Growth of plants and animals can be quite tricky to measure — there are different methods, but they all have pros and cons.

To work out if something's grown (i.e. increased in size), you need to take more than one measurement.

Method	What it involves	Advantages	Disadvantages
LENGTH	Just measure the length (or height) of a plant or animal.	Easy to measure.	It doesn't tell you about changes in width, diameter, number of branches, etc.
WET MASS	Weigh the plant or animal and bingo — you have the wet mass.	Easy to measure.	Wet mass is very changeable. For example, a plant will be heavier if it's recently rained because it will have absorbed lots of water. Animals will be heavier if they've just eaten or if they've got a full bladder.
DRY MASS	Dry out the organism before weighing it.	It's not affected by the amount of water in a plant or animal or how much an organism has eaten.	You have to kill the organism to work it out. This might be okay for an area of grass, but it's not so good if you want to know the dry mass of a person.

Dry mass is actually the best measure of growth in plants and animals — it's not affected by changes in water content and it tells you the size of the whole organism.

Human Growth has Different Phases

1) Humans go through five main phases of growth:

PHASE	DESCRIPTION
Infancy	Roughly the first two years of life. Rapid growth.
Childhood	Period between infancy and puberty. Steady growth.
Adolescence	Begins with puberty and continues until body development and growth are complete. Rapid growth.
Maturity/adulthood	Period between adolescence and old age. Growth stops.
Old age	Usually considered to be between age 65 and death.

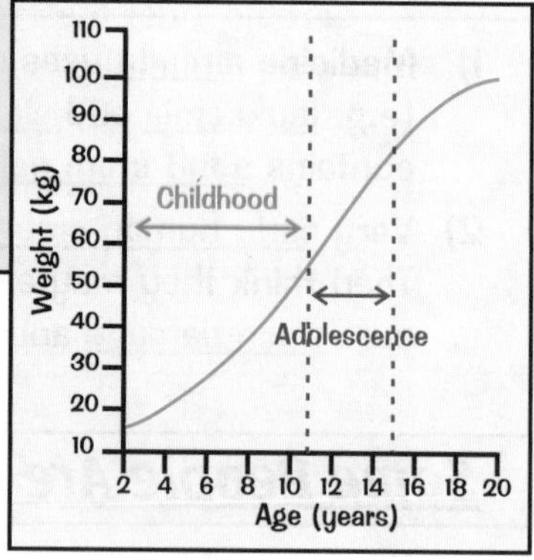

2) The two main phases of rapid growth take place just after birth and during adolescence. Growth stops when a person reaches adulthood.
3) The graph on the right is an example of a typical human growth curve. It shows how weight increases for boys between the ages of 2 and 20. When the line is steeper, growth is more rapid (e.g. during adolescence).

Certain Parts of the Body Grow Faster or Slower than Others

1) Organisms don't grow evenly. At different times, different parts of the body will grow at different rates.
2) For example, when a baby is developing in the womb, the brain grows at a greater rate than the rest of the body. This is because a large and well-developed brain gives humans a big survival advantage — it's our best tool for finding food, avoiding predators, etc.

I'm growing rather sick of this topic...

Listen, you think you're sick of reading these lame jokes? Just think how I feel, having to make them up.

Respiration

You need energy to keep your body going. Energy comes from food, and it's released by respiration.

Respiration is NOT "Breathing In and Out"

1) Respiration goes on in every cell in your body. It's the process of releasing energy from glucose.
2) The energy from respiration can't be used directly by cells — so it's used to make a substance called ATP.
3) ATP acts as the energy source for many cell processes and transports energy to where it's needed in a cell.
4) Respiration is controlled by enzymes. This means that the rate of respiration is affected by both temperature and pH (see page 49).
5) There are two types of respiration, aerobic and anaerobic.

Aerobic Respiration Needs Plenty of Oxygen

1) Aerobic respiration is what happens when there's plenty of oxygen available.
2) "Aerobic" just means "with oxygen" and it's the most efficient way to release energy from glucose.
3) This is the type of respiration that you're using most of the time.
4) You need to learn the word and chemical equations:

glucose + oxygen → carbon dioxide + water (+ ENERGY)

$$C_6H_{12}O_6 + 6O_2 \rightarrow 6CO_2 + 6H_2O \text{ (+ ENERGY)}$$

5) So, when respiration rate increases, both oxygen consumption and carbon dioxide production increase.
6) This means that the rate of oxygen consumption can be used to estimate metabolic rate (the amount of energy being used).

Anaerobic Respiration Doesn't Use Oxygen At All

1) When you do really vigorous exercise your body can't supply enough oxygen to your muscles for aerobic respiration — even though your heart rate and breathing rate increase as much as they can. Your muscles have to start respiring anaerobically as well.
2) "Anaerobic" just means "without oxygen". It's not the best way to convert glucose to energy because it releases much less energy per glucose molecule than aerobic respiration.
3) In anaerobic respiration, the glucose is only partially broken down, and lactic acid is also produced. The lactic acid builds up in the muscles, which gets painful and makes your muscles fatigued.

   You need to learn the word equation: Glucose → Lactic Acid (+ ENERGY)

4) The advantage is that at least you can keep on using your muscles.
5) After resorting to anaerobic respiration, when you stop exercising you'll have an oxygen debt. Basically you need extra oxygen to break down all the lactic acid that's built up in your muscles and to allow aerobic respiration to begin again.
6) This means you have to keep breathing hard for a while after you stop exercising — to repay the debt.
7) The lactic acid has to be carried to the liver to be broken down, so your heart rate has to stay high too.

The Respiratory Quotient

1) The respiratory quotient (RQ) can tell you whether someone is respiring aerobically or anaerobically. You can calculate it using this equation:

$$RQ = \frac{\text{Amount of } CO_2 \text{ produced}}{\text{Amount of } O_2 \text{ used}}$$

2) The RQ is usually between 0.7 and 1 — this means that the person is respiring aerobically. If the RQ value is greater than 1 then the person is short of oxygen and is respiring anaerobically, too.

I reckon aerobics classes should be called anaerobics instead...

You might get a question in the exam asking you to use data from experiments to compare respiration rates — just remember, increased oxygen consumption (or carbon dioxide production) means an increased respiration rate.

Functions of the Blood

Blood is very useful stuff. It's a big transport system for moving things around the body. The blood cells do good work too. Red blood cells, for example, are responsible for transporting oxygen about, and they carry 100 times more than could be moved just dissolved in the blood. Amazing.

Plasma is the Liquid Bit of Blood

It's basically blood minus the blood cells. Plasma is a pale yellow liquid which carries just about everything that needs transporting around your body:

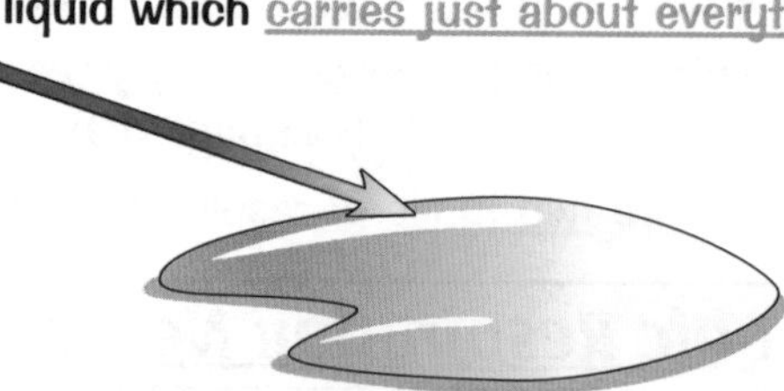

1) Red blood cells (see below), white blood cells, and platelets (used in blood clotting).
2) Water.
3) Digested food products like glucose and amino acids from the gut to all the body cells.
4) Carbon dioxide from the body cells to the lungs.
5) Urea from the liver to the kidneys (where it's removed in the urine).
6) Hormones — these act like chemical messengers.
7) Antibodies — these are proteins involved in the body's immune response.

Carbon dioxide and urea are both waste products, which need to be removed.

Red Blood Cells Have the Job of Carrying Oxygen

Red blood cells transport oxygen from the lungs to all the cells in the body. The structure of a red blood cell is adapted to its function:

1) Red blood cells are small and have a biconcave shape to give a large surface area to volume ratio for absorbing and releasing oxygen.
2) They contain haemoglobin, which is what gives blood its colour — it contains a lot of iron. In the lungs, haemoglobin combines with oxygen to become oxyhaemoglobin. In body tissues the reverse happens to release oxygen to the cells.
3) Red blood cells don't have a nucleus — this frees up space for more haemoglobin, so they can carry more oxygen.
4) Red blood cells are very flexible. This means they can easily pass through the tiny capillaries (see next page).

Biconcave is just a posh way to say they look a bit like doughnuts (see diagram below).

It's all blood, sweat and tears — kind of...

...without the sweat... or the tears... just the blood then... yep... anyway...

The average human body contains about six and a half pints of blood altogether, and every single drop contains millions of red blood cells — all of them perfectly designed for carrying plenty of oxygen to where its needed.

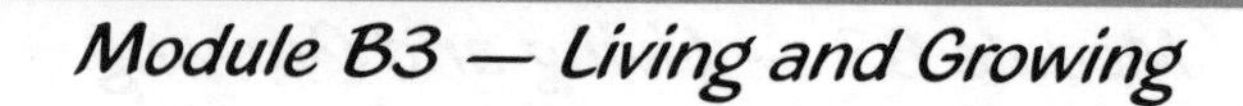

Blood Vessels

The blood has to get around the body somehow — which is what the blood vessels are for.

Blood Vessels are Designed for Their Function

There are three different types of blood vessel:

1) ARTERIES — these carry the blood away from the heart.
2) CAPILLARIES — these are involved in the exchange of materials at the tissues.
3) VEINS — these carry the blood to the heart.

Arteries Carry Blood Under Pressure

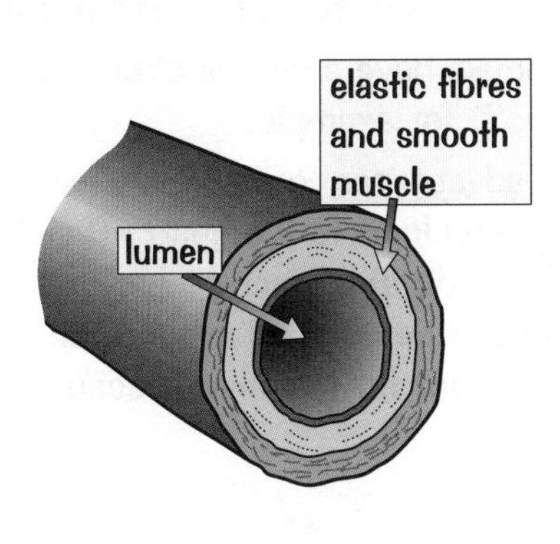

1) The heart pumps the blood out at high pressure so the artery walls are strong and elastic.
2) The walls are thick compared to the size of the hole down the middle (the "lumen" — silly name!). They contain thick layers of muscle to make them strong.

Capillaries are Really Small

thin wall — only one cell thick
very small lumen
nucleus of cell

1) Arteries branch into capillaries.
2) Capillaries are really tiny — too small to see.
3) They carry the blood really close to every cell in the body to exchange substances with them.
4) They have permeable walls, so substances can diffuse in and out. (See page 72 for more on diffusion.)

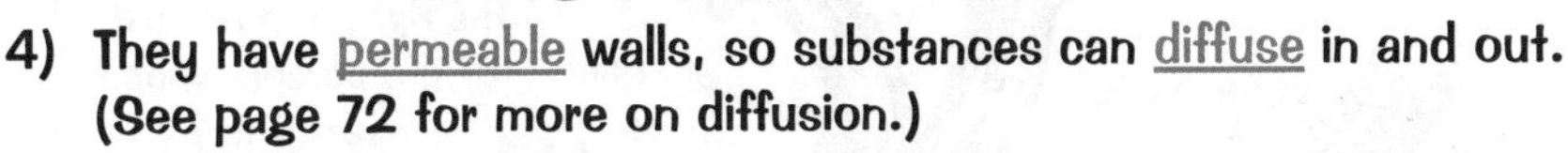

5) They supply food and oxygen, and take away wastes like CO_2.
6) Their walls are usually only one cell thick. This increases the rate of diffusion by decreasing the distance over which it occurs.

Veins Take Blood Back to the Heart

large lumen
elastic fibres and smooth muscle
valves

1) Capillaries eventually join up to form veins.
2) The blood is at lower pressure in the veins so the walls don't need to be as thick as artery walls.
3) They have a bigger lumen than arteries to help the blood flow despite the lower pressure.
4) They also have valves to help keep the blood flowing in the right direction.

Arteries don't need valves — the pressure in them is high enough to keep the blood flowing the right way.

Learn this page — don't struggle in vein...

Here's an interesting fact for you — your body contains about 60 000 miles of blood vessels. That's about six times the distance from London to Sydney in Australia. Of course, capillaries are really tiny, which is how there can be such a big length — they can only be seen with a microscope.

The Heart

Blood doesn't just move around the body on its own, of course. It needs a pump.

Mammals Have a Double Circulatory System

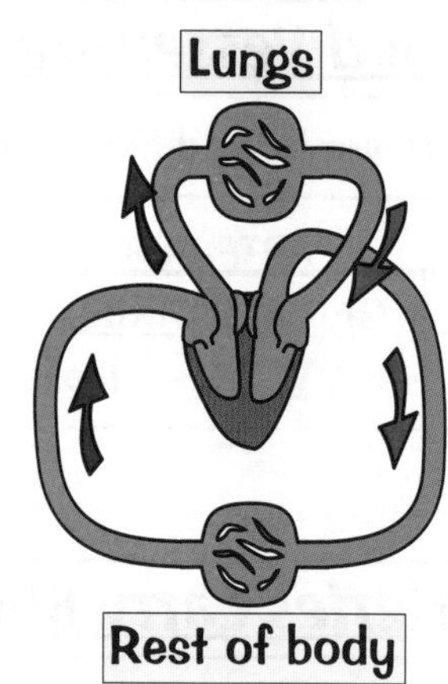

1) The first system connects the heart to the lungs. Deoxygenated blood is pumped to the lungs to take in oxygen. The blood then returns to the heart.
2) The second system connects the heart to the rest of the body. The oxygenated blood in the heart is pumped out to the body. It gives up its oxygen, and then the deoxygenated blood returns to the heart to be pumped out to the lungs again.
3) Not all animals have a double circulatory system — fish don't, for example.
4) There are advantages to mammals having a double circulatory system though. Returning the blood to the heart after it's picked up oxygen at the lungs means it can be pumped out around the body at a much higher pressure. This increases the rate of blood flow to the tissues (i.e. blood can be pumped around the body much faster), so more oxygen can be delivered to the cells. This is important for mammals because they use up a lot of oxygen maintaining their body temperature.

Learn This Diagram of the Heart with All Its Labels

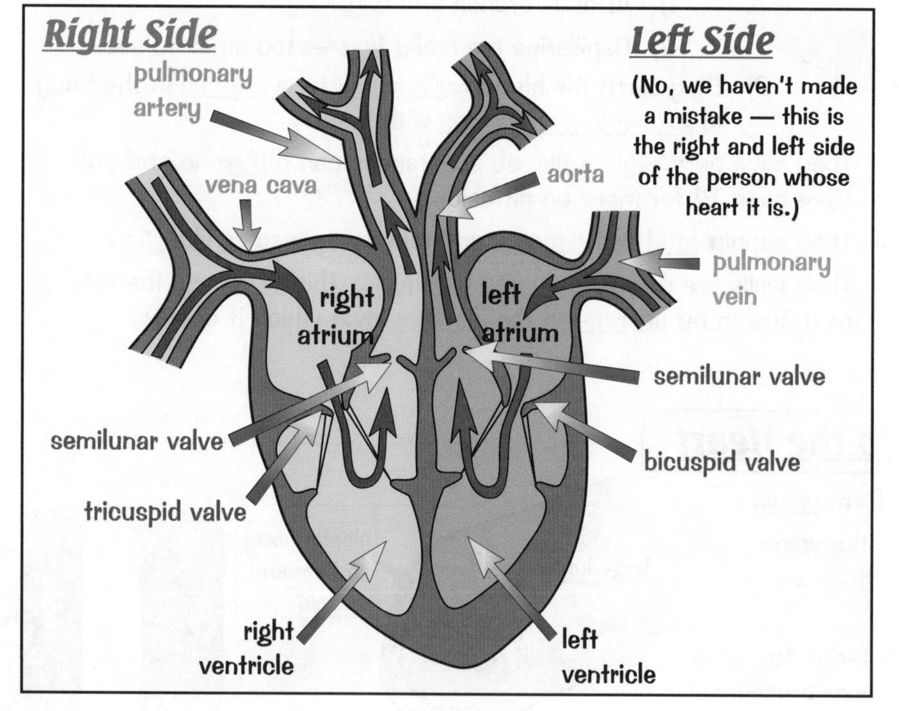

1) The right atrium of the heart receives deoxygenated blood from the body (through the vena cava).
(The plural of atrium is atria.)
2) The deoxygenated blood moves through to the right ventricle, which pumps it to the lungs (via the pulmonary artery).
3) The left atrium receives oxygenated blood from the lungs (through the pulmonary vein).
4) The oxygenated blood then moves through to the left ventricle, which pumps it out round the whole body (via the aorta).
5) The left ventricle has a much thicker wall than the right ventricle. It needs more muscle because it has to pump blood around the whole body, whereas the right ventricle only has to pump it to the lungs.
6) The semilunar, tricuspid and bicuspid valves prevent the backflow of blood.

Okay — let's get to the heart of the matter...

The human heart beats 100 000 times a day on average — it's exhausting just thinking about it. You can feel a pulse in your wrist or neck (where the vessels are close to the surface). This is the blood being pushed along by another beat. Doctors use a stethoscope to listen to your heart — it's actually the valves closing that they hear.

Selective Breeding

'Selective breeding' sounds like it has the potential to be a tricky topic, but it's actually dead simple. You take the best plants or animals and breed them together to get the best possible offspring. That's it.

Selective Breeding is Very Simple

Selective breeding is when humans artificially select the plants or animals that are going to breed and have their genes remain in the population, according to what we want from them. Organisms are selectively bred to develop the best features, which are things like:

- Maximum yield of meat, milk, grain etc.
- Good health and disease resistance.
- Other qualities like temperament, speed, attractiveness, etc.

This is the basic process involved in selective breeding:

1) From your existing stock select the ones which have the best characteristics.
2) Breed them with each other.
3) Select the best of the offspring, and breed them together.
4) Continue this process over several generations, and the desirable trait gets stronger and stronger.

EXAMPLE:

In agriculture (farming), selective breeding can be used to improve yields. E.g. to improve meat yields, a farmer could breed together the cows and bulls with the best characteristics for producing meat, e.g. large size. After doing this for several generations the farmer would get cows with a very high meat yield.

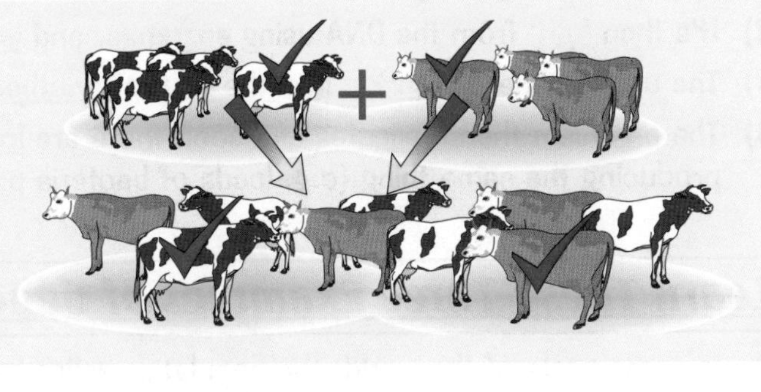

The Main Drawback is a Reduction in the Gene Pool

1) The main problem with selective breeding is that it reduces the gene pool — the number of different alleles (forms of a gene) in a population. This is because the farmer keeps breeding from the "best" animals or plants — which are all closely related. This is known as inbreeding.
2) Inbreeding can cause health problems because there's more chance of the organisms developing harmful genetic disorders when the gene pool is limited. This is because lots of genetic conditions are recessive — you need two alleles to be the same for it to have an effect. Breeding from closely related organisms all the time means that recessive alleles are more likely to build up in the population (because the organisms are likely to share the same alleles).

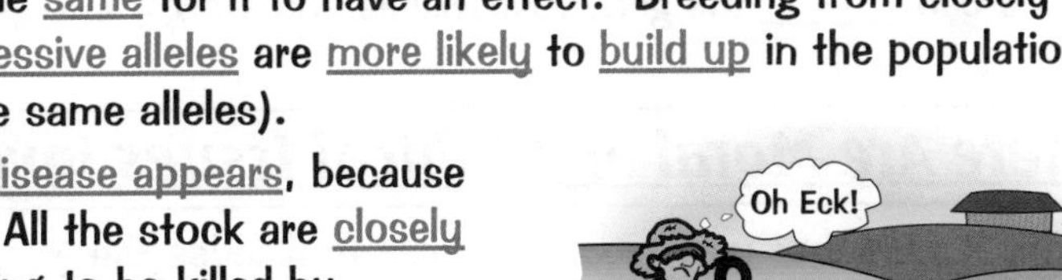

3) There can also be serious problems if a new disease appears, because there's not much variation in the population. All the stock are closely related to each other, so if one of them is going to be killed by a new disease, the others are also likely to succumb to it.

Selective Breeding → Reduction in the number of different alleles (forms of a gene) → Less chance of any resistant alleles being present in the population

I use the same genes all the time too — they flatter my hips...

Selective breeding's not a new thing. People have been doing it for absolutely yonks. That's how we ended up with something like a poodle from a wolf. Somebody thought 'I really like this small, woolly, yappy, wolf — I'll breed it with this other one'. And after thousands of generations, we got poodles. Hurrah.

Genetic Engineering

Genetic engineering — playing around with genes. Cool.

Genetic Engineering is Great — Hopefully

The basic idea behind genetic engineering is to move genes (sections of DNA) from one organism to another so that it produces useful biological products. You need to be able to explain some of the advantages and risks involved in genetic engineering.

1) The main advantage is that you can produce organisms with new and useful features very quickly. There are some examples of this below — make sure you learn them.
2) The main risk is that the inserted gene might have unexpected harmful effects. For example, genes are often inserted into bacteria so they produce useful products. If these bacteria mutated and became pathogenic (disease-causing), the foreign genes might make them more harmful and unpredictable. People also worry about the engineered DNA 'escaping' — e.g. weeds could gain rogue genes from a crop that's had genes for herbicide resistance inserted into it. Then they'd be unstoppable. Eeek.

Genetic Engineering Involves These Important Stages:

1) First the gene that's responsible for producing the desirable characteristic is selected (say the gene for human insulin).
2) It's then 'cut' from the DNA using enzymes, and isolated.
3) The useful gene is inserted into the DNA of another organism (e.g. a bacterium).
4) The organism then replicates and soon there are loads of similar organisms all producing the same thing (e.g. loads of bacteria producing human insulin).

Learn These Three Examples of Genetic Engineering:

1) In some parts of the world, the population relies heavily on rice for food. In these areas, vitamin A deficiency can be a problem, because rice doesn't contain much of this vitamin, and other sources are scarce. Genetic engineering has allowed scientists to take a gene that controls beta-carotene production from carrot plants, and put it into rice plants. Humans can then change the beta-carotene into vitamin A. Problem solved.
2) The gene for human insulin production has been put into bacteria. These are cultured in a fermenter, and the human insulin is simply extracted from the medium as they produce it. Great.
3) Some plants have resistance to things like herbicides, frost damage and disease. Unfortunately, it's not always the plants we want to grow that have these features. But now, thanks to genetic engineering, we can cut out the gene responsible and stick it into useful plants such as crops. Splendid.

There Are Moral and Ethical Issues Involved

All this is nice, but you need to be able to discuss the ethical issues surrounding genetic modification:

1) Some people think it's wrong to genetically engineer other organisms purely for human benefit. This is a particular problem in the genetic engineering of animals, especially if the animal suffers as a result.
2) People worry that we won't stop at engineering plants and animals. In the future, those who can afford genetic engineering might be able to decide the characteristics they want their children to have — and those who can't afford it may become a 'genetic underclass'.
3) The evolutionary consequences of genetic engineering are unknown, so some people think it's irresponsible to carry on when we're not sure what the impact on future generations might be.

If only they could genetically engineer you to be better at exams...

You can do great things with genetic engineering. But some people worry that we don't know enough about it, or that some maniac is going to come along and combine David Cameron with a grapefruit. Possibly.

Gene Therapy and Cloning Animals

If you thought that was it for genetic engineering, you'd be wrong. Next up is gene therapy...

Gene Therapy Could Be Used to Cure Genetic Disorders...

1) Gene therapy involves altering a person's genes in an attempt to cure genetic disorders. Scientists haven't got it to work properly yet, but they're working on it for the future.
2) There are two types of gene therapy:
   - The first would involve changing the genes in body cells, particularly the cells that are most affected by the disorder. For example, cystic fibrosis affects the lungs, so therapy for it would target the cells lining the lungs. This wouldn't affect the individual's gametes (sperm or eggs) though, so any offspring could still inherit the disease.
   - The second type of gene therapy would involve changing the genes in the gametes. This means that every cell of any offspring produced from these gametes will be affected by the gene therapy — and the offspring won't suffer from the disease. This type of therapy in humans is currently illegal though.
3) Gene therapy involving gametes is controversial.
   - For example, it might have unexpected consequences, which cause a whole new set of problems. These problems would then be inherited by all future generations.
   - There are fears that this kind of gene therapy could lead to the creation of 'designer babies' — where parents are able to choose the genes they want their children to have.

Now for something completely different — cloning...

Cloning is Making an Exact Copy of Another Organism

Learn what clones are:

Clones are genetically identical organisms.

Clones occur naturally in both plants and animals. Identical twins are clones of each other.

Cloning an Adult Animal is Done by Transferring a Cell Nucleus

The first mammal to be successfully cloned from an adult cell was a sheep called "Dolly". Dolly was produced using a method called nuclear transfer. This involves placing the nucleus of a body cell into an egg cell. Here's how it works:

1) The nucleus of a sheep's egg cell was removed — this left the egg cell without any genetic information.
2) Another nucleus was inserted in its place. This was a diploid nucleus from an udder cell of a different sheep (the one being cloned) and had all its genetic information.
3) The cell was given an electric shock so that it started dividing by mitosis (as if it was a normal fertilised egg).
4) The dividing cell (now an embryo) was implanted into the uterus of a surrogate mother sheep, to develop until it was ready to be born.
5) The result was Dolly, a clone of the sheep from which the udder cell came.

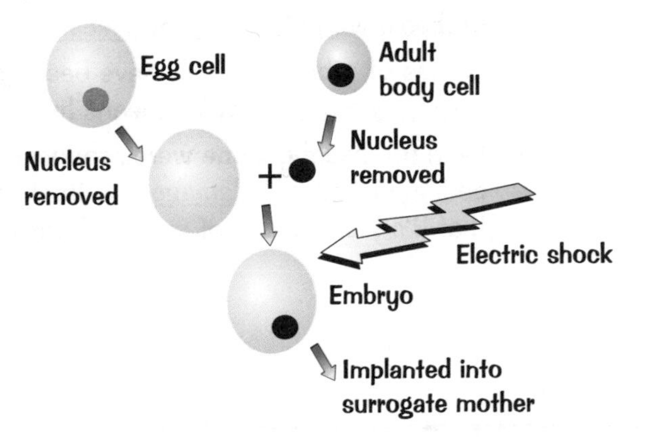

A whole lamb from a single cell? Pull the udder one...

Gene therapy is a bit of an ethical minefield. Most people would agree that treating diseases is a good thing, but there are concerns that it could lead to designer babies. The ethical issues of cloning are covered on the next page.

Uses and Risks of Cloning Animals

Cloning animals can lead to lots of potential benefits, for example, in medicine. But it can raise a lot of tricky issues, too — especially when the animals being cloned are humans.

There are Both Benefits and Risks Involved in Cloning

There are many possible BENEFITS of cloning:

1) Cloning allows you to mass produce animals with desirable characteristics, e.g.
   - Animals that can produce medicines in their milk could be developed by genetic engineering and then cloned. Researchers have managed to transfer human genes that produce useful proteins into sheep and cows. This means these animals can produce things like the blood clotting agent factor VIII (used for treating haemophilia).
   - Animals (like pigs) that have organs suitable for transplantation into humans could be developed by genetic engineering and then cloned. This would ensure a constant supply of organs for transplant — organs from human donors are currently in short supply. There are issues to consider with this type of transplant though — including concerns that viruses could be passed from the animals to humans.
2) Human embryos could be produced by cloning adult body cells. The embryos could then be used to supply stem cells for stem cell therapy (see page 53). These cells would have exactly the same genetic information as the patient, reducing the risk of rejection (a common problem with transplants).

But there are RISKS too:

1) There is some evidence that cloned animals might not be as healthy as normal ones.
2) Cloning is a new science and it might have consequences that we're not yet aware of.

Cloning Humans is a Possibility — with a Lot of Ethical Issues

Some people are worried that cloning animals is a short step away from using adult DNA to produce embryos which are allowed to grow into human clones.
There are ethical issues to consider with this...

1) There would have to be lots of surrogate pregnancies, probably with high rates of miscarriage and stillbirth.
2) Clones of other mammals have been unhealthy and often die prematurely — which means human clones might too.
3) Even if a healthy clone were produced, it might be psychologically damaged by the knowledge that it's just a clone of another human being.

An evil dictator might make an army of clones to rule the Galaxy...

That might be a good idea for a film, come to think of it. Cloning is exciting stuff — it's got loads of potential for helping to save lives, for one thing. But there are risks involved, as well as ethical issues, which shouldn't be ignored. You need to learn both the positives and the negatives of cloning for the exam.

Cloning Plants

More cloning here, I'm afraid, and this time it's all about plants. But this is the last page on it, I promise.

It's Fairly Easy to Clone Plants

1) Gardeners are familiar with taking cuttings from good parent plants, and then planting them to produce genetically identical copies — clones — of the parent plant.
2) Cloning plants is easier than cloning animals because many plant cells keep their ability to differentiate (see page 53) — animal cells lose this at an early stage.

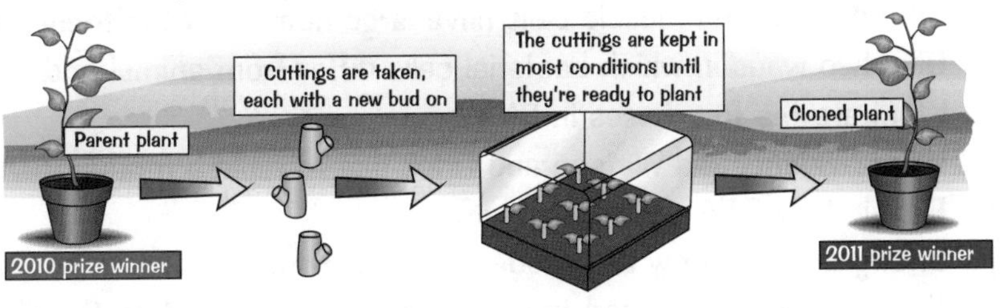

Commercial Cloning Often Involves Tissue Culture

1) First you choose the plant you want to clone based on its characteristics — e.g. a beautiful flower, a good fruit crop.
2) You remove several small pieces of tissue from the parent plant. You get the best results if you take tissue from fast-growing root and shoot tips.
3) You grow the tissue in a growth medium containing nutrients and growth hormones. This is done under aseptic (sterile) conditions to prevent growth of microbes that could harm the plants.
4) As the tissues produce shoots and roots they can be moved to potting compost to carry on growing.

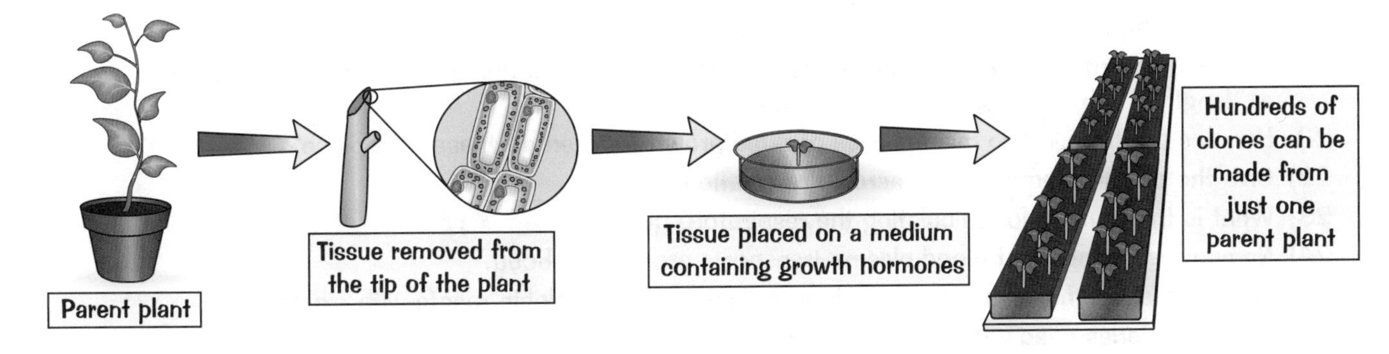

Commercial Use of Cloned Plants Has Pros and Cons

1) You can be fairly sure of the characteristics of the plant because it'll be genetically identical to the parent — so you'll only get good ones, and won't waste time and money growing duds.
2) It's possible to mass-produce plants that are hard to grow from seeds.
3) But, if the plants suffer from a disease or start doing badly because of a change in environment, they'll all have the same problems because they all have the same genes.
4) And there are the usual problems with lack of genetic variation (see page 59).

Stop cloning around — just learn it...

Plants are much better at being cloned than mammals are. They don't start dropping dead or having health problems, they just get on with it. And nobody seems that bothered about ethics when it's a tulip.

Revision Summary for Module B3

Here goes, folks — a beautiful page of revision questions to keep you at your desk studying hard until your parents have gone out and you can finally nip downstairs to watch TV. Think twice though before you reach for that remote control. These questions are actually pretty good — certainly more entertaining than 'Train Your Husband Like He's a Dog'. Question 14 is almost as good as an episode of 'Supernanny'. Question 4 is the corker though — like a reunion episode of 'Friends' but a lot funnier. Give the questions a go. Oh go on.

1) Why do liver and muscle cells have large numbers of mitochondria?
2) Give two ways in which bacterial cells differ from animal and plant cells.
3) What are the four bases in DNA?
4) What evidence did Watson and Crick use to build a model of DNA?
5) Explain how DNA replicates itself.
6) Briefly describe how DNA codes for a protein.
7) Name the molecule used to carry the code from DNA to the ribosomes.
8) Other than enzymes, give three different functions of proteins.
9) What are enzymes?
10) An enzyme with an optimum temperature of 37 °C is heated to 60 °C.
Suggest what will happen to the enzyme.
11) What does the Q_{10} value of an enzyme-controlled reaction show?
12) Why are mutations in an organism's DNA often harmful to that organism?
13) Give two things that increase the chance of mutation if you are exposed to them.
14) Give three advantages of being multicellular.
15) How many cells are produced after a mitotic division? Are they genetically identical?
16) How many cells are produced after a meiotic division? Are they genetically identical?
17) Give three ways that sperm cells are adapted for their function.
18) Describe two differences in the way plant cells and animal cells grow and develop.
19) Suggest why some people are against stem cell research.
20) Give one advantage and one disadvantage for each of the following ways of measuring growth:
a) length b) wet mass c) dry mass
21) Humans go through two main phases of rapid growth. When do these take place?
22) Give the chemical equation for aerobic respiration.
23) What is the formula for calculating the respiratory quotient?
24) Name seven things that blood plasma transports around the body.
25) Name the substance formed in red blood cells when haemoglobin reacts with oxygen.
26) Why do arteries need very muscular, elastic walls?
27) Explain how capillaries are adapted to their function.
28) Name the blood vessel that joins to the right ventricle of the heart. Where does it take the blood?
29) Why does the left ventricle have a thicker wall than the right ventricle?
30) What is selective breeding?
31) Give two disadvantages of selective breeding.
32) Give one advantage and one risk of genetic engineering.
33) Describe three examples of genetic engineering.
34) Describe the two types of gene therapy.
35) Why is gene therapy involving gametes controversial?
36) Describe the method of cloning that was used to produce Dolly the sheep.
37) Give two potential benefits and two potential risks of cloning animals.
38) Suggest three reasons why some people are concerned about cloning humans.
39) Describe how plants can be cloned using tissue culture.
40) Suggest two advantages and two disadvantages of the commercial use of cloned plants.

Estimating Population Sizes

1) A POPULATION is all the organisms of one species in a habitat (the place where an organism lives).
2) Populations of different species in a habitat make up a COMMUNITY.

Estimate Population Sizes by Scaling Up from a Small Sample Area

A quadrat is a square frame enclosing a known area. You can study the small area within a quadrat and scale up your findings to make estimates for larger areas:

1) Count all the organisms in a 1 m² quadrat.
2) Multiply the number of organisms by the total area (in m²) of the habitat.

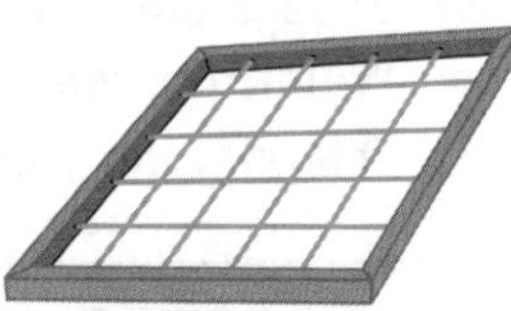
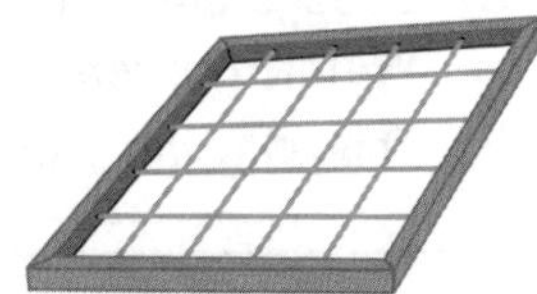

A quadrat

Example: Estimate the total populations of the various species in a 120 m² field if a 1 m² quadrat contained 90 grass plants, 30 buttercups and 25 daisies.

Answer: Multiply the figures for the 1 m² quadrat by 120 to estimate the populations in the whole field. So the field will contain about 10 800 grass plants, 3600 buttercups and 3000 daisies.

Estimate Population Sizes Using Capture-Recapture

To estimate population size using the capture-recapture method:

1) Capture a sample of the population and mark the animals in a harmless way.
2) Release them back into the environment.
3) Recapture another sample of the population. Count how many of this sample are marked.
4) Estimate population size using this equation:

$$\text{Population Size} = \frac{\text{number in first sample} \times \text{number in second sample}}{\text{number in second sample previously marked}}$$

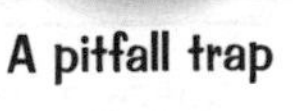

A pitfall trap

Example: A pitfall trap was set up in an area of woodland. 30 woodlice were caught in an hour and marked on their shell, before being released back into the environment. The next day, 35 woodlice were caught in an hour, only 5 of which were marked. Estimate the population size.

Answer: Multiply the number of woodlice in the first sample by the number in the second sample, then divide the answer by the number that were marked in the second sample. So the area of woodland will contain about (30 × 35) ÷ 5 = 210 woodlice.

A Few Important Points About These Methods:

1) The sample size affects the accuracy of the estimate — the bigger your sample, the more accurate your estimate of the total population is likely to be.
2) When you're using capture-recapture data you have to make the following assumptions:
   - There have been no changes in the population size due to deaths, immigration (individuals moving into the area) or emigration (individuals moving out of the area).
   - The sampling methods for the capture and recapture were identical (e.g. the pitfall trap was set up in the same way each time).
   - The marking hasn't affected the individuals' chances of survival (e.g. by making them more visible to predators).

Counting insects — avoid the pitfalls...

Whenever you're estimating the size of a population, you should make sure that your sample is representative of the whole population (i.e. what you find in your sample is broadly similar to what you'd find in the population).

Ecosystems and Distribution of Organisms

If you like getting down on your hands and knees and poking around at plants, you're in for a treat...

Ecosystems are Self-Supporting

1) An ecosystem is all the organisms living in a particular area, as well as all the non-living (abiotic) conditions, e.g. temperature, salinity and soil quality (see next page).
2) An ecosystem isn't the same as a habitat — a habitat is just the place where an organism lives.
3) Ecosystems are self-supporting — they contain (almost) everything they need to maintain themselves. Water, nutrients and essential elements like carbon all get recycled within the ecosystem.
4) The only thing that's needed from outside the ecosystem is an energy source. This is normally the Sun.

Transects are used to Investigate the Distribution of Organisms

1) Distribution is where organisms are found within a particular area.
2) You can investigate distribution using lines called transects.
3) To do a transect, you mark out a line using a tape measure and place quadrats next to each other all the way along the line. You then count and record the organisms you find in the quadrats.

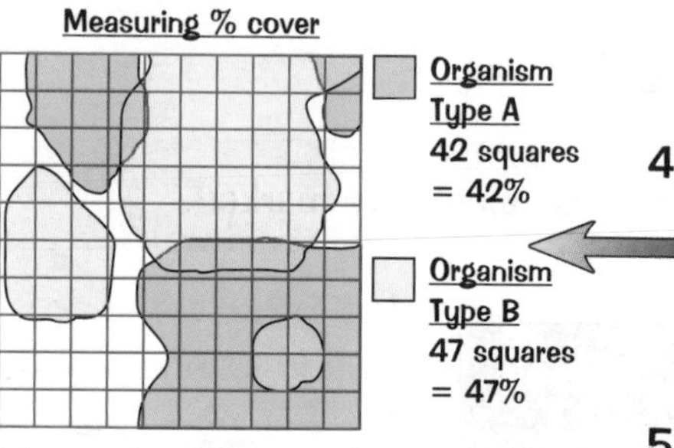

You count a square if it's more than half covered.

4) If it's difficult to count all the individual organisms in the quadrat (e.g. if they're grass) you can calculate the percentage cover. This means estimating the percentage area of the quadrat covered by a particular type of organism, e.g. by counting the number of little squares covered by the organisms.
5) You can plot the results of a transect in a kite diagram (see below). This allows you to map the distribution of organisms in an area.

Kite Diagrams Show the Abundance and Distribution of Organisms

The kite diagram below shows the distribution and abundance (number) of organisms along a transect in coastal sand dunes:

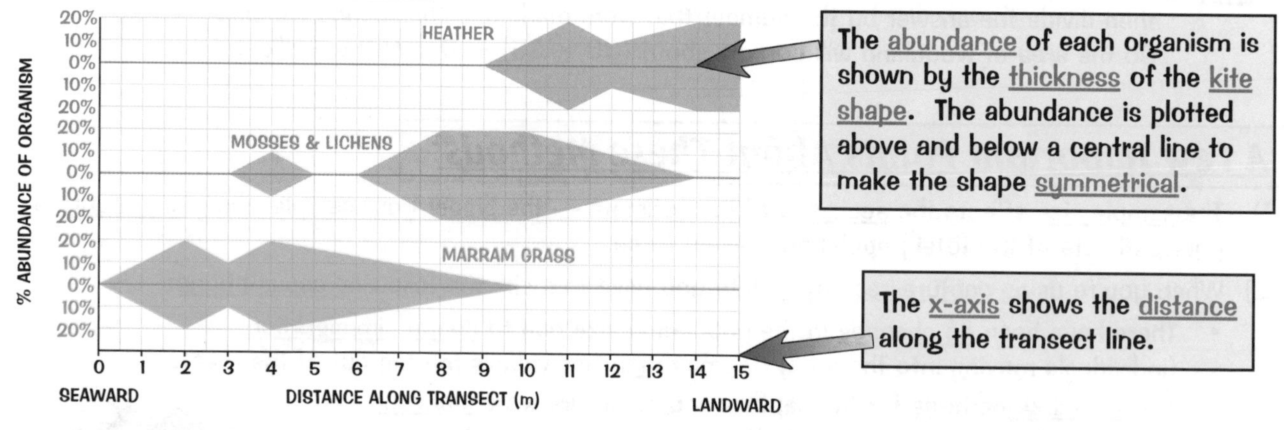

From the kite diagram you can see that marram grass was distributed between 0 and 10 m along the transect. At 2 m along the transect the abundance of marram grass was 20% (i.e. it covered 20% of the quadrat). At 7 m the abundance of marram grass was 10%.

Kite diagrams — to show your parents exactly how it got stuck in the tree...

Granted — this isn't the most adrenaline-fuelled wonder-page — but you still need to know it. Making sure you know the basics from this page and the previous one will make the rest of this section seem a lot easier.

Zonation

You need to know the factors that affect where organisms are found. You also need to know about a thing called zonation — thankfully, here's a page that'll tell you just that.

The Distribution of Organisms is Affected by Abiotic Factors

1) Abiotic factors are all the non-living, physical factors in an environment — e.g. light, temperature, water, oxygen, salinity (salt level) and soil quality.
2) The distribution of organisms is affected by abiotic factors because:

- Organisms are adapted to live in certain physical conditions. This means they're more likely to survive and reproduce in areas with these conditions. E.g. woodland ferns are adapted to living in shade, so you don't often find them growing in sunny, open spaces.
- Many organisms can only survive in the conditions they're adapted to. E.g. mosquitoes are adapted to live in warm climates — they can't survive in extreme cold.

Changes in Abiotic Factors Can Lead to Zonation

ZONATION IS THE GRADUAL CHANGE IN THE DISTRIBUTION OF SPECIES ACROSS A HABITAT.

A gradual change in abiotic factors can lead to the zonation of organisms in a habitat. For example, in a coastal habitat, changes in salinity and soil depth result in zones where different types of plants grow:

1) Few plants can grow in zone 1 because salinity is very high — marram grass can grow because it is adapted to the salty conditions.

2) In zone 2, lichens and mosses can grow. They out-compete the marram grass because they're better adapted to the less saline conditions.

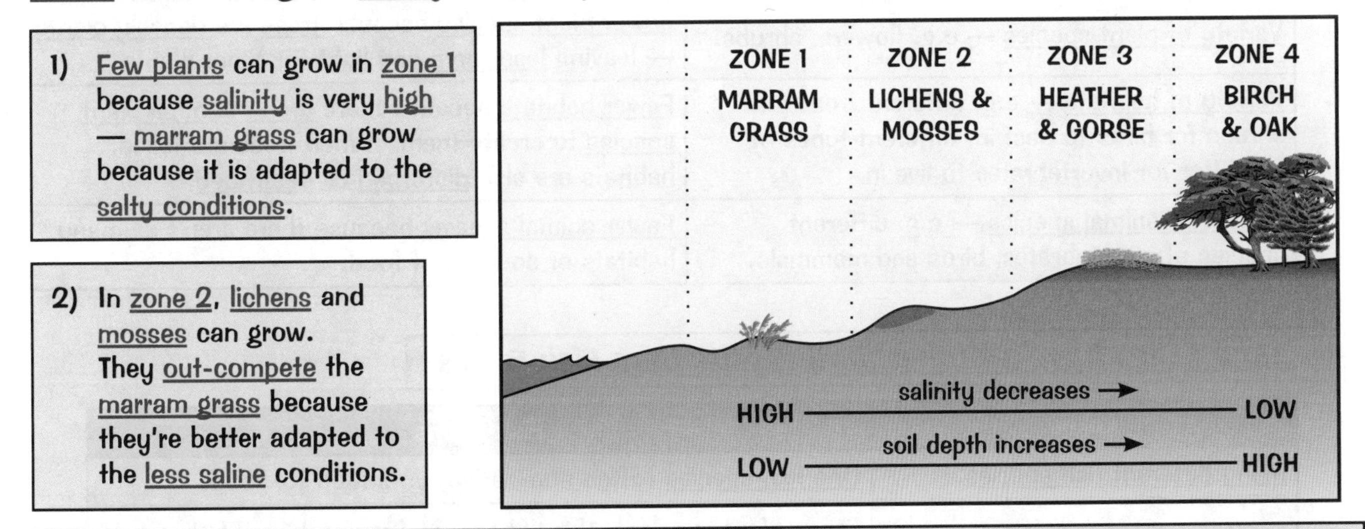

3) In zone 3, shrubs such as heather and gorse can grow and they out-compete the lichens and mosses. This is because they're better adapted to the lower salinity and deeper soil further away from the shore.

4) In zone 4, trees such as birch and oak can grow and they out-compete the shrubs. This is because they're better adapted to the very low salinity and deep soil that's found even further inland.

Believe it or not — there's a reason that penguins don't live in the Sahara...

...and giraffes don't live in the sea. It sounds pretty straightforward, but make sure you can explain everything on this page — even the really tricky stuff, like the zonation bit. Sketching out the diagram should help.

Biodiversity

Biological + diversity = Biodiversity. Simple. There's a bit more to it than that actually — enjoy.

Biodiversity is a Measure of the Variety of Life in an Area

Biodiversity includes:

1) The amount of variation between individuals of the same species in an area.
2) The number of different species in an area.
3) The number of different habitats in an area.

Biodiversity is important — ecosystems with a high level of biodiversity are healthier than those without. This is because more diverse ecosystems are better able to cope with changes in the environment.

Natural Ecosystems have a Higher Biodiversity than Artificial Ones

1) Natural ecosystems maintain themselves without any major interference from humans — e.g. native woodlands and natural lakes.
2) Artificial ecosystems are created and maintained by humans — e.g. forestry plantations and fish farms.

Native Woodlands have a Higher Biodiversity than Forestry Plantations...

Native Woodlands	Forestry Plantations
Variety of tree species — e.g. birch, hazel, oak.	One species of tree (often non-native) is planted for timber — e.g. Corsican pine or Douglas fir.
Trees are different sizes and ages.	Blocks of trees are planted at the same time — so many trees are the same age.
Variety of plant species — e.g. flowers, shrubs.	Fewer plant species because trees are densely planted — leaving less room and light for other plants.
Variety of habitats — e.g. different trees and shrubs for birds to nest in, different types of leaf litter for invertebrates to live in.	Fewer habitats because there aren't enough plant species to create them. When trees are felled, habitats are also disturbed or destroyed.
Variety of animal species — e.g. different species of invertebrates, birds and mammals.	Fewer animal species because there aren't as many habitats or sources of food.

...and Lakes have a Higher Biodiversity than Fish Farms

Lakes	Fish Farms
Many different fish species.	One fish species (often non-native) is farmed for food.
Variety of plant species.	Fewer plant species. This is because fish food is added and the food waste can cause algal blooms (rapid algal growth). The blooms block out the light, killing plants.
Variety of animal species, e.g. invertebrates, birds, mammals.	Fewer animals species. Predators (e.g. herons, otters) are kept out and pests (e.g. fish lice) are killed. There's also less food and fewer habitats because of the lack of plants.

Biodiversity — sounds like a washing powder...

Getting your head around exactly what biodiversity actually is is really important. Lots of people make the mistake of thinking that it's just the total number of species in a particular habitat. Luckily — you know better.

Photosynthesis

There's a fair old bit to learn about photosynthesis, so make sure you've had a snack before you start.

Photosynthesis is a Two-Stage Process

1) Photosynthesis uses energy from the Sun to change carbon dioxide and water into glucose and oxygen.
2) It takes place in chloroplasts in plant cells — they contain pigments like chlorophyll that absorb light energy.
3) The overall balanced symbol equation for photosynthesis is:

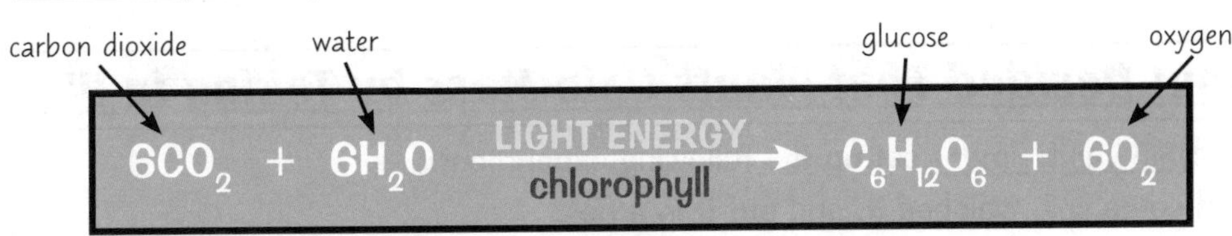

4) Even though the equation above looks like a single chemical reaction, photosynthesis actually happens in two main stages.
5) First, light energy is used to split water into oxygen gas and hydrogen ions.
6) Carbon dioxide gas then combines with the hydrogen ions to make glucose and water.
7) Watch out though — water isn't one of the overall products of photosynthesis (because more gets used up in the first stage than is made in the second stage).

Glucose is Converted into Other Substances

Here's how plants use the glucose they make:

For Respiration ①

Plants use some of the GLUCOSE for RESPIRATION. This releases energy so they can convert the rest of the glucose into various other useful substances.

Making Cell Walls ②

GLUCOSE is converted into CELLULOSE for making cell walls, especially in a rapidly growing plant.

Stored in Seeds ③

GLUCOSE is turned into LIPIDS (fats and oils) for storing in seeds. Sunflower seeds, for example, contain a lot of oil — we get cooking oil and margarine from them.

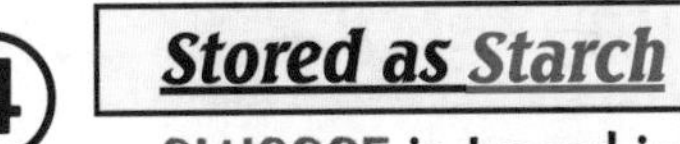

Stored as Starch ④

GLUCOSE is turned into STARCH and stored in roots, stems and leaves, ready for use when photosynthesis isn't happening, like at night.

STARCH is INSOLUBLE, which makes it good for storing. This is because:

- It can't dissolve in water and move away from storage areas in solution.
- It doesn't affect the water concentration inside cells — soluble substances would bloat the storage cells by drawing in water.

Making Proteins ⑤

GLUCOSE is combined with nitrates (collected from the soil) to make amino acids, which are then made into PROTEINS. These are used for growth and repair.

Convert this page into stored information...

Photosynthesis is important. All the energy we get from eating comes from it. When we eat plants, we're consuming the energy they've made, and when we eat meat, we're eating animals who got their energy from eating plants, or from eating animals that have eaten other animals who have... and so on.

Understanding Photosynthesis

We now know that plants get their food from photosynthesis — but it's taken us a while to work it out.

Greek Scientists Concluded That Plants Gain Mass from Soil Minerals

1) Around 350 BC Greek scientists (including Aristotle) studied plant growth.
2) They observed that the only thing touching plants was soil, so they decided that plants must grow and gain mass by taking in minerals from the soil (air touches plants too, but they couldn't see that).

Van Helmont Decided That Plants Gain Mass by Taking in Water

1) In the 1600s Jan van Helmont set up the following experiment:
   - He dried some soil, weighed it, and put it in a pot.
   - He planted a willow tree weighing 2.2 kg in the soil.
   - He added rainwater to the pot whenever it was dry.
2) 5 years later van Helmont removed the tree from the pot:
   - The tree weighed 76.7 kg — so it had gained 74.5 kg of mass.
   - He dried the soil and weighed it — its mass had changed very little (it weighed about 60 g less).
3) Van Helmont concluded that because the weight of the soil had changed so little, the tree must have gained mass from another source. Because he only added water to the tree, he concluded the tree must have gained mass by taking in water.
4) Today we know that plants also gain mass using CO_2 from the air — but this experiment was important because it introduced the idea that plants don't just gain mass by taking in minerals from the soil.

2.2 kg — 5 years — 76.7 kg

Priestley's Experiments Showed that Plants Produce Oxygen

1) In the early 1770s Joseph Priestley did the following experiment:

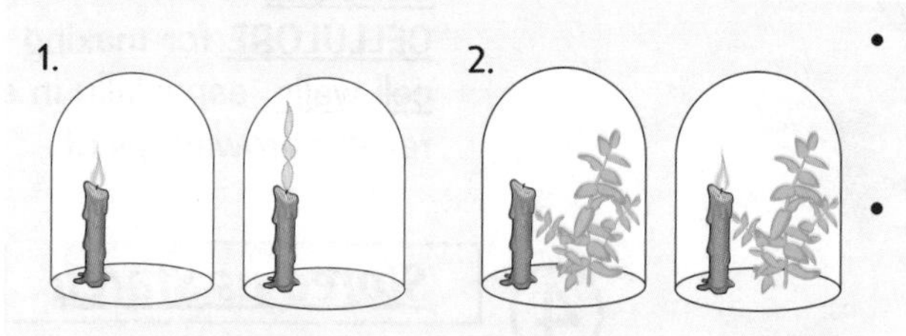

   - He placed a burning candle in a sealed container and observed that the flame went out after a short time. The candle couldn't be re-lit while in the container.
   - He then placed a burning candle and a living plant in the container. The flame went out after a short time, but after a few weeks the candle could be re-lit.
2) He decided that the burning candle used up something in the container — and that this made the flame go out. He also decided that the living plant 'restored the air' so the candle could burn again.
3) Priestley also did this experiment:
   - He filled a sealed container with exhaled air. He put a mouse in the container, and observed that it only survived for a few seconds.
   - He filled another sealed container with exhaled air. He put a living plant in the container and waited for a few days. He then put a mouse in the container — this time it survived for several minutes (lucky thing).

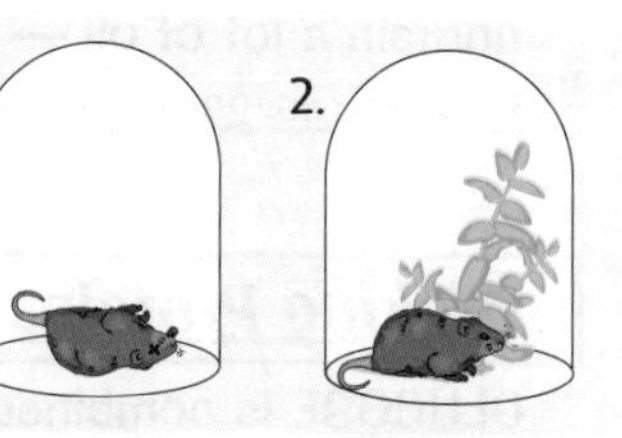

4) He thought that the mouse couldn't survive for long in the exhaled air because breathing had taken something out of the air. Again, he decided that the living plant 'restored the air' — this time allowing the mouse to survive for longer.
5) From these experiments, Priestley concluded that plants restore something to the air that burning and breathing take out. Today we know that this substance is oxygen — a product of photosynthesis.

I don't understand 'Understanding Photosynthesis'...

Putting a mouse in a jar of carbon dioxide and noticing that it dies doesn't sound like a particularly cutting-edge investigation — but the experiments on this page all contributed hugely to our understanding of photosynthesis.

More on Photosynthesis

Here's some other wonderful stuff that scientists have worked out about photosynthesis.

The Oxygen Produced in Photosynthesis Comes From Water

1) Scientists realised that plants release oxygen during photosynthesis, but they didn't know whether the oxygen came from carbon dioxide or water (both of which contain oxygen atoms).
2) To find out where the oxygen came from, a scientist supplied plants with water containing an isotope of oxygen called oxygen-18. The carbon dioxide the plants received contained ordinary oxygen-16.
3) It was found that when the plants photosynthesised, they released oxygen-18.
4) This showed that the oxygen came from the water that was supplied to the plant, not the carbon dioxide.

Isotopes are just different forms of the same element.

There are Three Limiting Factors that Control the Rate of Photosynthesis

1) Not Enough LIGHT Slows Down the Rate of Photosynthesis

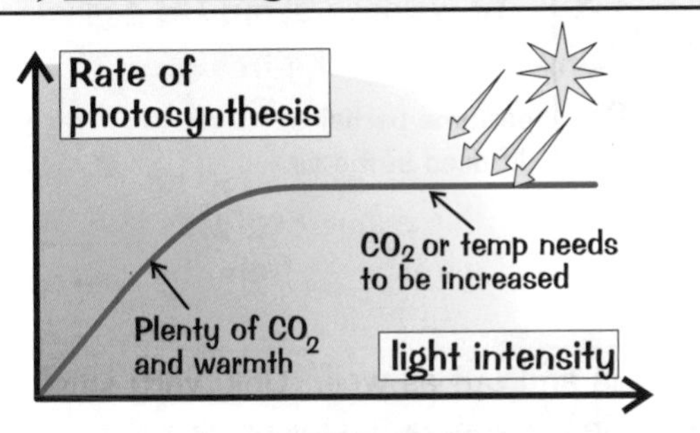

Light provides the energy needed for photosynthesis.

1) If the light level is raised, the rate of photosynthesis will increase, but only up to a certain point.
2) Beyond that, it won't make any difference because then it'll be either the temperature or the CO_2 level which is now the limiting factor.

2) Too Little CARBON DIOXIDE Also Slows It Down

CO_2 is one of the raw materials needed for photosynthesis — only 0.04% of the air is CO_2, so it's pretty scarce as far as plants are concerned.

1) As with light intensity, the amount of CO_2 will only increase the rate of photosynthesis up to a point. After this the graph flattens out, showing that CO_2 is no longer the limiting factor.
2) As long as light and CO_2 are in plentiful supply then the factor limiting photosynthesis must be temperature.

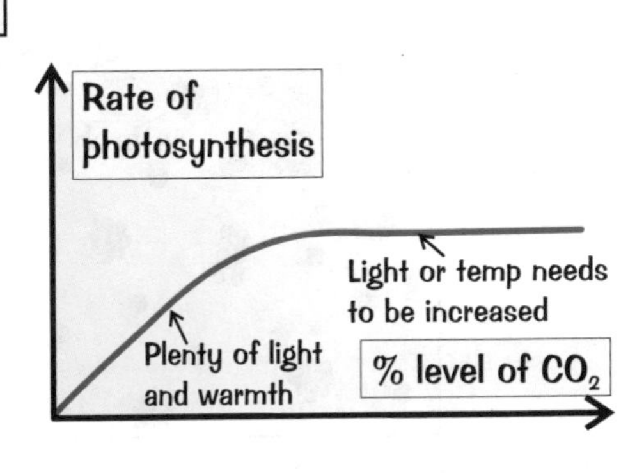

3) The TEMPERATURE Has to be Just Right

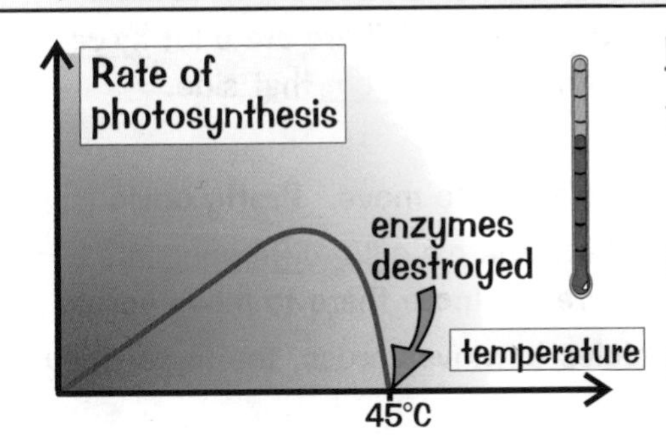

Photosynthesis works best when it's warm but not too hot.

1) As the temperature increases, so does the rate of photosynthesis. But if the temperature is too high, the plant's enzymes will be denatured (see page 49), so the rate rapidly decreases.
2) This happens at about 45 °C (which is pretty hot for outdoors, though greenhouses can get that hot if you're not careful).
3) Usually though, if the temperature is the limiting factor it's because it's too low, and things need warming up a bit.

Life isn't all fun and sunshine...

There are three limiting factors, a graph for each and an explanation of why the rate of photosynthesis levels off or falls abruptly. After you've read over the page, cover it up and jot down the graphs and explain why they're the shapes that they are. It's not my idea of fun (honest) but it's the best way to get stuff lodged in your brain.

Diffusion

Particles move about randomly, and after a bit they end up evenly spaced. And that's how most things move about in our bodies — by "diffusion".

Don't be Put Off by the Fancy Word

"Diffusion" is simple. It's just the gradual movement of particles from places where there are lots of them to places where there are fewer of them. That's all it is — just the natural tendency for stuff to spread out. Unfortunately you also have to learn the fancy way of saying the same thing, which is this:

DIFFUSION is the NET MOVEMENT OF PARTICLES from an area of HIGHER CONCENTRATION to an area of LOWER CONCENTRATION

Diffusion happens in both liquids and gases — that's because the individual particles in these substances are free to move about randomly. The simplest type is when different gases diffuse through each other. This is what's happening when the smell of perfume diffuses through the air in a room:

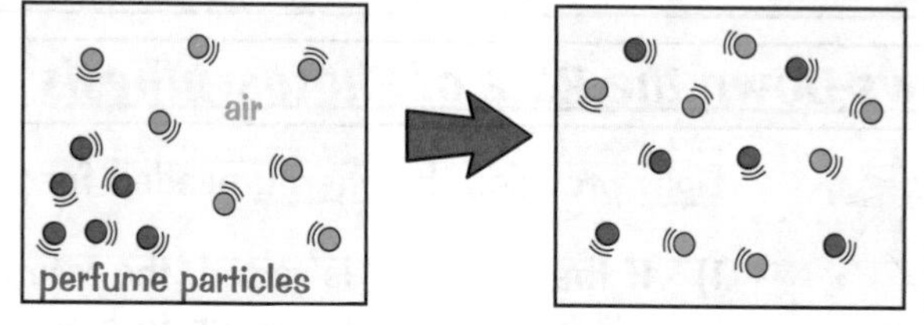

Cell Membranes are Kind of Clever...

They're clever because they hold the cell together BUT they let stuff in and out as well. Only very small molecules can diffuse through cell membranes though — things like simple sugars, water or ions. Big molecules like starch and proteins can't pass through the membrane.

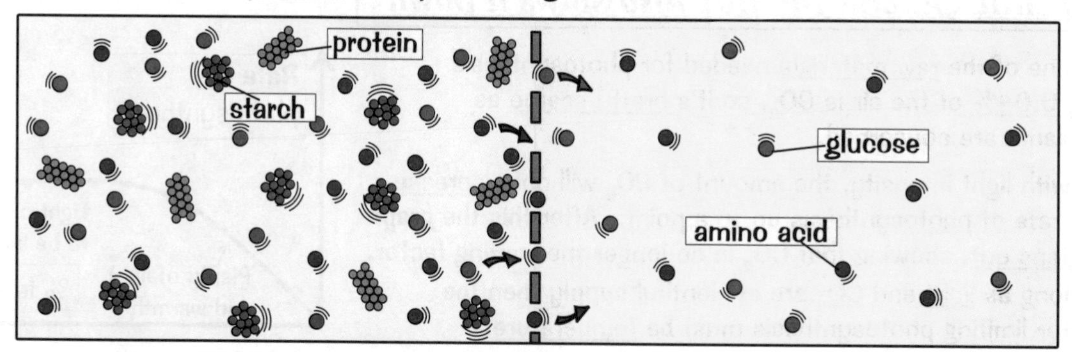

1) Just like with diffusion in air, particles flow through the cell membrane from where there's a higher concentration (a lot of them) to where there's a lower concentration (not such a lot of them).
2) They're only moving about randomly of course, so they go both ways — but if there are a lot more particles on one side of the membrane, there's obviously an overall movement from that side.
3) The rate of diffusion depends on three main things:
   a) Distance — substances diffuse more quickly when they haven't as far to move. Pretty obvious.
   b) Concentration difference (gradient) — substances diffuse faster if there's a big difference in concentration. If there are lots more particles on one side, there are more there to move across.
   c) Surface area — the more surface there is available for molecules to move across, the faster they can get from one side to the other.

Whoever smelt it dealt it... Whoever said the rhyme did the crime...

Because, of course, it's not just perfume that diffuses through a room. Anyway. All living cells have membranes, and their structure allows sugars, water and the rest to drift in and out as needed. Don't forget, the membrane doesn't control diffusion, it happens all by itself — but the membrane does stop large molecules passing through.

Leaves and Diffusion

This page is all about leaves, what they get up to in the dark, and how they exchange gases.

You Need to Learn The Structure of A Leaf

Let's start with the basics. You need to know all the different parts of a typical leaf shown on the diagram:

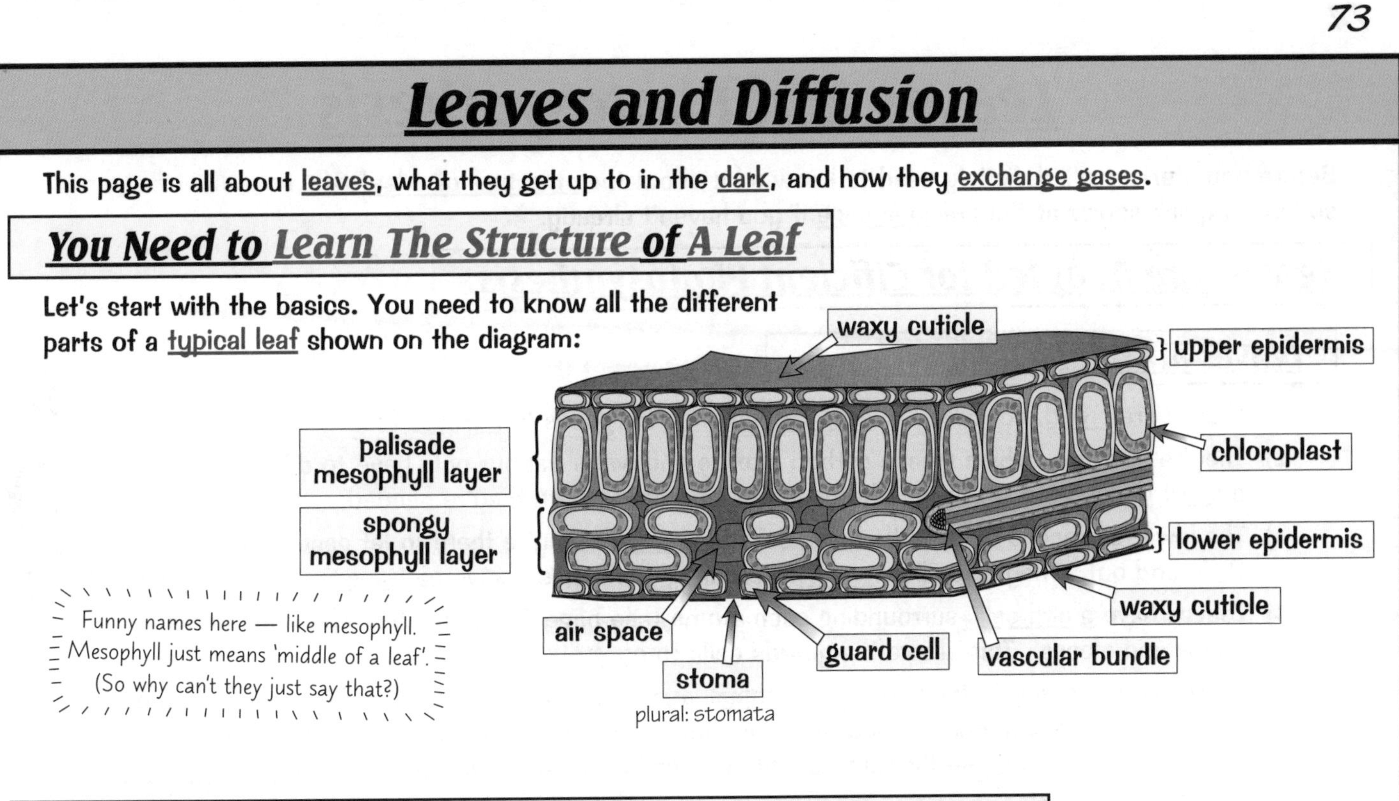

Plants Carry Out Both Photosynthesis and Respiration

1) Photosynthesis and respiration are opposite processes:

   Photosynthesis: carbon dioxide + water → glucose + oxygen (Requires energy)

   Respiration: glucose + oxygen → carbon dioxide + water (Energy released)

2) Photosynthesis only happens during the day (i.e. when there's light available). But plants must respire all the time, day and night to get the energy they need to live.
3) During the day, plants make more oxygen by photosynthesis than they use in respiration. So in daylight, they release oxygen and take in carbon dioxide.
4) At night though, plants only respire — there's no light for photosynthesis. This means they take in oxygen and release carbon dioxide — just like us.

For more on respiration, see page 55.

Plants Exchange Gases by Diffusion

Diffusion of gases in the leaves is vital for both photosynthesis and respiration. Here's how it works:

PHOTOSYNTHESIS

1) When the plant is photosynthesising it uses up lots of carbon dioxide, so there's hardly any inside the leaf.
2) Luckily this makes more carbon dioxide move into the leaf by diffusion (from an area of higher concentration to an area of lower concentration).
3) At the same time lots of oxygen is being made as a waste product of photosynthesis.
4) Some is used in respiration, and the rest diffuses out of the leaf (moving from an area of higher concentration to an area of lower concentration).

RESPIRATION

1) At night it's a different story — there's no photosynthesis going on because there's no light. Lots of carbon dioxide is made in respiration and lots of oxygen is used up.
2) There's a lot of carbon dioxide in the leaf and not a lot of oxygen, so now it's mainly carbon dioxide diffusing out and oxygen diffusing in.

I tried really hard to leaf the dodgy jokes out of this page...

... and I got so close. Oh well — sorry about that. Remember: photosynthesis uses energy from light so it can only take place during the day. Respiration releases energy for life processes — it takes place all the time.

Leaves and Photosynthesis

Before you start, you'll definitely need to know a bit about the structure of a leaf — so have a quick squizz at the previous page if you haven't already.

Leaves are Adapted for Efficient Photosynthesis:

Leaves are Adapted for Diffusion

1) Leaves are broad, so there's a large surface area for gases to diffuse.
2) They're also thin, which means carbon dioxide and water vapour only have to diffuse a short distance to reach the photosynthesising cells where they're needed.
3) The lower surface is full of little holes called stomata. They're there to let gases like CO_2 and O_2 in and out. They also allow water to escape — which is known as transpiration (see page 77).
4) Leaves have guard cells surrounding each stoma (see page 78) to control when the stoma opens and closes. This allows the guards cells to control gas exchange.
5) There are air spaces in the spongy mesophyll layer. This allows gases like CO_2 and O_2 to move between the stomata and the photosynthesising cells. This also means there's a large surface area for gas exchange — the technical phrase for this is "they have a very big internal surface area to volume ratio".

Leaves are Adapted to Absorb Light

1) The leaves being broad also means there's a large surface area exposed to light.
2) Leaves contains lots of chloroplasts. Chloroplasts contain chlorophyll and other photosynthetic pigments to absorb light energy.
3) Different pigments absorb different wavelengths of light, so plant cells can make the most of the Sun's energy by absorbing as much of it as possible. The table below shows four different pigments found in plants and the wavelengths of light they absorb:

You might get asked to interpret data on the absorption of light in the exam.

Pigment:	Absorbs wavelengths of:
Chlorophyll a	400-450 nm and 650-700 nm
Chlorophyll b	450-500 nm and 600-650 nm
Carotene	400-550 nm
Xanthophyll	400-530 nm

'nm' stands for 'nanometre' — a really small unit of length.

4) The cells that contain the most chloroplasts are arranged in the palisade layer near the top of the leaf where they can get the most light.
5) The upper epidermis is transparent so that light can pass through it to the palisade layer.

Leaves Have a Network of Vascular Bundles

The vascular bundles are the transport vessels, xylem and phloem (see page 76). They deliver water and other nutrients to every part of the leaf and take away the glucose produced by photosynthesis. They also help to support the leaf structure.

If you don't do much revision, it's time to turn over a new leaf...

So how do they know all this stuff? Well, scientists know how leaves are adapted for photosynthesis because they've looked and seen the structure of leaves and the cells inside them. Not with the naked eye, of course — they used microscopes. So they're not just making it up, after all.

Osmosis

Trust me — osmosis really isn't as scary as it sounds. This page tells you everything you need to know.

Osmosis is a Special Case of Diffusion, That's All

> Osmosis is the net movement of water molecules across a partially permeable membrane from a region of higher water concentration (i.e. a dilute solution) to a region of lower water concentration (i.e. a concentrated solution).

1) A partially permeable membrane is just one with very small holes in it. So small, in fact, that only tiny molecules (like water) can pass through them, and bigger molecules (e.g. sucrose) can't.
2) The water molecules actually pass both ways through the membrane during osmosis. This happens because water molecules move about randomly all the time.
3) But because there are more water molecules on one side than on the other, there's a steady net flow of water into the region with fewer water molecules, i.e. into the stronger sucrose solution.
4) This means the concentrated sucrose solution gets more dilute. The water acts like it's trying to 'even up' the concentration either side of the membrane.
5) Osmosis is a type of diffusion — net movement of particles from an area of higher concentration to an area of lower concentration.

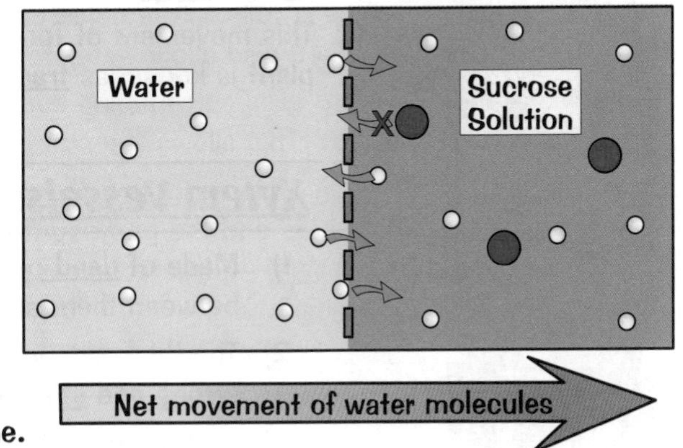

Turgor Pressure Supports Plant Tissues

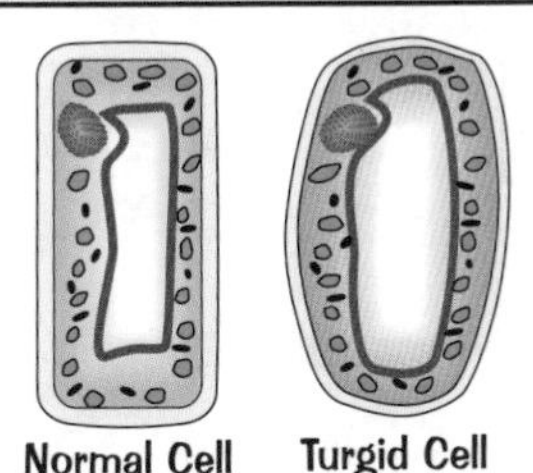

1) When a plant is well watered, all its cells will draw water in by osmosis and become plump and swollen. When the cells are like this, they're said to be turgid.
2) The contents of the cell push against the inelastic cell wall — this is called turgor pressure. Turgor pressure helps support the plant tissues.
3) If there's no water in the soil, a plant starts to wilt (droop). This is because the cells start to lose water and so lose their turgor pressure. They're then said to be flaccid.
4) If the plant's really short of water, the cytoplasm inside its cells starts to shrink and the membrane pulls away from the cell wall. The cell is now said to be plasmolysed. The plant doesn't totally lose its shape though, because the inelastic cell wall keeps things in position. It just droops a bit.

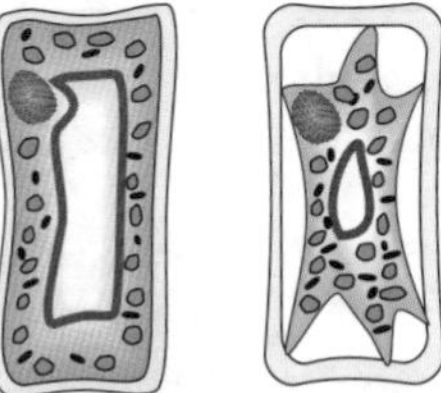

Animal Cells Don't Have an Inelastic Cell Wall

Turgid plant cell

Animal cell bursting

Plant cells aren't too bothered by changes in the amount of water because the inelastic cell wall keeps everything in place.

It's different in animal cells because they don't have a cell wall. If an animal cell takes in too much water, it bursts — this is known as lysis. If it loses too much water it gets all shrivelled up — this is known as crenation.

What all this means is that animals have to keep the amount of water in their cells pretty constant or they're in trouble, while plants are a bit more tolerant of periods of drought.

Revision by osmosis — you wish...

Wouldn't that be great — if all the ideas in this book would just gradually drift across into your mind, from an area of higher concentration (in the book) to an area of lower concentration (in your mind — no offence). Actually, that probably will happen if you read it again. Why don't you give it a go...

Transport Systems in Plants

Plants have two transport systems. They have two separate types of vessel — xylem and phloem — for transporting stuff around. Both types of vessel go to every part of the plant in a continuous system, but they're totally separate.

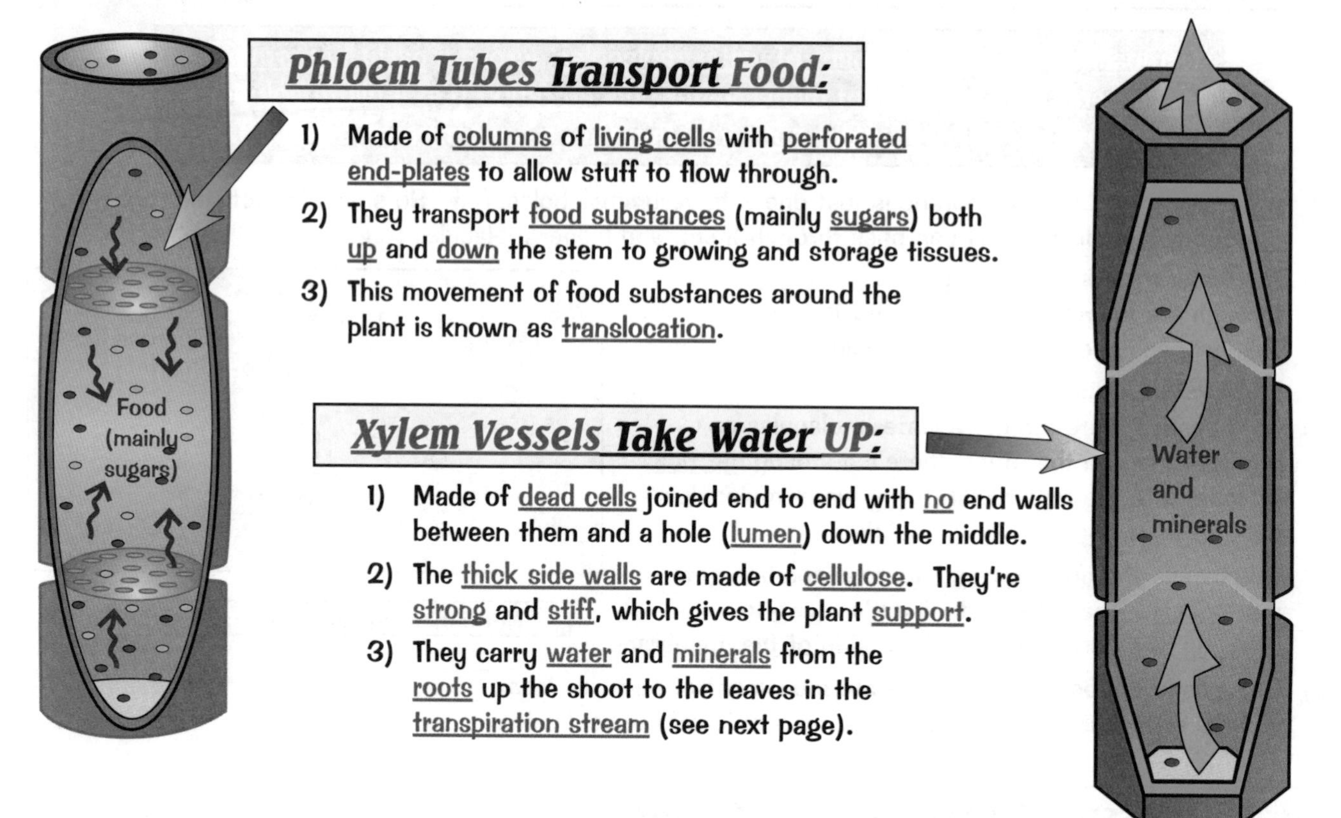

Phloem Tubes Transport Food:

1) Made of columns of living cells with perforated end-plates to allow stuff to flow through.
2) They transport food substances (mainly sugars) both up and down the stem to growing and storage tissues.
3) This movement of food substances around the plant is known as translocation.

Xylem Vessels Take Water UP:

1) Made of dead cells joined end to end with no end walls between them and a hole (lumen) down the middle.
2) The thick side walls are made of cellulose. They're strong and stiff, which gives the plant support.
3) They carry water and minerals from the roots up the shoot to the leaves in the transpiration stream (see next page).

You can Recognise Xylem and Phloem by Where They Are

1) They usually run alongside each other in vascular bundles (like veins).
2) Where they're found in each type of plant structure is related to xylem's other function — support.

You need to learn these three examples:

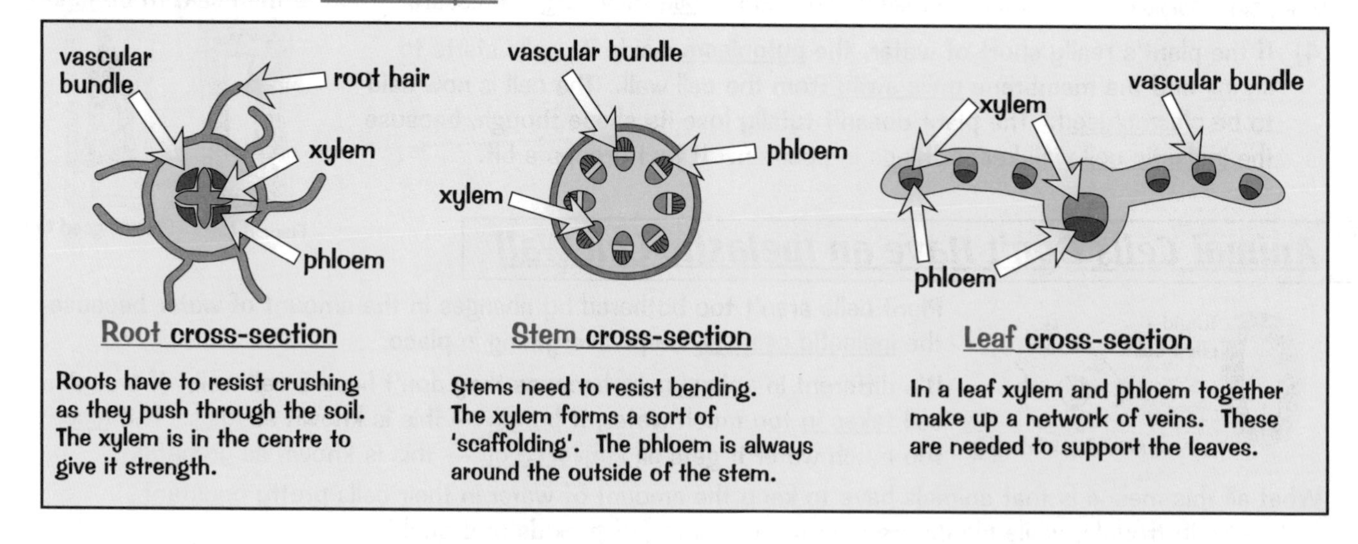

Root cross-section

Roots have to resist crushing as they push through the soil. The xylem is in the centre to give it strength.

Stem cross-section

Stems need to resist bending. The xylem forms a sort of 'scaffolding'. The phloem is always around the outside of the stem.

Leaf cross-section

In a leaf xylem and phloem together make up a network of veins. These are needed to support the leaves.

Don't let revision stress you out — just go with the phloem...

You've probably done that really dull experiment where you stick a piece of celery in a beaker of water with red food colouring in it. Then you stare at it for half an hour, and once the time is up, hey presto, the red has reached the top of the celery. That's because it travelled there in the xylem. Unbelievable.

Water Flow Through Plants

If you don't water a house plant for a few days it starts to go all droopy. Then it dies, and the people from the Society for the Protection of Plants come round and have you arrested. Plants need water.

Root Hairs Take in Water by Osmosis

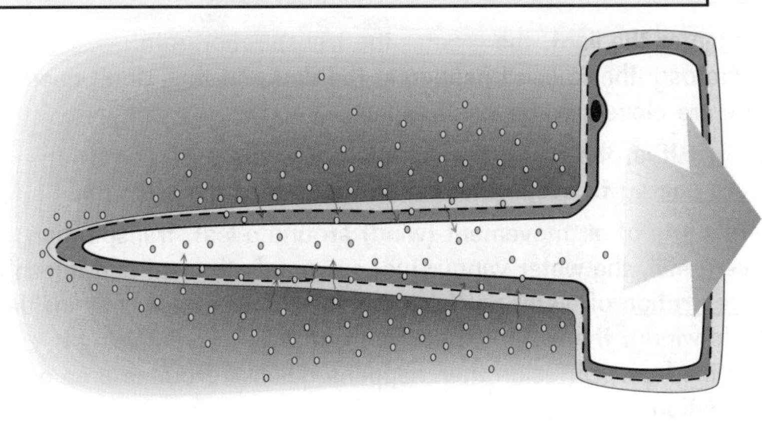

1) The cells on plant roots grow into long 'hairs' which stick out into the soil.
2) Each branch of a root will be covered in millions of these microscopic hairs.
3) This gives the plant a big surface area for absorbing water from the soil.
4) There's usually a higher concentration of water in the soil than there is inside the plant, so the water is drawn into the root hair cell by osmosis (see page 75).

Transpiration is the Loss of Water from the Plant

1) Transpiration is caused by evaporation and diffusion of water vapour from inside the leaves.
2) This creates a slight shortage of water in the leaf, and so more water is drawn up from the rest of the plant through the xylem vessels (see previous page) to replace it.
3) This in turn means more water is drawn up from the roots, and so there's a constant transpiration stream of water through the plant.

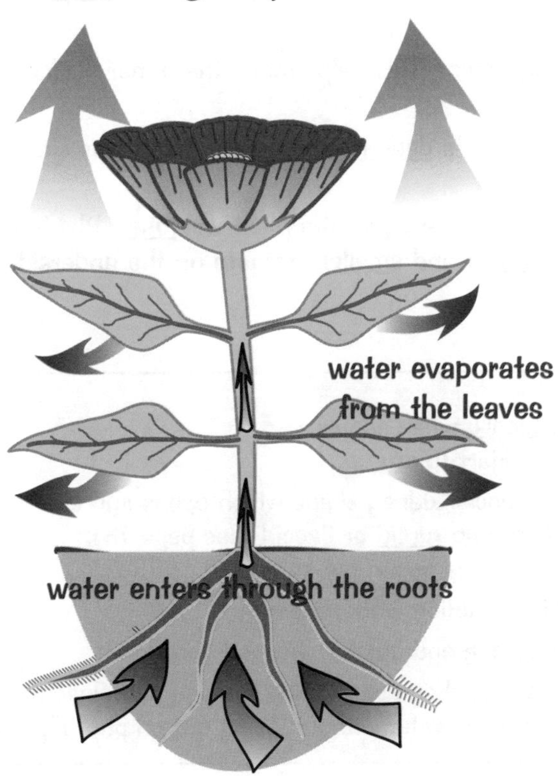

Transpiration is just a side-effect of the way leaves are adapted for photosynthesis. They have to have stomata in them so that gases can be exchanged easily (see page 74). Because there's more water inside the plant than in the air outside, the water escapes from the leaves through the stomata.

The transpiration stream does have some benefits for the plants, however:

1) The constant stream of water from the ground helps to keep the plant cool.
2) It provides the plant with a constant supply of water for photosynthesis.
3) The water creates turgor pressure in the plant cells, which helps support the plant and stops it wilting (see page 75).
4) Minerals needed by the plant (see page 79) can be brought in from the soil along with the water.

Transpiration — the plant version of perspiration...

Here's an interesting fact — a biggish tree loses about a thousand litres of water from its leaves every single day. That's as much water as the average person drinks in a whole year, so the roots have to be very effective at drawing in water from the soil. Which is why they have all those root hairs, you see.

Water Flow Through Plants

If you thought that page on transpiration was interesting, you're not gonna believe your luck — here's another page all about water transport in plants.

Transpiration Rate is Increased by Four Main Things

1) AN INCREASE IN LIGHT INTENSITY — the brighter the light, the greater the transpiration rate. Stomata begin to close as it gets darker. Photosynthesis can't happen in the dark, so they don't need to be open to let CO_2 in. When the stomata are closed, water can't escape.
2) AN INCREASE IN TEMPERATURE — the warmer it is, the faster transpiration happens. When it's warm the water particles have more energy to evaporate and diffuse out of the stomata.
3) AN INCREASE IN AIR MOVEMENT — if there's lots of air movement (wind) around a leaf, transpiration happens faster. If the air around a leaf is very still, the water vapour just surrounds the leaf and doesn't move away. This means there's a high concentration of water particles outside the leaf as well as inside it, so diffusion doesn't happen as quickly. If it's windy, the water vapour is swept away, maintaining a low concentration of water in the air outside the leaf. Diffusion then happens quickly, from an area of high concentration to an area of low concentration.
4) A DECREASE IN AIR HUMIDITY — if the air around the leaf is very dry, transpiration happens more quickly. This is like what happens with air movement. If the air is humid there's a lot of water in it already, so there's not much of a difference between the inside and the outside of the leaf. Diffusion happens fastest if there's a really high concentration in one place, and a really low concentration in the other.

Plants Need to Balance Water Loss with Water Uptake

Transpiration can help plants in some ways (see previous page), but if it hasn't rained for a while and you're short of water it's not a good idea to have it rushing out of your leaves. So plants have adaptations to help reduce water loss from their leaves.

1) Leaves usually have a waxy cuticle covering the upper epidermis. This helps make the upper surface of the leaf waterproof.
2) Most stomata are found on the lower surface of a leaf where it's darker and cooler. This helps slow down diffusion of water out of the leaf (see above).
3) The bigger the stomata and the more stomata a leaf has, the more water the plant will lose. Plants in hot climates really need to conserve water, so they have fewer and smaller stomata on the underside of the leaf and no stomata on the upper epidermis.

Stomata Open and Close Automatically

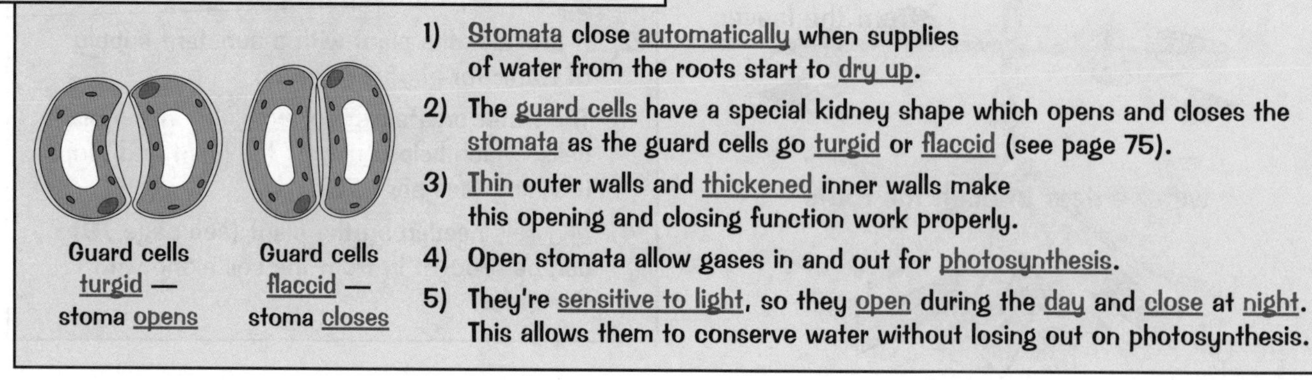

1) Stomata close automatically when supplies of water from the roots start to dry up.
2) The guard cells have a special kidney shape which opens and closes the stomata as the guard cells go turgid or flaccid (see page 75).
3) Thin outer walls and thickened inner walls make this opening and closing function work properly.
4) Open stomata allow gases in and out for photosynthesis.
5) They're sensitive to light, so they open during the day and close at night. This allows them to conserve water without losing out on photosynthesis.

It always helps if you're quick on the uptake...

In the exam they might ask you to interpret some data from experiments about transpiration rate. Don't panic — as long as you remember the four factors that affect the transpiration rate, you should be able to say something intelligent and get some valuable marks in the bag.

Minerals Needed for Healthy Growth

Plants are important in food chains and nutrient cycles because they can take minerals from the soil and energy from the Sun and turn it into food. And then, after all that hard work, we eat them.

Plants Need Three Main Minerals

Plants need certain elements so they can produce important compounds. They get these elements from minerals in the soil. If there aren't enough of these minerals in the soil, plants suffer deficiency symptoms.

1) Nitrates

Contain nitrogen for making amino acids and proteins. These are needed for cell growth. If a plant can't get enough nitrates, its growth will be poor and it'll have yellow older leaves.

2) Phosphates

Needed for respiration and growth. Contain phosphorus for making DNA and cell membranes. Plants without enough phosphate have poor root growth and discoloured older leaves.

3) Potassium

To help the enzymes needed for photosynthesis and respiration. If there's not enough potassium in the soil, plants have poor flower and fruit growth and discoloured leaves.

Magnesium is Also Needed in Small Amounts

The three main minerals are needed in fairly large amounts, but there are other elements which are needed in much smaller amounts. Magnesium is one of the most significant as it's required for making chlorophyll (needed for photosynthesis). Plants without enough magnesium have yellow leaves.

Root Hairs Take in Minerals Using Active Transport

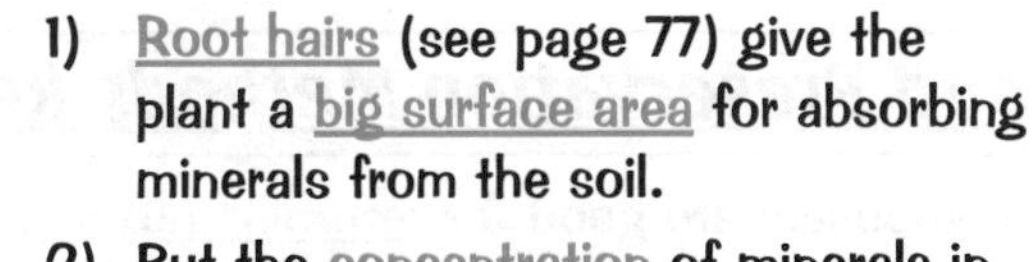

1) Root hairs (see page 77) give the plant a big surface area for absorbing minerals from the soil.
2) But the concentration of minerals in the soil is usually pretty low. It's normally higher in the root hair cell than in the soil around it.
3) So normal diffusion doesn't explain how minerals are taken up into the root hair cell.
4) They should go the other way if they followed the rules of diffusion.
5) The answer is that a different process called 'active transport' is responsible.
6) Active transport uses energy from respiration to help the plant pull minerals into the root hair against the concentration gradient (from low concentrations to high concentrations).

Nitrogen and phosphorus and potassium — oh my...

When a farmer or a gardener buys fertiliser, that's pretty much what he or she is buying — nitrates, phosphates and potassium. A fertiliser's NPK label tells you the relative proportions of nitrogen (N), phosphorus (P) and potassium (K) it contains, so you can choose the right one for your plants and soil.

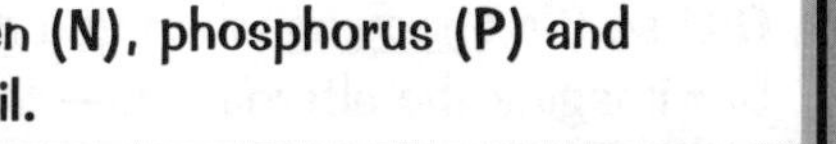

Decay

Microorganisms are great because they break down plant and animal remains which are lying around and looking unsightly. But they also break down plant and animal remains that we just bought at the shops.

Things Decay Because of Microorganisms

1) Living things are made of materials they take from the world around them.
2) When they die and decompose, or release material as waste, the elements they contain are returned to the soil or air where they originally came from.
3) Nearly all decomposition is done by microorganisms like soil bacteria and fungi (known as decomposers).
4) The rate of decay depends on three main things:

   a) Temperature — a warm temperature makes things decay faster because it speeds up respiration in microorganisms.
   b) Amount of water — things decay faster when they're moist because microorganisms need water.
   c) Amount of oxygen (air) — decay is faster when there's oxygen available. The microorganisms can respire aerobically (see page 55), providing more energy.

5) When these factors are at optimum levels (i.e. warm, moist, plenty of O_2), microorganisms grow and reproduce more quickly. This means there'll be more of them to decay other living things.

Detritivores and Saprophytes Feed on Decaying Material

Detritivores and saprophytes are both types of organism that are important in decay. They're grouped into those two types depending on how they feed:

1) Detritivores feed on dead and decaying material (detritus). Examples of detritivores include earthworms, maggots and woodlice. As these detritivores feed on the decaying material, they break it up into smaller bits. This gives a bigger surface area for smaller decomposers to work on and so speeds up decay.
2) Saprophytes also feed on decaying material, but they do so by extracellular digestion — i.e. they feed by secreting digestive enzymes on to the material outside of their cells. The enzymes break down the material into smaller bits, which can then be absorbed by the saprophyte. Many saprophytes are fungi.

Food Preservation Methods Reduce the Rate of Decay

Decomposers are good for returning nutrients to the soil, but they're not so good when they start decomposing your lunch. So people have come up with ways to stop them:

1) Canning — basically, this involves putting food in an airtight can. This keeps the decomposers out.
2) Cooling — putting food in a fridge slows down decay because it slows the decomposers' reproduction rate.
3) Freezing — food lasts longer in the freezer than in the fridge because the decomposers can't reproduce at all at such low temperatures.
4) Drying — dried food lasts longer because decomposers need water to carry out cell reactions. Lots of fruits are preserved by drying them out, and sometimes meat is too.
5) Adding salt/sugar — if there's a high concentration of salt or sugar around decomposers, they'll lose water by osmosis. This damages them and means they can't work properly. Things like tuna and olives are often stored in brine (salt water).
6) Adding vinegar — mmm, pickled onions. Vinegar is acidic, and the acid kills the decomposers.

Decomposers — they're just misunderstood...

OK, so it's annoying when you go to the cupboard and find that everything has turned a funny green colour. But imagine the alternative — there'd be no nutrients in the soil and we'd be up to our eyes in dead things. Eww.

Intensive Farming

Farming's a noisy, tiring and often smelly pastime. You can understand why farmers would want to make it as efficient as possible — that's where intensive farming comes in. There are two sides to the story though...

Intensive Farming is Used to Produce More Food

Intensive farming means trying to produce as much food as possible from your land, animals and plants. Farmers can do this in different ways — the following methods all involve reducing the energy losses that happen at each stage in a food chain (making the transfer of energy between organisms in a food chain more efficient):

1) Using herbicides to kill weeds. This means that more of the energy from the Sun falling on fields goes to the crops, and not to any other competing plants that aren't wanted.
2) Using pesticides to kill insects that eat the crops. This makes sure no energy is transferred into a different food chain — it's all saved for growing the crops.
3) Battery farming animals. The animals are kept close together indoors in small pens, so that they're warm and can't move about. This saves them wasting energy as they move around, and stops them using up so much energy keeping warm.

Intensive farming allows us to produce a lot of food from less and less land, which means a huge variety of top quality foods, all year round, at cheap prices.

Hydroponics is Where Plants are Grown Without Soil

1) Hydroponics is another method of intensive farming. It's where plants are grown in nutrient solutions (water and fertilisers) instead of in soil.
2) Hydroponics is often used to grow glasshouse tomatoes on a commercial scale, as well as to grow plants in areas with barren soil.
3) There are advantages and disadvantages of growing plants using hydroponics rather than in soil:

ADVANTAGES	DISADVANTAGES
Mineral levels can be controlled more accurately.	Lots of fertilisers need to be added.
Diseases can be controlled more effectively.	There's no soil to anchor the roots and support the plants.

Intensive Farming Can Destroy the Environment

Intensive farming methods are efficient, but they sometimes raise ethical dilemmas because they can damage the world we live in, making it polluted, unattractive and devoid of wildlife. The main effects are:

1) Removal of hedges to make huge great fields destroys the natural habitat of wild creatures. It can also lead to serious soil erosion.
2) Careless use of fertilisers can pollute rivers and lakes (known as eutrophication).
3) Pesticides disturb food chains — see next page.
4) Lots of people think that intensive farming of animals such as battery-hens is cruel because they have very little space or freedom to move around.

Intensive farming — sounds like hard work...

So. Intensive farming allows us to produce lots of food, cheaply and efficiently, but it sometimes raises ethical dilemmas. For some environmentally friendly alternatives to these intensive farming methods, see page 83.

Pesticides and Biological Control

Biological control is growing more popular, as people get fed up with all the problems caused by pesticides.

Pesticides Disturb Food Chains

1) Pesticides are sprayed onto crops to kill the creatures that damage them (pests), but unfortunately they can also kill organisms that aren't pests, like bees and ladybirds.
2) This can cause a shortage of food for animals further up the food chain.
3) Some pesticides are persistent — they tend to stick around in ecosystems and are hard to get rid of.
4) There's a danger of pesticides being passed along the food chain and killing the animals further up.

This is well illustrated by the case of otters which were almost wiped out over much of crop-dominated southern England by a pesticide called DDT in the early 1960s. The diagram shows the food chain which ends with the otter. DDT (like most pesticides) can't be excreted — so it accumulates along the food chain and the otter ends up with most of the DDT collected by all the other animals.

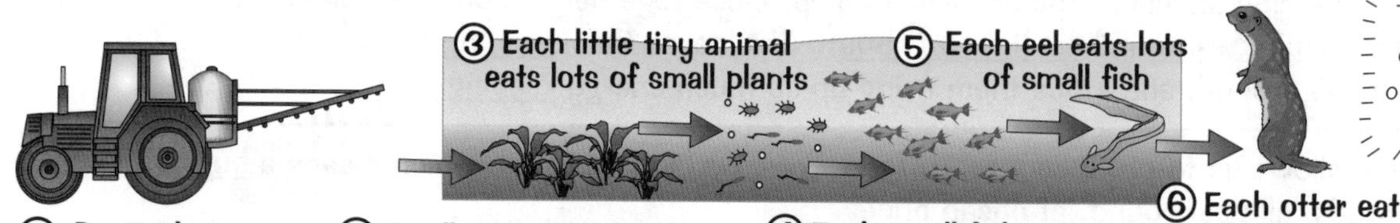

The concentration of pesticide in the organisms increases at each stage.

① Pesticide seeps into the river
② Small water plants take up a little pesticide
④ Each small fish eats lots of tiny animals
⑥ Each otter eats lots of eels and ends up with lots of pesticide

You Can Use Biological Control Instead of Pesticides

Biological control means using living things instead of chemicals to control a pest.
You could use a predator, a parasite or a disease to kill the pest. For example:

1) Aphids are a pest because they eat roses and vegetables. Ladybirds are aphid predators, so people release them into their fields and gardens to keep aphid numbers down.
2) Certain types of wasps and flies produce larvae which develop on (or in, yuck) a host insect. This eventually kills the insect host. Lots of insect pests have parasites like this.
3) Myxomatosis is a disease which kills rabbits. The *Myxoma virus* was released in Australia as a biological control when the rabbit population there grew out of control and ruined crops.

You need to be able to explain the advantages and disadvantages of biological control:

ADVANTAGES:

- No chemicals are used, so there's less pollution, disruption of food chains and risk to people eating the food that's been sprayed.
- There's no need to keep repeating the treatment — like you would with chemical pesticides.

DISADVANTAGES:

- The predator that you introduce might not eat the pest — making it useless.
- The predator could eat useful species e.g. pollinators or seed dispersers.
- The predator's population might increase and get out of control.
- The predator might not stay in the area where it's needed.

Remember that removing an organism from a food web, whether you use biological control or pesticides, can affect all the other organisms too. For example, if you remove a pest insect, you're removing a source of food from all the organisms that normally eat it. These might die out, and another insect that they normally feed on could breed out of control and become a pest instead. You have to be very careful.

Don't get bugged by biological pest control...

There's a fair ol' bit of information on this page, but you really do need to know it. So make sure you do.

Alternatives to Intensive Farming

Intensive farming can allow farmers to produce lots of food — but it isn't always possible and it isn't always the best approach. Some farmers are sticking with the good old fashioned 'hard graft' approach.

Lots of Farmers Use Organic Farming Methods

Modern intensive farming produces lots of food and we all appreciate it on the supermarket shelves. But traditional organic farming methods do still work (amazingly!), and they have their benefits too. You need to know about these organic farming techniques:

1) Use of organic fertilisers (i.e. animal manure and compost). This recycles the nutrients left in plant and animal waste. It doesn't work as well as artificial fertilisers, but it is better for the environment.

2) Crop rotation — growing a cycle of different crops in a field each year. This stops the pests and diseases of one crop building up, and stops nutrients running out (as each crop has slightly different needs). Most crop rotations include a nitrogen-fixing crop, such as legume plants (usually peas or beans). These help put nitrates back in the soil. (See page 79 for more on nitrates.)

Eeugh. I feel so dizzy.

Me too.

3) Weeding — this means physically removing the weeds, rather than just spraying them with a herbicide. Obviously it's a lot more labour intensive, but there are no nasty chemicals involved.

4) Varying seed planting times — sowing seeds later or earlier in the season will avoid the major pests for that crop. This means the farmer won't need to use pesticides.

5) Biological control — this is covered on the previous page.

Organic Farming Methods Have Their Advantages and Disadvantages

You also need to be able to explain the advantages and disadvantages of organic farming. Here are some of the main ones:

Advantages

1) Organic farming uses fewer chemicals, so there's less risk of toxic chemicals remaining on food.
2) It's better for the environment. There's less chance of polluting rivers with fertiliser. Organic farmers also avoid using pesticides, so don't disrupt food chains and harm wildlife.
3) For a farm to be classed as organic, it will usually have to follow guidelines on the ethical treatment of animals. This means no battery farming.

Disadvantages

1) Organic farming takes up more space than intensive farming — so more land has to be farmland, rather than being set aside for wildlife or for other uses.
2) It's more labour-intensive. This provides more jobs, but it also makes the food more expensive.
3) You can't grow as much food. But on the other hand, Europe over-produces food these days anyway.

Crop rotation — it's just like editing your digital photos...

Organic farming might be much better for the environment than intensive farming, but it still has its disadvantages. Make sure you're able to explain both the pros and the cons for the exam.

Revision Summary for Module B4

What a nice leafy section that was. Things started to get a bit mouldy at one point, but that's life I suppose. Now, just to make sure you've taken in all the leafiness and mouldiness, here's a little revision summary so you can check what you've learned. You know the routine by now — whizz through the questions and make a note of any you can't answer. Then go back and find the answer in the section. It's actually kind of fun, like a treasure hunt... well, okay, it's not — but it works.

1) Explain the terms 'community' and 'population'.
2)* Estimate the total ant population in a 4000 m^2 car park if a 1 m^2 area contained 80 ants.
3)* You catch 23 woodlice one day and mark their shells. The next day you catch 28 woodlice and find that four of them are marked. Estimate the population size.
4) Explain the meaning of the word 'ecosystem'. How is an ecosystem different to a habitat?
5) Describe how you'd carry out a transect to investigate the distribution of plant species in a field.
6) What are 'abiotic factors'?
7) What is zonation?
8) What is biodiversity?
9) Describe how the biodiversity is different in a native woodland compared to a forestry plantation.
10) Write down the balanced symbol equation for photosynthesis.
11) Explain why starch rather than glucose is used for storage in plants.
12) Describe van Helmont's experiment with a willow tree. What did it show?
13) What were the conclusions of Priestley's experiments with mice and plants?
14) Explain how experiments with isotopes have contributed to our understanding of photosynthesis.
15) What are the three limiting factors in photosynthesis? Sketch graphs to illustrate their effect on the rate of photosynthesis.
16) Write a definition of the word 'diffusion'.
17) Why can't starch pass through a partially permeable membrane?
18) What is usually found covering the upper epidermis layer of a leaf?
19) Why does oxygen tend to move into leaves during the night?
20) Describe how leaves are adapted for efficient diffusion.
21) Describe how leaves are adapted to absorb light energy.
22) Explain what osmosis is.
23) What is turgor pressure?
24) How are xylem vessels adapted to their function?
25) What do phloem tubes transport?
26) Where are the xylem and phloem found in a root?
27) What is the advantage to a plant of having root hairs?
28) Give three ways that the transpiration stream benefits a plant.
29) How is the transpiration rate affected by: a) increased temperature, b) increased air humidity?
30) What causes stomata to close when a plant is short of water? How does this benefit the plant?
31) Name the three main minerals plants need for healthy growth.
32) What is magnesium needed for in a plant?
33) Give an example of a detritivore.
34) Why does pickling food in vinegar help it to last for longer without decaying?
35) Give three ways that intensive farming methods reduce the energy lost at each stage in a food chain.
36) Give three problems associated with intensive farming.
37) Explain how pesticides can accumulate in a food chain.
38) List the advantages and disadvantages of biological pest control.
39) What is meant by the term 'hydroponics'?
40) Give two advantages and two disadvantages of organic farming methods.

* Answers on page 124.

Bones and Cartilage

Bones and joints are pretty darned important — without them you wouldn't be able to move around at all.

If You Didn't Have a Skeleton, You'd be Jelly-like

1) The job of a skeleton is to support the body and allow it to move — as well as protect vital organs.
2) Fish, amphibians, reptiles, birds and mammals are all vertebrates — they all have an internal skeleton including a backbone. Some animals (e.g. insects) have an external skeleton — their skeleton is on the outside of their bodies.
3) An internal skeleton has certain advantages compared to an external skeleton:
   - It can easily grow with the body.
   - It's easy to attach muscles to it.
   - It's more flexible than an external skeleton.
   - It gives the body support and provides a framework.

Bones are Living Tissues...

Bones are a lot cleverer than they might look...

1) Bones are made up of living cells — so they grow, and can repair themselves if they get damaged.

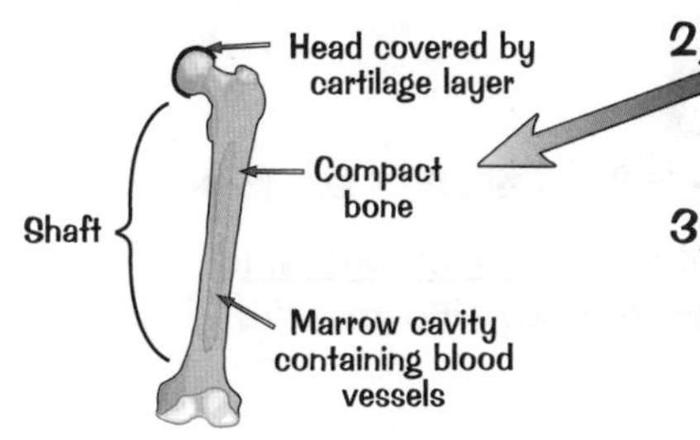

2) Long bones (e.g. the big one in your thigh) are actually hollow — this makes them lighter than solid bones of the same size (and stronger than solid bones of the same mass). This makes movement far more efficient.
3) The hole in the middle of some long bones is filled with bone marrow. Bone marrow is a spongy substance that makes new blood cells — meaning your bones are actually a kind of blood factory.

...That Start Off Life as Cartilage

1) Bones start off as cartilage in the womb. Cartilage is living tissue that looks and feels a bit rubbery. It can grow and repair itself too (although not as easily as bone).
2) As you grow, a lot of your cartilage is replaced by bone. Blood vessels deposit calcium and phosphorus in the cartilage — which eventually turns it into bone. This process is called ossification.
3) You can tell if someone is still growing by looking at how much cartilage is present — if there's a lot, they're still growing.
4) Even when you're fully grown, the ends of bones remain covered with cartilage (to stop bones rubbing together at joints — see next page).

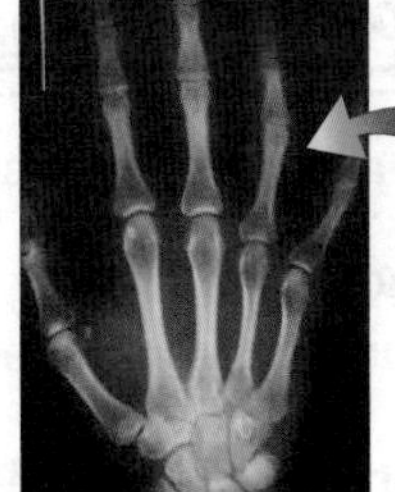

Bones show up on an X-ray, but cartilage doesn't.

X-rays can also show where fractures are.

Bones and Cartilage Can Get Damaged

1) Cartilage and bone are both made up of living tissue, and so can get infected.
2) Even though bones are really strong, they can be fractured (broken) by a sharp knock. Elderly people are more prone to breaking bones as they often suffer from osteoporosis — a condition where calcium is lost from the bones. (Osteoporosis makes the bones softer, more brittle and more likely to break — it can be treated with calcium supplements.)
3) A broken bone can easily injure nearby tissue — so you shouldn't move anyone who might have a fracture. That's especially true for someone with a suspected spinal fracture (broken back) — moving them could damage their spinal cord (basically an extension of the brain running down the middle of the backbone). Damage to the spinal cord can lead to paralysis.

What do skeletons say before eating?... bone appetit...

Bones are all too easily thought of as just organic scaffolding. They're pretty amazing really, and painful if you break one. But bones usually mend pretty easily — if you hold them still, a break will knit itself together.

Joints and Muscles

Like it says in the song, the knee bone's connected to the thigh bone. And it's done with a joint. Read on.

Joints Allow the Bones to Move

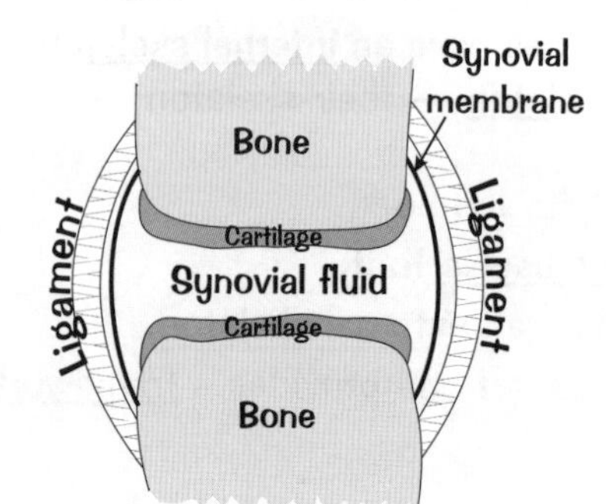

1) Synovial joints (e.g. the knee) are the main type of joint in the body.
2) The bones at a synovial joint are held together by ligaments. Ligaments have a high tensile strength (i.e. you can pull them and they don't snap easily), but are pretty elastic (stretchy).
3) The ends of bones are covered with cartilage to stop the bones rubbing together. And because cartilage can be slightly compressed, it can act as a shock absorber.
4) The synovial membrane releases synovial fluid to lubricate the joints, allowing them to move more easily.
5) Different kinds of joints move in different ways. For example...

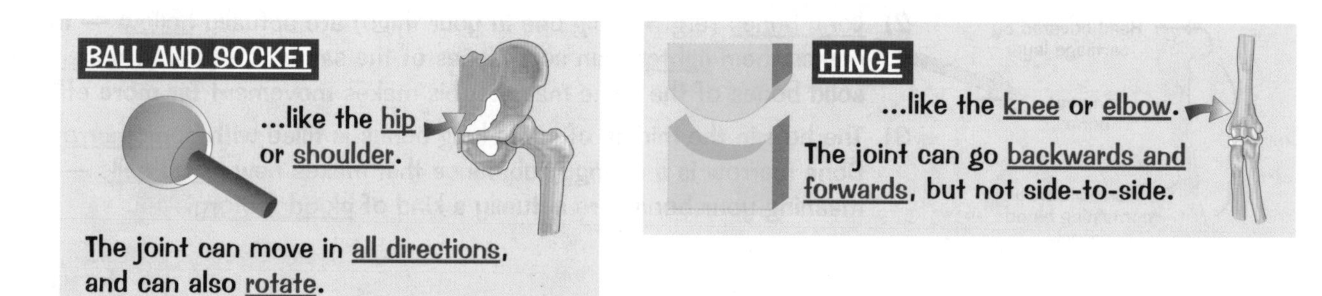

Muscles Pull on Bones to Move Them

1) Bones are attached to muscles by tendons.
2) Muscles move bones at a joint by contracting (becoming shorter). They can only pull on bones to move a joint — they can't push.
3) This is why muscles usually come in pairs (called antagonistic pairs). When one muscle in the pair contracts, the joint moves in one direction. When the other muscle contracts, it moves in the opposite direction.

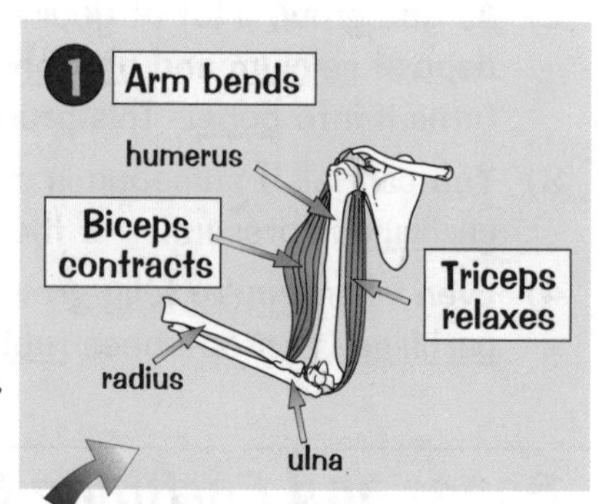

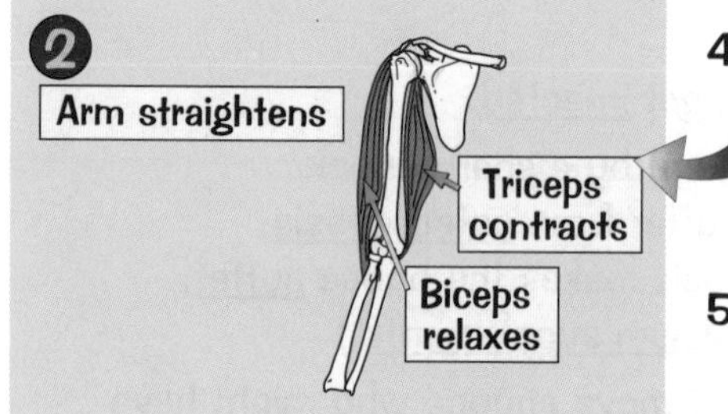

4) The biceps and triceps are an antagonistic pair of muscles. When the biceps contracts it pulls the lower arm upwards. This bends the arm. And when the triceps contracts the lower arm is pulled back down. This straightens the arm.
5) Together, they make the arm work as a lever, where the elbow is the pivot (fulcrum).

What's a skeleton's favourite instrument?... a trom-bone...

Different joints have different ranges of movement. And if you do something that makes the bone move further than its range of movement (like fall on it), then you could dislocate it. Painful. Make sure you learn the different parts of the synovial joint, as well as exactly what each bit does.

Circulatory Systems

If the circulatory system sounds familiar, that's because you covered it back in Module B3. You need to know about it for this module, too — but in a bit more detail. My heart's all of a flutter just thinking about it...

Lots of Animals Need a Blood Circulatory System

See page 72 for more on diffusion.

1) All living cells need to be supplied with materials like oxygen and glucose. They also need to get rid of waste materials like carbon dioxide.
2) In single-celled organisms these materials just diffuse in and out of the cell. But multicellular organisms like animals are much larger. Diffusion through all the cells would be too slow — so animals need a blood circulatory system to transport materials efficiently around their bodies.
3) In any circulatory system (so this goes for humans, dogs, fish, etc.), the heart acts as a pump. The heart contracts, pushing blood round the body. Blood flows away from the heart along arteries, through capillaries at the organs, and then back to the heart through veins.
4) As blood travels round the body through blood vessels it loses pressure. So arteries have the highest pressure, veins have the lowest and capillaries are in between.

Humans Have a Double Circulatory System

1) Animals with gills (e.g. fish), have a single circulatory system — one circuit of blood vessels from the heart.
2) For this, you need a two-chambered heart — one chamber to receive blood and one to pump blood out to the gills and the rest of the body.

3) Humans (and other mammals) have a double circulatory system. It has two circuits from the heart — one to the body and the other to the lungs.
4) In a double circulatory system, you need a four-chambered heart This allows the blood to be pumped separately to the lungs and the body, which is important for maintaining a high pressure (see below).
5) Unborn babies don't need a double-circulatory system. They get their oxygen from their mother via the placenta, so their blood doesn't need to travel to the lungs. As a result, all unborn babies have a 'hole in the heart' (a gap between the atria), which allows blood to bypass the lungs. It closes soon after birth.

(See page 90 for more on different types of hole in the heart.)

Blood is Under a Higher Pressure In a Double Circulatory System

1) In animals with a single circulatory system, the blood loses pressure as its pumped to the gills and then around the rest of the body. This means the overall pressure of the blood is fairly low.
2) In a double circulatory system, blood pressure is much higher. The blood loses pressure in the lungs, but returns to the heart before being pumped to the rest of the body. This increases the pressure of the blood going to the body.
3) Keeping the blood at a higher pressure allows materials to be transported around the body more quickly.

The heart — it's all just pump and circumstance...

In the exam you might be asked to interpret data on pressure changes in the arteries, veins and capillaries. Remember that pressure goes from high to low in the alphabetical order of their names — so arteries have the highest pressure, then capillaries have medium pressure and veins have the lowest pressure. Simple.

The Cardiac Cycle and Circulation

The chambers of the heart work together to pump blood around your body — and you need to know how.

The Cardiac Cycle is How the Heart Contracts

1) The heart pumps blood around the body by contracting and relaxing the atria and ventricles in sequence.
2) Blood is prevented from flowing in the wrong direction through the heart by the atrio-ventricular and semilunar valves.
3) The sequence of events in one complete heartbeat is called the cardiac cycle:

If you've forgotten what atria and ventricles are, have a look at page 58.

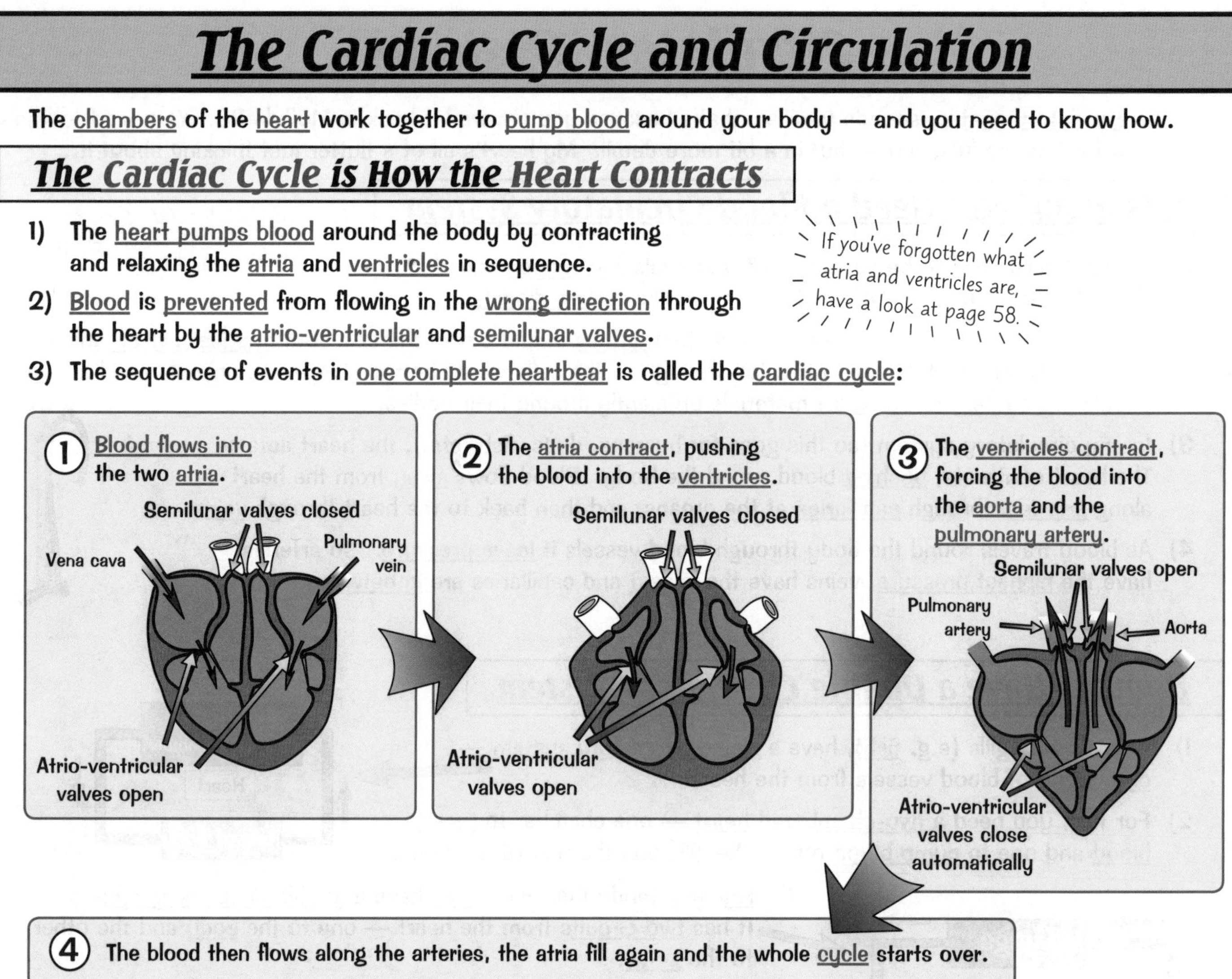

4 The blood then flows along the arteries, the atria fill again and the whole cycle starts over.

We Haven't Always Known This Much About the Heart

CLAUDIUS GALEN (ancient Greece).

1) He cut up animals to study them, and so knew about chambers in the heart.
2) He thought arterial blood was made by the heart, while blood in veins was made by the liver, sucked through veins by the heart and consumed by the organs.

WILLIAM HARVEY (1578-1657).

Before Harvey, scientists still believed more or less the same as Galen. Harvey changed all this. He showed that:

- the heart valves stopped the back flow of blood,
- the heart is a pump (rather than something that sucks),
- the pulse is caused by the heart pumping blood into the arteries,
- the same blood was circulated around the body over and over again — not manufactured and consumed.

Blood vessels — a vampire's favourite type of ship...

If you're given data in the exam on the cardiac cycle, don't panic — so long as you understand how the heart pumps blood around the body, you'll be just fine. And no matter how bad it looks, at least it isn't in Greek...

Heart Rate

The heart has a regular beat — and this page explains why. So keep reading...

Heart Rate Changes According to Activity

1) When you exercise, your muscles need more oxygen to work harder, so you need to breathe faster. Your heart also pumps faster to deliver more oxygenated blood to your muscles. (And when you stop exercising your heart gradually returns to normal.)

What happens is that your muscles produce more carbon dioxide — this change is detected by the brain, which tells your body to breathe faster.

2) Hormones can also affect your heart rate, e.g. adrenaline is released when you get a shock or you're in danger (it causes the 'fight or flight' response which revs your body up to run away from danger). It increases heart rate to make sure the muscles have plenty of oxygen.

The Heart Has a Pacemaker

1) The heart is told how fast to beat by a group of cells called the pacemakers.
2) These cells produce a small electric current which spreads to the surrounding muscle cells, causing them to contract.
3) There are two clusters of these cells in the heart:
   - The sino-atrial node (SAN) stimulates the atria to contract.
   - The atrio-ventricular node (AVN) stimulates the ventricles to contract.

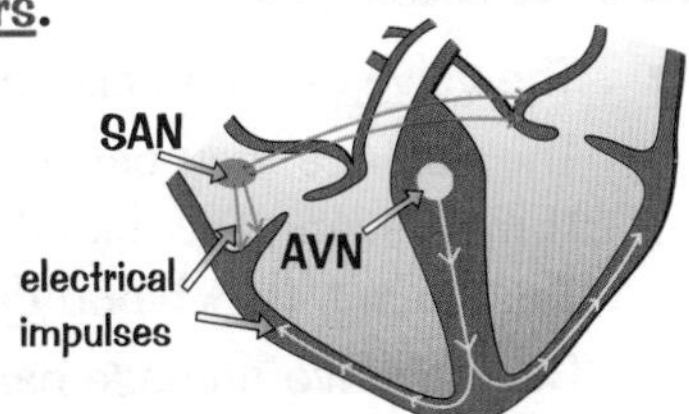

4) In one complete heartbeat the SAN produces an electric current first, which spreads to the atria (making them contract). The current stimulates the AVN to produce an electric current (causing the ventricles to contract). This process ensures that the atria always contract before the ventricles.
5) An artificial pacemaker is often used to control heartbeat if the pacemaker cells don't work properly. It's a little device that's implanted under the skin and has a wire going to the heart. It produces an electric current.

ECGs and Echocardiograms Measure the Heart

Doctors can measure how well the heart is working (heart function) in two main ways.

1) Electrocardiogram (ECG) — showing the electrical activity of the heart. They can show:
   - heart attacks — e.g. if you're having a heart attack, or are about to have one,
   - irregular heartbeats and general health of the heart.

This is what a healthy person's ECG looks like...

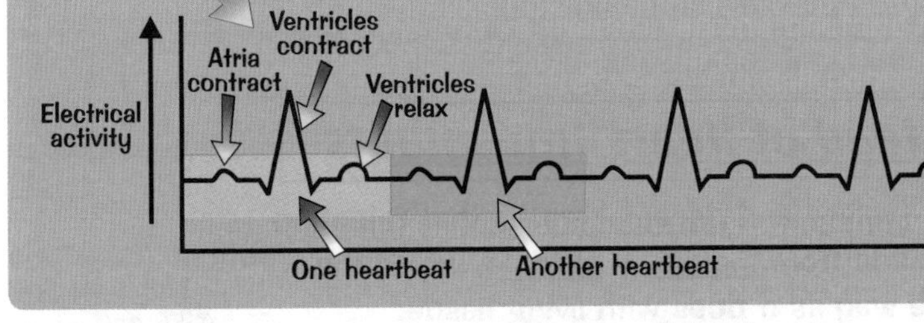

...and here are some unhealthy ones.

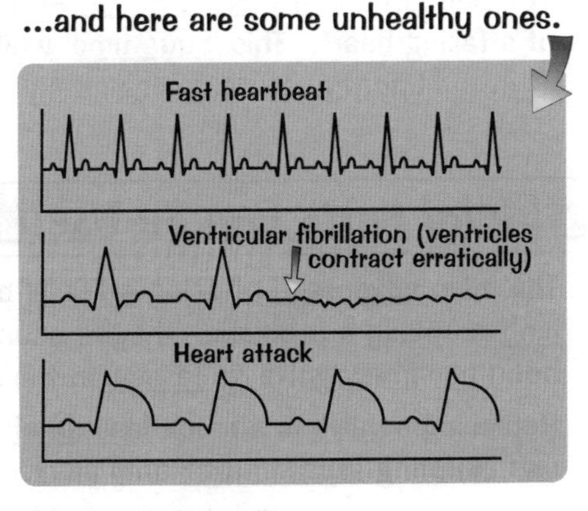

2) Echocardiogram — an ultrasound scan of the heart, which can show:
   - an enlarged heart — this could indicate heart failure,
   - decreased pumping ability — this could indicate a disease called cardiomyopathy,
   - valve function — torn, infected or scarred heart valves can cause problems.

A stitch — the best running pacemaker in the world...

In the exam you might be asked to interpret an ECG — they look scary but they're not too difficult... If a peak is missing, then that part of the heart isn't contracting. If the peaks are close together, the heart's beating faster. But if everything is going haywire, then it could be a heart attack or fibrillation.

Heart Disease

Some types of heart disease are getting more common — but there are new ways of treating them...

There are Three Main Ways Your Heart Can Go Wrong

1) HOLE IN THE HEART

- A hole in the heart is a gap in the wall separating either the two ventricles or the two atria.
- It allows blood to move directly from one side of the heart to the other. This allows deoxygenated and oxygenated blood to mix, which reduces the amount of oxygen in the blood being pumped to the body.
- A hole in the heart sometimes needs to be corrected by surgery.

All unborn babies have a hole in the heart, which usually closes up after birth — see page 87 for more.

2) VALVE DAMAGE

- The valves in the heart can be damaged or weakened by heart attacks, infection or old age.
- The damage may cause the valve not to open properly, causing high blood pressure. It may even allow blood to flow in both directions rather than just forward. This means that blood doesn't circulate as effectively as normal.
- Severe valve damage can be treated by replacing the valve with an artificial one.

3) CORONARY HEART DISEASE (CHD)

- Coronary heart disease is when the coronary arteries supplying blood to the heart muscle get blocked by fatty deposits.
- This reduces blood flow to the heart muscle and often results in a heart attack.
- It can be treated by a coronary bypass operation, where a piece of blood vessel is taken from another part of the body and inserted to 'bypass' the blockage.

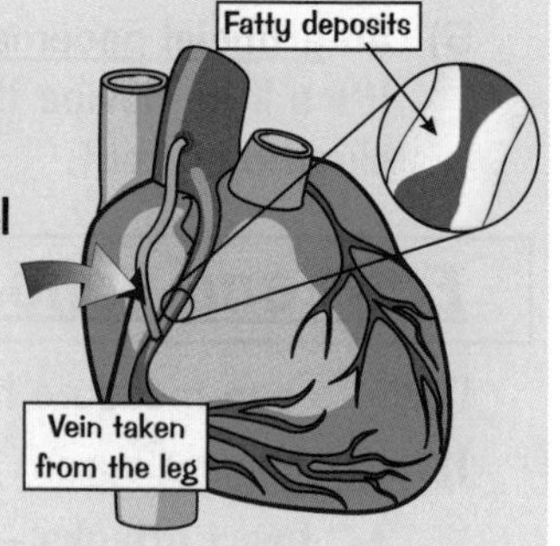

You can have surgery to put a lot of heart problems right. For example...

- You can have a heart transplant — an entirely new heart from a donor.
- You can also get new bits fitted, such as valves and pacemakers (see below).
- You can get a heart assist device — this takes over the pumping duties of a failing heart. This 'buys time' while the patient waits for a transplant.

Artificial Parts Can Be Used Instead of Heart Transplants

1) The main advantage of using artificial parts (valves and pacemakers) is that rejection isn't normally a problem. They're usually made from metals or plastics, which the body can't recognise as foreign in the same way as it does with living tissue.
2) Replacing a valve is a much less drastic procedure than a transplant, and inserting a pacemaker only involves an overnight stay in hospital.
3) However, the main disadvantage is that the new valves and pacemakers might not last very long and need replacing as a result.

See page 92 for more on organ rejection.

There's no treatment for a broken heart...

Heart disease is serious stuff, but scientists have developed lots of ways of treating it. Heart transplants have been an option since the 1960s and today artificial devices can also be used to keep the old tickers working.

Blood Clotting and Transfusions

If you get a cut, you don't want all your blood to drain away — this is why clotting is so handy. Sometimes injuries are so bad you lose a lot of blood and you need to replace it — that's where transfusions come in.

Blood Sometimes Doesn't Clot Properly

1) When you're injured, your blood clots to prevent too much bleeding. A clot is a mesh of protein fibres (called fibrin fibres) that 'plugs' the damaged area. Clots are formed by a series of chemical reactions that take place when platelets in your blood are exposed to damaged blood vessels.

PLATELETS
These are small fragments of cells that help blood clot.

2) Too little clotting could mean you bleed to death (well, you're more likely to get loads of bruises). Too much clotting can cause strokes and deep vein thrombosis (DVT).
3) People who are at risk of stroke and DVT can take drugs to reduce their risk. Warfarin, heparin and aspirin all help prevent the blood from clotting.
4) Haemophilia is a genetic condition where the blood doesn't clot easily because a clotting factor can't be made by the body — this missing clotting factor can be injected.

Blood Type is Important in Transfusions

1) If you're in an accident or having surgery, you may lose a lot of blood — this needs to be replaced by a blood transfusion, using blood from a blood donor. But you can't just use any old blood...
2) People have different blood groups or types — you can be any one of: A, B, O or AB. These letters refer to the type of antigens on the surface of a person's red blood cells. (An antigen is a substance that can trigger a response from a person's immune system.)
3) Red blood cells can have A or B antigens (or neither, or both) on their surface.
4) And blood plasma can contain anti-A or anti-B antibodies. (Plasma's the pale liquid in blood that actually carries all the different bits — e.g. the blood cells, antibodies, hormones, etc.)
5) If an anti-A antibody meets an A antigen, the blood clumps together. This is known as agglutination (and it's not good). The same thing happens when an anti-B antibody meets a B antigen.
6) This table explains which blood groups can donate blood to which other blood groups.

Blood Group	Antigens	Antibodies	Can give blood to	Can get blood from
A	A	anti-B	A and AB	A and O
B	B	anti-A	B and AB	B and O
AB	A, B	none	only AB	anyone
O	none	anti-A, anti-B	anyone	only O

For example, if your blood group is type O, your blood can be given to anyone — there are no antigens on your blood cells, so any anti-A or anti-B antibodies have nothing to 'attack'. You can only receive blood from other type O people though — your antibodies would attack the antigens in type A, B or AB blood.

I think I need an information transfusion... *from this book to my brain...*

You might get asked a question on who can donate blood to whom in the exam. Just look at what blood type the donor is and think about what antigens and antibodies they have in their blood. It's hard, and you need to think carefully about it (I do anyway), but it does make sense.

Transplants and Organ Donation

If an organ is severely damaged, it can be removed and replaced by one from someone else — this known as an organ transplant. Unfortunately though, it's not as simple as just whacking in a new kidney...

Organs Can Come From Living or Dead Donors

1) Living donors can donate whole (or parts of) certain organs. For example, you can live with just one of your two kidneys and donate the other, or you can donate a piece of your liver.
2) Organs from people who have recently died can also be transplanted.
3) To be an organ donor, a person must meet certain criteria...

All donors must be:
- Relatively young so that the organ is as fit and healthy as possible.
- A similar body weight to the patient needing the transplant, so the organ is a good 'fit'.
- A close tissue match to the patient to prevent problems with rejection (see below). For a living donor, this usually means being a close family member of the patient.

Living donors must be over the age of 18.

Donors who have died must have done so very recently — this is because organs only stay usable for a few hours outside the body. Close relatives of the dead donor must give their permission.

4) Success rates of transplants depend on a lot of things — e.g. the type of organ (e.g. the heart is riskier than a kidney), the age of the patient, the skill of the surgeon, etc.

Transplants Can Be Rejected

1) One of the main problems with organ transplants is that the patient's immune system often recognises the new organ as 'foreign' and attacks it — this is called rejection.
2) To reduce the chances of this happening, the donor should have a similar tissue type to the patient (i.e. have similar antigens on their cell surfaces). This is what's meant by being a 'close tissue match'.
3) Doctors use immuno-suppressive drugs that suppress the patient's immune system to help stop the donor organ being rejected — but it leaves the patient more vulnerable to infections.

There are Ethical Issues Surrounding Organ Donation

1) Some people think for religious reasons that a person's body should be buried intact (so giving organs is wrong). Others think life or death is up to God (so receiving organs is wrong).
2) Others worry that doctors might not save them if they're critically ill and their organs are needed for transplant. There are safeguards in place that should prevent this though.
3) There are also worries that people may get pressured into being a 'living donor' (e.g. donating a kidney to a close relative). But doctors try to ensure that it's always the donor's personal choice.

I think I need a brain transplant to learn all this lot...

Did you know that if you transplant a piece of a liver it can actually grow back to normal size within a few weeks. Impressive. Changing the subject slightly... one donor (if they're dead) can donate several organs — e.g. their heart, kidneys, liver, lungs, pancreas... And on top of that, other tissues (e.g. skin, bone, tendons, corneas...) can also be donated. It's absolutely amazing really, when you think about it.

Organ Donation and Organ Replacement

Organ transplants can save lives — but there are more people who need replacement organs than there are donors. Sometimes mechanical replacements can be used instead — but they're not perfect, either...

There Are Problems With the Supply of Donor Organs

1) The UK has a shortage of organs available for donation...

- You can join the NHS Organ Donor Register to show you're willing to donate organs after you die. However, doctors still need your family's consent before they can use the organs for a transplant.
- Some people say it should be made easier for doctors to use the organs of people who have died. One suggestion is to have an 'opt-out' system instead — this means anyone's organs can be used unless the person has registered to say they don't want them to be donated.

2) The shortage of donors means that a person needing a transplant usually has to wait for an organ to become available.
3) The wait can last a long time because the organ donor must meet so many different criteria (see previous page).

You Can Get Mechanical Replacements for Organs

1) Sometimes, temporary mechanical replacements for organs can be used to keep someone alive. This could be for anything from a few hours (e.g. during an operation), to several months or even years (e.g. if they're waiting for a suitable organ donor).
2) Mechanical replacements can be used inside or outside of the body. Here are a few examples of mechanical replacements used outside of the body...

HEART-LUNG MACHINES

These keep a patient's blood oxygenated and pumping during heart or lung surgery.

KIDNEY DIALYSIS MACHINES

These can filter a patient's blood (e.g. while they wait for a kidney transplant).

MECHANICAL VENTILATORS

These are used to push air in and out of a patient's lungs if they stop breathing.

3) There are problems in using mechanical replacements though, e.g.

- They usually need a constant power supply.
- They're often large and difficult to move around.
- They must be made from materials that won't harm the body and won't degrade (i.e. break down or rust).
- Even if they're made from the right materials, they can occasionally cause inflammation or allergic reactions in the patient.

I haven't got an organ to donate — but I've got a piano...

Organ donation can save lives, but some people feel strongly about what happens to their body after they die — and you need to make sure you can discuss the advantages and disadvantages of an organ register in the exam. Mechanical replacements don't raise so many ethical issues, but they're not perfect — and you need to know why.

The Respiratory System

The respiratory system is the posh name for the breathing system — all things to do with the lungs.

We Need to Take In Oxygen and Remove Carbon Dioxide

1) When we breathe, we take in oxygen for respiration and release carbon dioxide.
2) Carbon dioxide is a waste product of respiration. At a high level, CO_2 is toxic — which is why it must be removed from the body through breathing.
3) When the brain detects a rise in the CO_2 level in the blood, it responds by increasing the rate of breathing.

Ventilation (Breathing) Uses Muscles

Inspiration (or Breathing In)...

1) Your intercostal muscles (between the ribs) and diaphragm (the muscle beneath the lungs) contract, and increase the volume of the thorax (the bit of your body containing your lungs).
2) This expands the lungs and decreases the pressure inside them, which draws air in.

air goes in
muscles between ribs pull ribcage and sternum up and out
sternum
in
in
ribcage
diaphragm flattens out

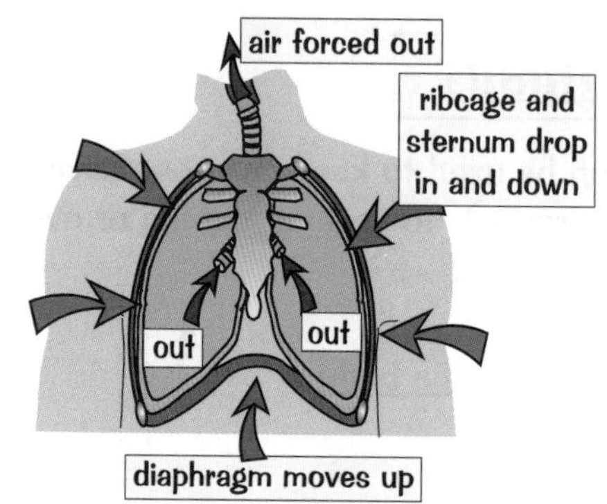

...and Expiration (or Breathing Out)

1) Intercostals and diaphragm relax.
2) The thorax volume decreases.
3) This increases the pressure in the lungs and air is forced out.

Lung Capacity Can be Measured with a Spirometer

Doctors measure lung capacity using a machine called a spirometer — it can help diagnose and monitor lung diseases.

The patient breathes into the machine (through a tube) for a few minutes, and the volume of air that is breathed in and out is measured and plotted on a graph (called a spirogram) — like this one...

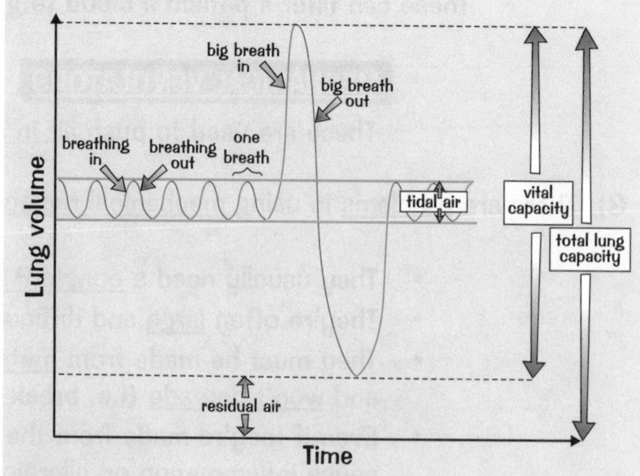

1) The total volume of air you can fit in your lungs is your total lung capacity (usually about 6 litres).
2) The volume of air you breathe in (or out) in one normal breath is called your tidal air.
3) Even if you try to breathe out really hard there's always some air left (just over a litre) in your lungs to make sure that they stay open — this is called the residual air.
4) Total lung capacity minus residual air gives you vital capacity air — the amount of usable air (or the maximum volume of air that can be breathed in or out).

Spirograms... aren't they those fancy drawing machines...

If the values on a spirogram are low the person might have a lung disease. If the tidal volume increases (i.e. if they're breathing deeper), then they're probably exercising. Simple really.

More on the Respiratory System

All living organisms need to exchange gases for respiration — but they do it in very different ways...

In Humans, Gaseous Exchange Happens in the Lungs

1) The lungs contain millions of little air sacs called alveoli — these air sacs are where gas exchange takes place.
2) The blood passing next to the alveoli has just returned to the lungs from the rest of the body, so it contains lots of carbon dioxide and very little oxygen. As a result:
   - Oxygen diffuses out of the alveolus (an area of high O_2 concentration) into the blood (an area of low O_2 concentration).
   - Carbon dioxide diffuses out of the blood (high concentration) into the alveolus (low concentration) to be breathed out.

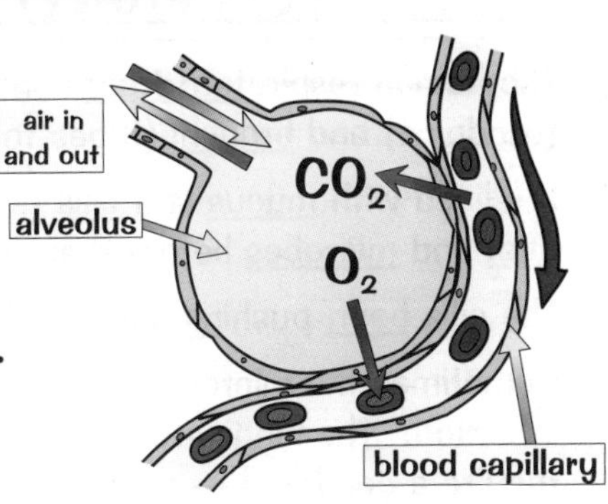

See page 72 for more on diffusion.

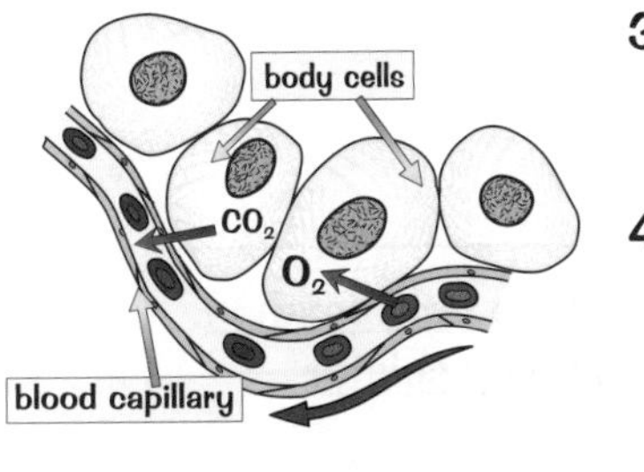

3) When the blood reaches body cells which need oxygen it is released from the red blood cells (where there's a high concentration) and diffuses into the body cells (where the concentration is low).
4) At the same time, carbon dioxide diffuses out of the body cells (where there's a high concentration) into the blood (where there's a low concentration). It's then carried back to the lungs.

The Alveoli Are Adapted for Gas Exchange

To make gaseous exchange as efficient as possible the alveoli have:
- a very large surface area to increase the rate of diffusion,
- a moist surface to help oxygen and carbon dioxide dissolve,
- a permeable surface to help gases exchange easily,
- a thin lining (only one cell thick) so gases don't have to diffuse very far,
- a good blood supply.

All gaseous exchange surfaces have similar adaptations.

Other Organisms Exchange Gas Differently...

1) Adult amphibians have simple lungs, but their skin also plays an important part in gaseous exchange.
2) Oxygen moves into the animal and carbon dioxide moves out through their permeable skin (as well as via the lungs). To help with this, an adult amphibian's skin has to be kept moist.
3) However, this means the skin can't be waterproof. This lack of waterproofing means the amphibian would lose too much water if it lived in a dry environment — it must have a moist habitat.

1) In fish, gas exchange occurs at the gills (organs at the sides of the head). A constant supply of oxygen-rich water flows through the open mouth of the fish and is then forced over the gill filaments when the mouth closes.
2) Water helps support the gills — it keeps the gill filaments separated from each other. If fish weren't in water their gills would stick together and they would suffocate (which is why fish can only breathe when they're in water).

blood vessels

gill filaments

What did the fish say when it swam into a wall? Dam...

It's not the most interesting stuff but you need to learn this page — or you'll be a fish out of water on exam day.

Lung Disease

Without your lungs you'd be stuffed, so it's a good thing they've got ways of protecting themselves from little nasties like dust and microbes. Even so, your lungs are still susceptible to diseases.

Cilia and Mucus Protect the Lungs

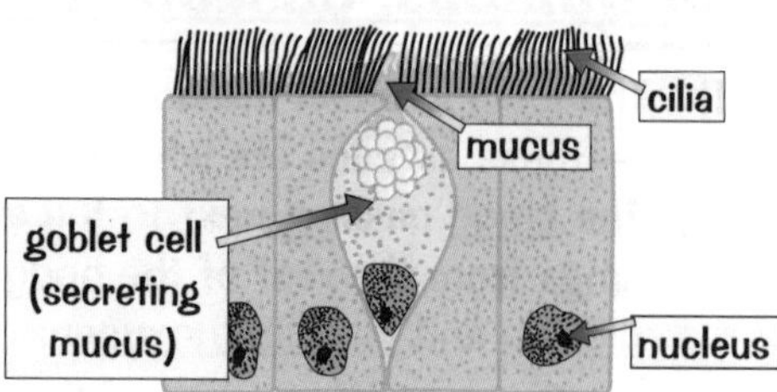

Ciliated cells in the trachea and bronchi.

1) The human respiratory tract consists of the trachea (windpipe) and bronchi (tubes to the lungs).
2) It's lined with mucus and cilia (little hairs), which catch dust and microbes before they reach the lungs.
3) The cilia beat, pushing microbe-filled mucus out of the lungs as phlegm.
4) Sometimes the microbes get past the body's defences and cause infection. The lungs are particularly prone to infections because they're a dead end — microbes can't easily be flushed out.

Lung Disease Can be Caused by Lots of Things

INDUSTRIAL MATERIALS

E.g. asbestos. Asbestos can cause a disease called asbestosis — this is where inflammation and scarring in the lungs limits gas exchange. Asbestos used to be used as an insulator in roofs, floors, furnaces, etc. Its use is more tightly controlled now.

GENETIC CAUSES

E.g. cystic fibrosis is an inherited lung condition. A single defective gene causes the lungs to produce a really thick, sticky mucus that clogs up the bronchioles (small tubes in the lungs) — this makes breathing difficult and can lead to life-threatening infections.

LIFESTYLE CAUSES

E.g. smoking can cause lung cancer. This is where cells divide out of control, forming a tumour and reducing the surface area in the lungs.

ASTHMA

1) Asthmatics' lungs are overly sensitive to certain things (e.g. pet hair, pollen, dust, smoke...).
2) When they encounter these things the muscles around the bronchioles contract, constricting the airways.
3) The lining of the airways becomes inflamed and fluid builds up in the airways, making it hard to breathe (an asthma attack).
4) Symptoms of an attack are:
   - difficulty breathing,
   - wheezing,
   - a tight chest.
5) When symptoms appear a muscle relaxant drug is inhaled (from an inhaler) to open up the airways.
6) Some people also take drugs to stop attacks happening in the first place (but there's no actual cure.)

Stop huffing and puffing and just LEARN it..

There are lots of different types of lung disease, and some of them, like asthma, can be managed quite easily. Lung cancer on the other hand is pretty nasty — but you can lower your chances of getting it by not smoking. Make sure you learn the examples on this page and way the lungs protect themselves from disease for the exam.

Digestion

Digestion is the breaking down of the nutrients in your food, so that they can be absorbed.
There are two types of digestion — physical and chemical.

Big Molecules are Broken Down into Smaller Ones

1) The aim of the game is break down the large insoluble molecules in food into small soluble molecules so you can absorb them into your blood plasma or lymph (a type of fluid that carries the products of fat digestion).
2) First the big lumps of food are physically digested — this basically means chewing them in the mouth, then churning them about in the stomach. Physical digestion allows food to pass easily through the digestive system and provides a larger surface area for chemical digestion (the next step).
3) Chemical digestion involves enzymes — biological catalysts that speed up reactions. Digestive enzymes break down molecules that are too big to pass through cell membranes.

There are Three Main Types of Digestive Enzyme

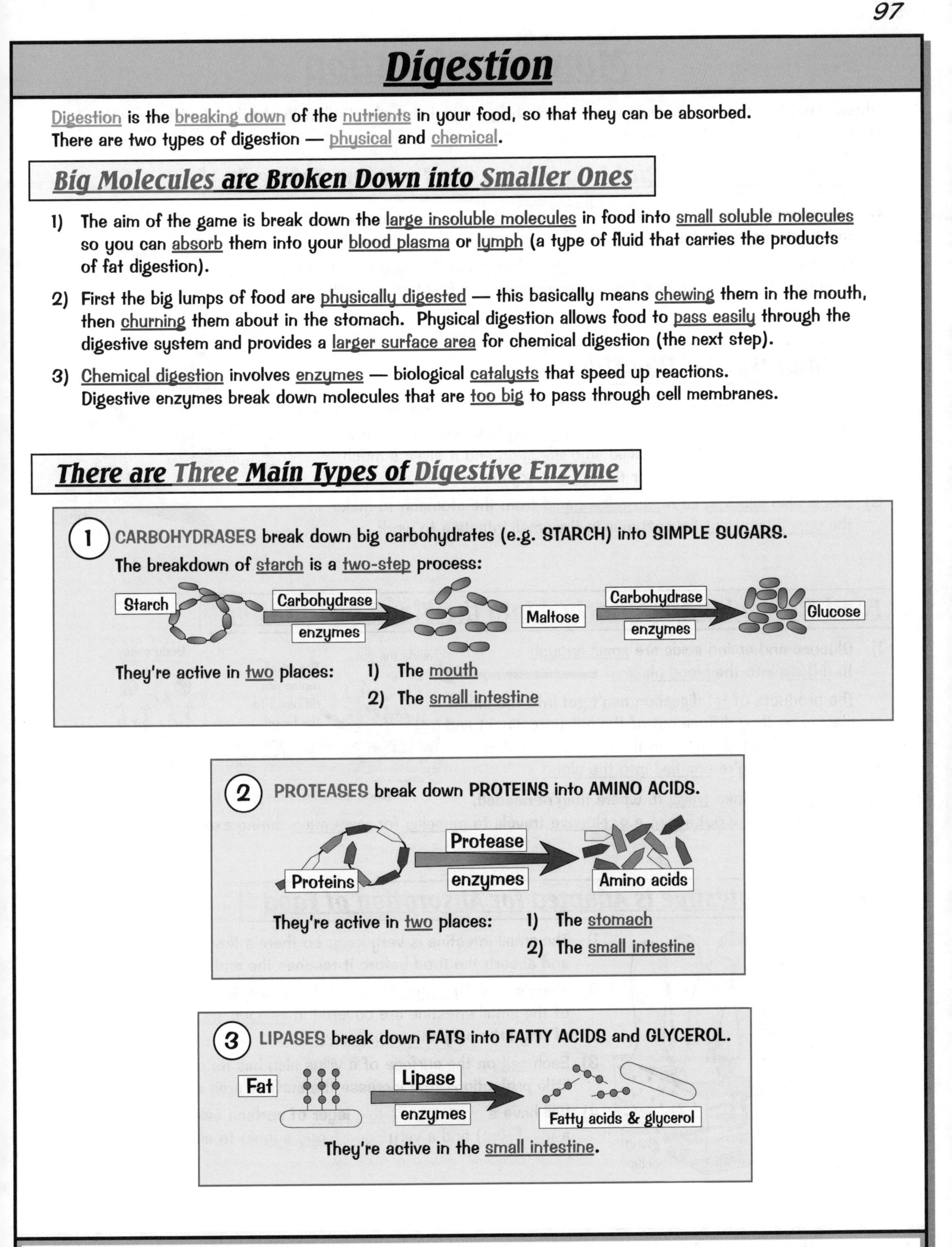

Now get digesting those facts...

Revision is a lot like digestion if you think about it — you break down the big topics into manageable chunks and then absorb the information. Imagine if you could eat this book and absorb all the facts in one sitting... it'd make life easier. But it probably wouldn't be as tasty as scoffing baked beans on toast. Mmmm toast...

More on Digestion

Phew. That last page on digestion was so much fun, I just thought, "What the heck, let's have another". So here you have it. Read on and enjoy...

Enzymes Need the Right Conditions to Function Properly

1) The pH in the stomach is very acidic (about pH 1-2). It's maintained at this level to provide the optimum pH for protease enzymes to work.
2) Other enzymes have higher optimum pHs. The pH in the mouth and small intestine is alkaline or neutral so that the enzymes there can function properly.

For more on enzymes and optimum pH, see page 49.

Bile Improves Fat Digestion

1) Bile is made in the liver and stored in the gall bladder.
2) It helps fat digestion in the small intestine by breaking the fat down into tiny droplets. This is called emulsification and it gives a much bigger surface area of fat for the lipase enzymes to work on.
3) Bile is also alkaline, so it neutralises acid from the stomach to make the conditions right for enzymes in the small intestine to work.

liver
bile duct
gall bladder
small intestine

Food Molecules Are Absorbed into the Blood by Diffusion

1) Glucose and amino acids are small enough to diffuse into the blood plasma.
   The products of fat digestion can't get into the blood plasma so they diffuse out of the gut (intestines) and into a fluid called lymph, in the lymphatic system. From here they're emptied into the blood.
2) The nutrients then travel to where they're needed, and then diffuse out again, e.g. glucose travels to muscles for respiration during exercise.

Inside the gut
The small molecules diffuse into the blood...
Body cells
...and then out again somewhere else...
Blood vessel

Blood flows from the gut to the body cells.

The Small Intestine is Adapted for Absorption of Food

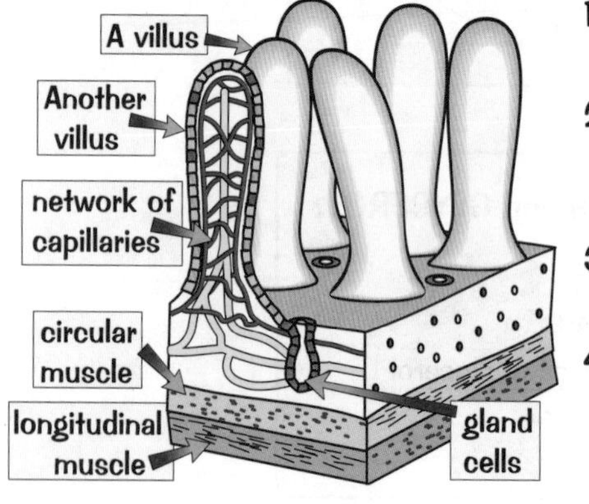

1) The small intestine is very long, so there's time to break down and absorb the food before it reaches the end.
2) There's a really big surface area for absorption, because the walls of the small intestine are covered in millions and millions of tiny little projections called villi.
3) Each cell on the surface of a villus also has its own microvilli — little projections that increase the surface area even more.
4) Villi have a single permeable layer of surface cells (which form a thin lining) and a very good blood supply to allow quick absorption.

You don't have to bust a gut to revise this page...

Just think. That lovely piece of toast you had for breakfast this morning will be making its way through your digestive system as we speak. Eventually it'll end up in the perfectly adapted small intestine, where all the tiny toasty molecules will be absorbed into your bloodstream by diffusion through the villi. Amazing really.

The Kidneys

The kidney is involved in excretion (the removal of waste products from the body).

The Kidneys are Excretion Organs

The kidneys perform three main roles:

1) Removal of urea from the blood. Urea is produced in the liver from excess amino acids.
2) Adjustment of salt levels in the blood.
3) Adjustment of water content of the blood.

They do this by filtering stuff out of the blood under high pressure, and then reabsorbing the useful things. The end product is urine.

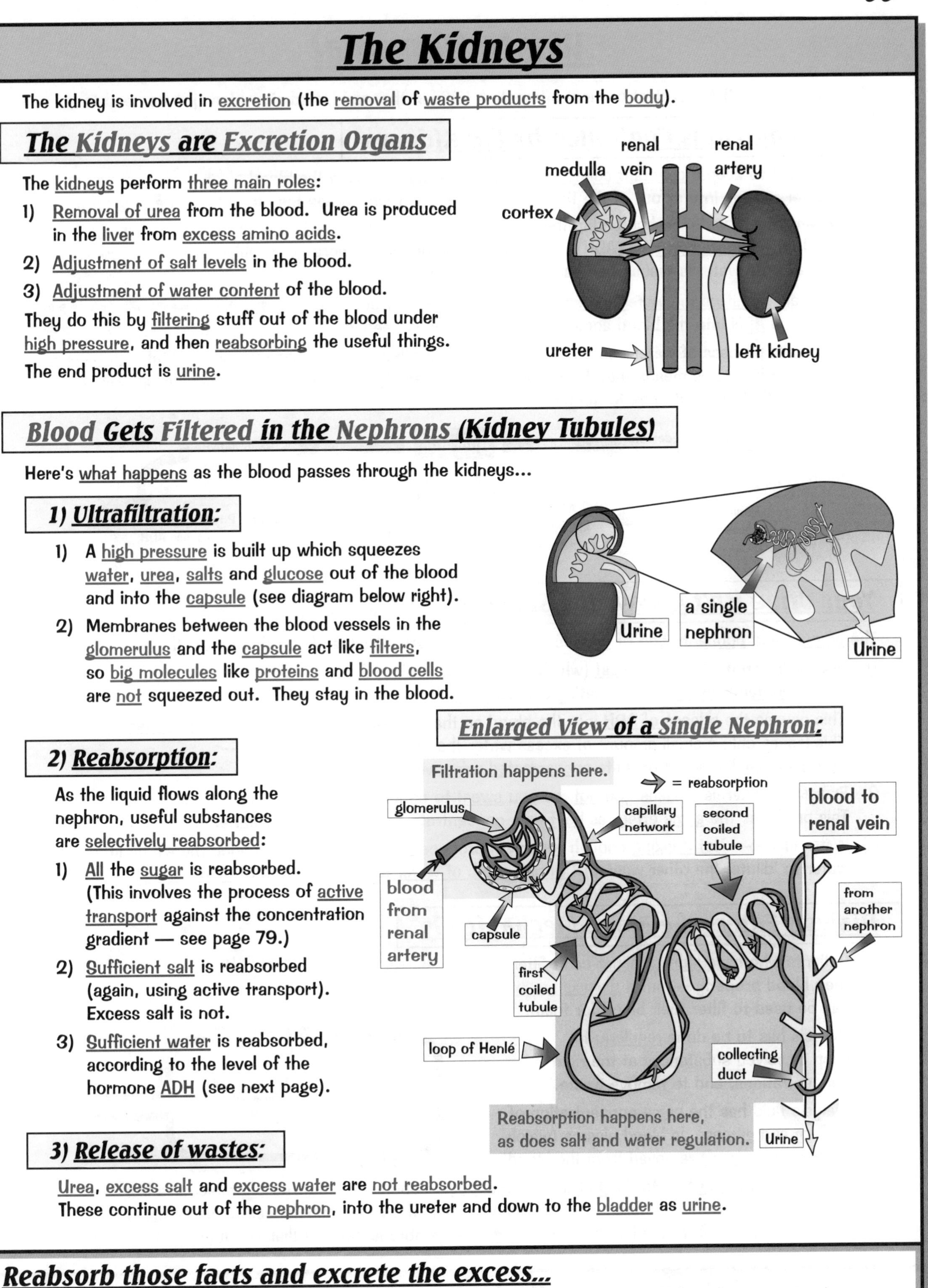

Blood Gets Filtered in the Nephrons (Kidney Tubules)

Here's what happens as the blood passes through the kidneys...

1) Ultrafiltration:

1) A high pressure is built up which squeezes water, urea, salts and glucose out of the blood and into the capsule (see diagram below right).
2) Membranes between the blood vessels in the glomerulus and the capsule act like filters, so big molecules like proteins and blood cells are not squeezed out. They stay in the blood.

Enlarged View of a Single Nephron:

2) Reabsorption:

As the liquid flows along the nephron, useful substances are selectively reabsorbed:

1) All the sugar is reabsorbed. (This involves the process of active transport against the concentration gradient — see page 79.)
2) Sufficient salt is reabsorbed (again, using active transport). Excess salt is not.
3) Sufficient water is reabsorbed, according to the level of the hormone ADH (see next page).

3) Release of wastes:

Urea, excess salt and excess water are not reabsorbed. These continue out of the nephron, into the ureter and down to the bladder as urine.

Reabsorb those facts and excrete the excess...

On average, the kidneys filter 1500 litres of blood a day (you only have 4-6 litres of blood in your body — it just goes through the kidneys about 300 times). And the kidneys excrete 1.5 litres of urine a day — so that's 547.5 litres of wee a year... that's five baths full... not that I'm suggesting you put it there.

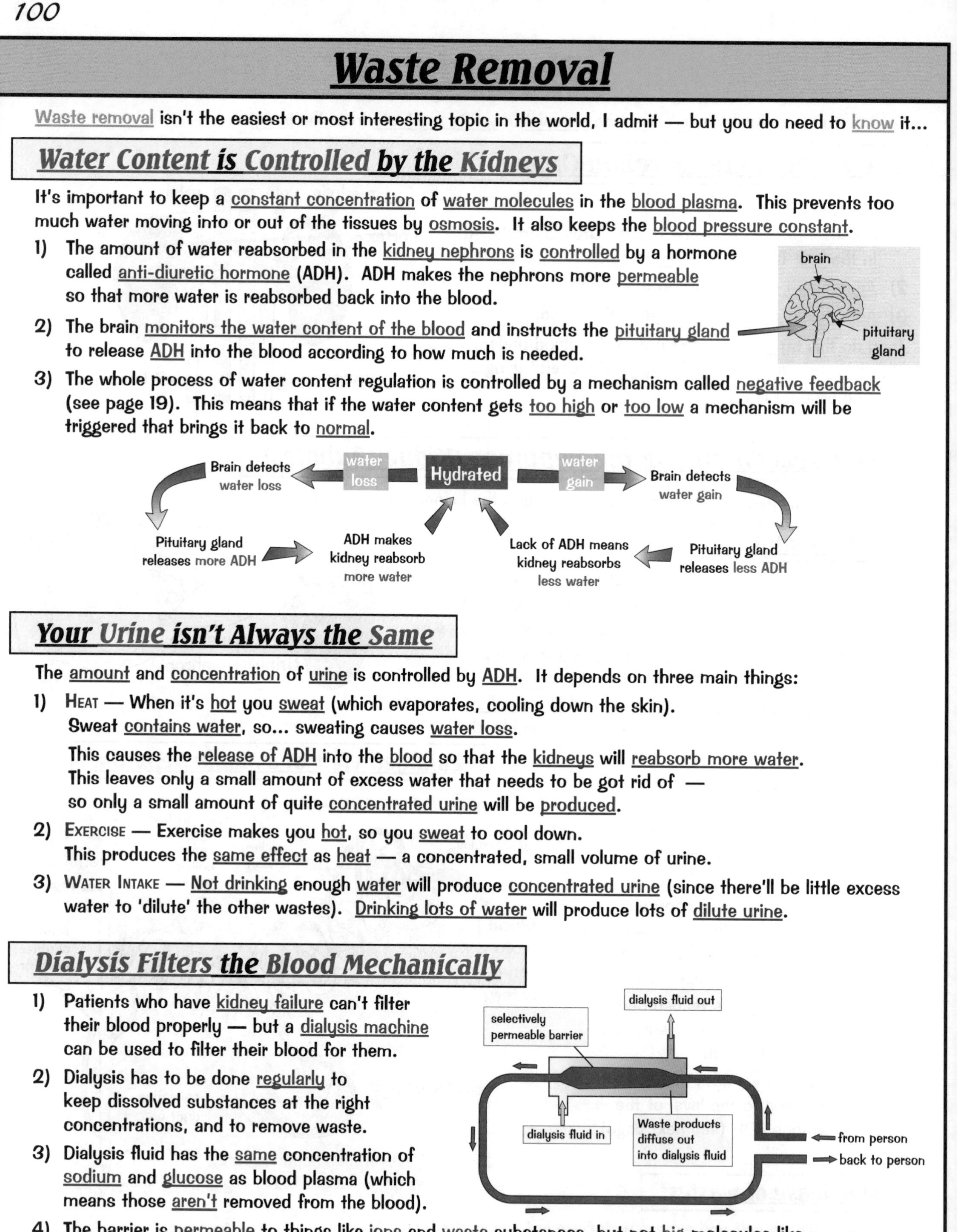

Waste Removal

Waste removal isn't the easiest or most interesting topic in the world, I admit — but you do need to know it...

Water Content is Controlled by the Kidneys

It's important to keep a constant concentration of water molecules in the blood plasma. This prevents too much water moving into or out of the tissues by osmosis. It also keeps the blood pressure constant.

1) The amount of water reabsorbed in the kidney nephrons is controlled by a hormone called anti-diuretic hormone (ADH). ADH makes the nephrons more permeable so that more water is reabsorbed back into the blood.
2) The brain monitors the water content of the blood and instructs the pituitary gland to release ADH into the blood according to how much is needed.
3) The whole process of water content regulation is controlled by a mechanism called negative feedback (see page 19). This means that if the water content gets too high or too low a mechanism will be triggered that brings it back to normal.

Your Urine isn't Always the Same

The amount and concentration of urine is controlled by ADH. It depends on three main things:

1) HEAT — When it's hot you sweat (which evaporates, cooling down the skin). Sweat contains water, so... sweating causes water loss.
   This causes the release of ADH into the blood so that the kidneys will reabsorb more water. This leaves only a small amount of excess water that needs to be got rid of — so only a small amount of quite concentrated urine will be produced.
2) EXERCISE — Exercise makes you hot, so you sweat to cool down. This produces the same effect as heat — a concentrated, small volume of urine.
3) WATER INTAKE — Not drinking enough water will produce concentrated urine (since there'll be little excess water to 'dilute' the other wastes). Drinking lots of water will produce lots of dilute urine.

Dialysis Filters the Blood Mechanically

1) Patients who have kidney failure can't filter their blood properly — but a dialysis machine can be used to filter their blood for them.
2) Dialysis has to be done regularly to keep dissolved substances at the right concentrations, and to remove waste.
3) Dialysis fluid has the same concentration of sodium and glucose as blood plasma (which means those aren't removed from the blood).

4) The barrier is permeable to things like ions and waste substances, but not big molecules like proteins (just like the membranes in the kidney). So.. the waste substances (such as urea) and excess water from the blood move across the membrane into the dialysis fluid.

Simon says touch urea... actually don't...

Kidney failure patients often have high blood pressure because diseased kidneys can't control the water content of the blood. This excess water is removed during dialysis (up to 5 litres of fluid can be removed in one session).

The Menstrual Cycle

The monthly release of an egg from a woman's ovaries is part of the menstrual cycle.

The Menstrual Cycle Has Four Stages

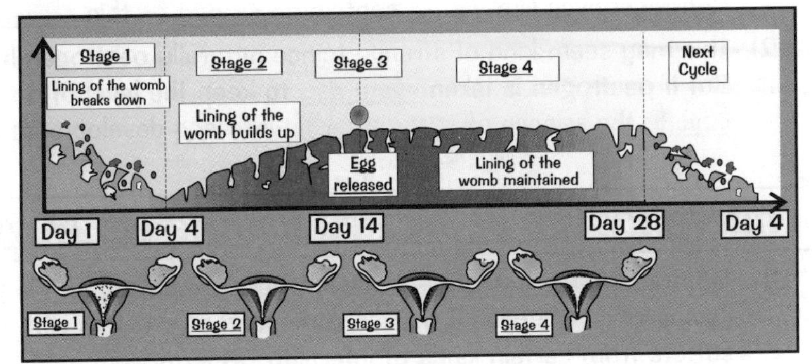

Stage 1 Day 1 — menstruation starts. The uterus lining breaks down for about four days.

Stage 2 The uterus lining builds up again, from day 4 to day 14, into a thick spongy layer full of blood vessels, ready to receive a fertilised egg.

Stage 3 An egg develops and is released from the ovary at day 14 — this is called ovulation.

Stage 4 The wall is then maintained for about 14 days until day 28. If no fertilised egg has landed on the uterus wall by day 28, the spongy lining starts to break down and the whole cycle starts again.

It's Controlled by Four Hormones

1. FSH (follicle-stimulating hormone)

1) Produced in the pituitary gland.
2) Causes an egg to develop in one of the ovaries.
3) Stimulates the ovaries to produce oestrogen.

2. Oestrogen

1) Produced in the ovaries.
2) Causes the lining of the uterus to repair (thicken and grow).
3) Stimulates the production of LH (which causes the release of an egg) and inhibits production of FSH.

3. LH (luteinising hormone)

1) Produced by the pituitary gland.
2) Stimulates the release of an egg at day 14 (ovulation).
3) Indirectly stimulates progesterone production.

4. Progesterone

1) Produced in the ovaries.
2) Maintains the lining of the uterus. When the level of progesterone falls, the lining breaks down.
3) Inhibits the production of LH.

Negative Feedback Mechanisms Affect Hormone Production

1) The production of hormones in the menstrual cycle is controlled by negative feedback (see page 19).
2) When the concentration of one hormone becomes too high, the release of another hormone will return it to a lower level.

Example 1:

1) FSH stimulates the ovary to release oestrogen.
2) Oestrogen inhibits the release of FSH.

So when there's lots of FSH, oestrogen is released and FSH production is inhibited. This causes the FSH level to fall.

Example 2:

1) LH indirectly stimulates the production of progesterone.
2) Progesterone inhibits the release of LH.

When there's lots of LH, progesterone is released. LH production is inhibited and the LH level falls.

Which came first — the chicken or the luteinising hormone...

You need to know what hormone does what for the exam — and where negative feedback comes in. So learn it.

Controlling Fertility

The artificial use of sex hormones like oestrogen and FSH can be used to control human fertility.

Female Hormones Can Be Used to Reduce Fertility For Contraception

1) Contraceptives like the pill contain oestrogen — this prevents the release of an egg (ovulation).
2) This may seem kind of strange (since naturally oestrogen helps stimulate the release of eggs). But if oestrogen is taken every day to keep the level of it permanently high, it mimics pregnancy and inhibits the release of FSH. After a while egg development and production stop and stay stopped.

Infertility Can be Treated in Different Ways

1) Artificial Insemination (AI) — this is where a man's sperm is placed into a woman's uterus without having sex. It's used if there's some kind of problem with the sperm reaching the egg, or if the man suffers from certain kinds of infertility. Sperm from a donor can also be used if necessary.
2) FSH Injections — some women have very low levels of the hormone FSH, so their eggs don't develop properly and they can't get pregnant. FSH injections can increase fertility by stimulating egg production — making fertilisation more likely.
3) In Vitro Fertilisation (IVF) — this is where a woman's eggs are fertilised outside the body. The woman is given hormones to stimulate egg production. Several eggs are then collected and mixed with the man's sperm, and a few fertilised eggs are implanted back into the woman's uterus.

   So... for IVF you need sperm, eggs and a healthy uterus. Any of these can come from someone else:
   - Some women can't produce eggs. But they can still have a baby by using donated eggs.
   - Some women can produce eggs but always miscarry. The couple's fertilised eggs can be implanted into another woman (called a surrogate mother), who gives birth to their baby.
4) Ovary Transplants — some women don't have ovaries (e.g. due to surgery for ovarian cancer) or they have damaged ones that don't produce any eggs (again, often due to cancer treatment). A relatively new (and rare) way to treat this is to transplant a healthy ovary donated by someone else.

Not Everyone Agrees with Infertility Treatment

Infertility treatment can give an infertile couple a child — a pretty obvious benefit. But some people argue against using some of these fertility treatments, either for ethical or practical reasons.

1) In IVF not all the fertilised eggs are implanted back into the woman. Some people think that throwing away these extra fertilised eggs (embryos) is denying a life and so morally wrong.
2) IVF increases the chance of multiple pregnancies (e.g. twins). This can be a danger to the mother's health and possibly a financial burden to the parents.

Foetuses Can be Screened to See If They're Healthy

1) Doctors can screen a foetus for genetic disorders (see page 61) before it's born. They can check for various problems, e.g. Down's syndrome and cystic fibrosis.
2) The main screening method is amniocentesis — where doctors use a long needle to remove some of the fluid that surrounds the baby. This contains skin cells from the baby, and the chromosomes in these can be analysed.
3) Like with infertility treatments, there are ethical issues surrounding screening. For example...
   - If the foetus has a genetic defect, the parents may consider whether or not to continue the pregnancy.
   - Foetal screening like amniocentesis can increase the risk of miscarriage.

Too many initials to learn — FSH, AI, IVF, CIA, DVD...

Foetal screening isn't done on every pregnant woman — just those at risk of having babies with genetic defects.

More on Growth

Growth is pretty important. Without growth, we'd still be an egg-sperm fusion, and that's about it.

Growth is Influenced by Many Things

Growth happens when cells divide (by mitosis, see page 51 — producing new cells identical to the originals.

1) The size an adult reaches is mainly due to genetic factors, but it can be influenced by external factors.

   E.g., **1. Diet** is important, especially for children who are growing. A poor diet, particularly if it's low in proteins (needed to make new cells) or minerals (for bone growth), may mean that a child doesn't grow as much as its genes would allow.

   2. Exercise can also affect growth. Exercise builds muscle, and weight-bearing exercise can increase bone mass. Exercise also stimulates the release of growth hormone.

   Human growth hormone is produced by the pituitary gland (see page 100). It stimulates the growth of the whole body, but especially growth of the long bones.

2) Sometimes hormonal or genetic factors affect growth. Gigantism (extreme height) is often the result of a tumour of the pituitary in childhood, which causes too much growth hormone to be produced. Dwarfism (extreme short stature) is caused by genetic factors, and results in stunted bone growth.

A Baby's Growth is Monitored

1) Different parts of a baby (and foetus) grow at different rates, e.g. a baby's head grows relatively quickly (see page 54).
2) A baby's growth is regularly monitored after birth to make sure it's growing normally and provide an early warning of any growth problems. Three measurements are taken — length, mass and head size. These results are plotted on average growth charts, like this...
3) The chart shows a number of 'percentiles'. E.g. the 50th percentile shows the mass that 50% of babies will have reached at a certain age.
4) Babies vary in size, so doctors aren't usually concerned unless a baby's size is above the 98th percentile or below the 2nd percentile, or if there's an inconsistent pattern (e.g. a very small baby with a very large head).

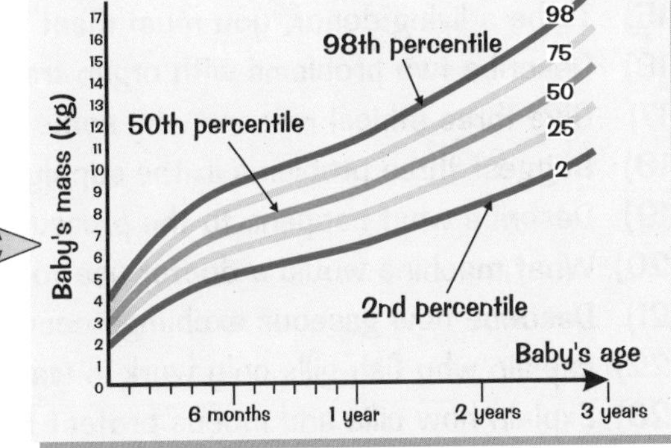

Growth charts can pick up things like obesity, malnutrition, dwarfism, water on the brain, and so on.

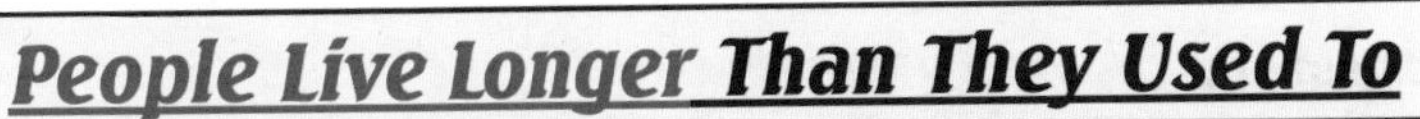

People Live Longer Than They Used To

Life expectancy in the UK has increased loads over the last century...
There are many reasons for this, such as:

1) medical advances mean previously fatal conditions can be treated,
2) places of work and housing are much safer and healthier,
3) people are better off and can afford a healthier diet and lifestyle,
4) there's less industrial disease.

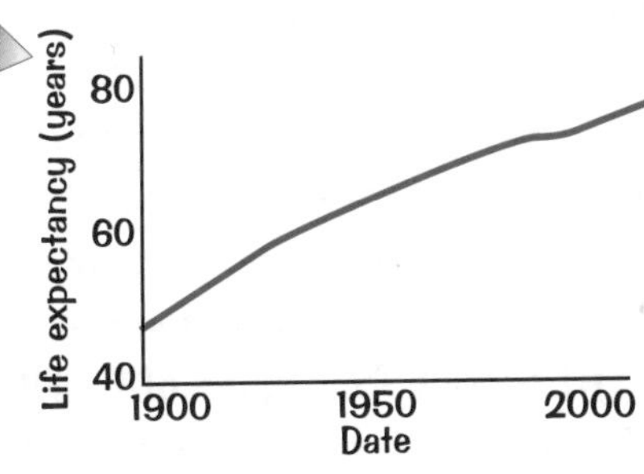

There are problems that come with people living longer, however.
(No one's saying it's a bad thing — only that we need to think about it...)

1) The population grows, leading to possible shortages of housing and more environmental pollution.
2) The number of older people increases, and the state might not be able to give pensions to everyone.
3) Older people have more medical problems and need more care, increasing costs to the taxpayer.

From cell division to babies to old-age pensioners — what a page...

It's a big worry, this whole people living longer lark. By the time you're a senior citizen, you'll have to work until you're in your 70s as there just won't be enough money to give everyone pensions. Poor you.

Revision Summary for Module B5

It's the end of the section. And that can only mean one thing. Yep... it's time for a good ol' revision summary. That's right — it's time to see how much you've learnt. Which had better be everything, frankly — or you're going to have to go back and learn the stuff again — properly, this time. So heads down, eyes open — and get ready to see how much revision you need, or don't need, to do...

1) List three advantages of an internal skeleton over an external skeleton.
2) Why is it unwise to move someone with a broken bone?
3) Sketch and label a diagram of a synovial joint.
4) What happens to the lower arm when the triceps contracts?
5) Describe the circulatory system of humans. How is it different from the circulatory system of fish?
6) Explain why the blood is under higher pressure in a double circulatory system.
7) Describe the sequence of events in the cardiac cycle.
8) Name three contributions Harvey made to our understanding of the circulatory system.
9) Name the two clusters of pacemaker cells in the heart. What do they do?
10) What does ECG stand for? Describe what a healthy person's ECG should look like.
11) Explain what's going wrong if someone has a hole in the heart.
12) Give one advantage and one disadvantage of the use of heart pacemakers and heart valves over heart replacement.
13) What exactly is happening when blood clots?
14) Explain what would happen if a person with type A blood was given a transfusion of type B blood.
15) To be a living donor, you must meet four criteria. What are they?
16) Describe two problems with organ transplants.
17) Give three ethical reasons why some people are concerned about organ transplants.
18) Suggest three problems in the supply of donor organs.
19) Describe what happens to the pressure and volume in the lungs when you breathe in and out.
20) What machine would a doctor use to measure lung capacity? Why would you want to measure it?
21) Describe how gaseous exchange occurs in human alveoli.
22) Explain why fish gills only work in water.
23) Explain how cilia and mucus protect the lungs.
24) List the four main causes of lung disease. Which of these is the most likely to result in lung cancer?
25) Give two functions of physical digestion.
26) Name three types of digestive enzyme and state the name of the type of molecule they break down.
27) Describe how stomach pH aids digestion.
28) Give three ways that villi are adapted to aid digestion.
29) Describe the three main roles of the kidneys.
30) Explain how a kidney works.
31) Describe three things that affect the amount and concentration of urine produced.
32) How does a dialysis machine work? Which substances does it remove from the blood?
33) Which four hormones control the menstrual cycle? What exactly do they do?
34) How does negative feedback control the concentration of hormones in the menstrual cycle?
35) Describe four types of fertility treatment.
36) List three reasons why people may argue that fertility treatment is wrong.
37) Name a method of foetal screening.
    Explain two ethical issues to do with foetal screening.
38) How can diet and exercise affect a person's growth?
39) What three measurements do doctors make to check a baby is growing normally?
40) Why are people living longer these days? What problems is this trend likely to cause?

Bacteria

You've already met bacteria in B3, but you need to know a bit more about them for B6 — so here goes...

Bacterial Cells are Usually Smaller and Simpler than Animal Cells

1) Bacterial cells have a cell wall to help them keep their shape and stop them from bursting.
2) They have a strand of DNA in the cytoplasm that controls the cell's activities and replication. Some also have several small loops of DNA called plasmids.
3) They sometimes have a flagellum (tail) to help them move.
4) They come in 4 shapes: rods, curved rods, spheres and spirals.
5) Bacteria can consume a huge range of organic nutrients from their surroundings. This provides them with energy. Some types of bacteria can even produce their own nutrients.
6) This means that different bacteria can survive in almost any habitat, e.g. soil, water, air, the human body and food.

A typical bacterial cell:

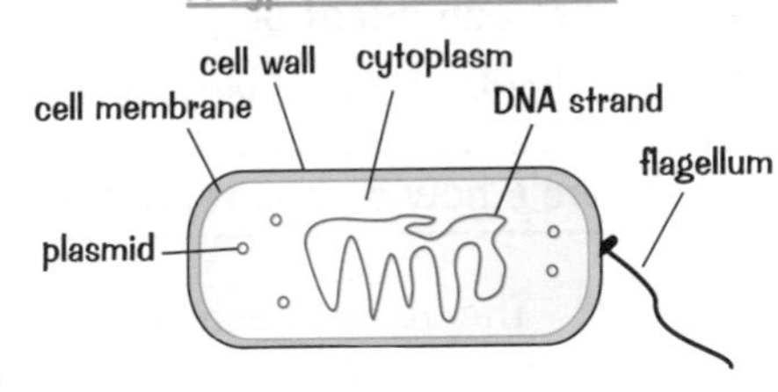

Bacteria Reproduce by Asexual Reproduction

1) Bacteria reproduce by asexual reproduction — they're clones of each other. They reproduce by a process called binary fission (a posh way of saying 'they split in two').
2) Bacteria reproduce very quickly. If disease-causing bacteria enter your body, they can reproduce and cause disease before your body has a chance to respond.
3) Bacteria reproduce faster when it's warm and there's a good source of nutrients. This is why it's important to store food carefully. E.g. If you leave some meat on a warm kitchen top, bacteria on the meat will reproduce very quickly and cause it to spoil (go off). In a fridge, the cold temperature would slow down the bacteria's reproduction and it wouldn't spoil as quickly.

Aseptic Technique Should be Used for Culturing Bacteria

1) You can culture (grow) bacteria on an agar plate — a Petri dish containing agar jelly. Bacteria can be transferred to the plate from a sample using a wire inoculation loop.
2) When you culture bacteria, it's important to use aseptic technique to protect yourself from infection and to stop the agar from being contaminated by other microbes. This involves:
   - Wearing gloves and keeping long hair tied back (so it doesn't fall in your culture).
   - Sterilising equipment before and after use — e.g. passing the inoculation loop through a Bunsen burner flame to kill any unwanted bacteria on it.
   - Sealing the dish once you've transferred the bacteria onto it.
   - Disposing of cultures safely after use — usually done by pressure sterilising in an autoclave.

We Can Use Bacteria to Make Useful Things Like Yoghurt

1) The equipment is sterilised to kill off any unwanted microorganisms.
2) Then the milk is pasteurised (heated up to 72 °C for 15 seconds) — again to kill off any unwanted microorganisms. Then the milk's cooled.
3) A starter culture of *Lactobacillus* bacteria is added. The mixture is incubated (heated to about 40 °C) in a vessel called a fermenter. The bacteria break down the lactose sugar in the milk into lactic acid. The lactic acid causes the milk to clot and solidify into yoghurt.
4) A sample is taken to make sure it's at the right consistency. Then flavours (e.g. fruit) and colours are sometimes added and the yoghurt is packaged.

Yoghurt — bacteria and gone-off milk... mmm...yummy...

Bacteria are also used to make cheese, vinegar, silage (for animal feed) and compost (for your garden). Bacteria that can make Belgian chocolates, caviar and profiteroles haven't been discovered yet.

Microorganisms and Disease

There are different kinds of microorganism, e.g. bacteria, viruses, fungi and protozoa. Some are useful, while others are pretty harmful if you get infected. This page focuses on the nasty ones...

Viruses Can Only Reproduce Inside Living Cells

1) Viruses aren't cells. They're usually no more than a protein coat around a strand of genetic material.
2) They can only reproduce inside living cells, so they must infect other organisms in order to multiply.
3) Viruses can infect plant, animal and bacterial cells.
4) A particular type of virus will only attack specific cells.

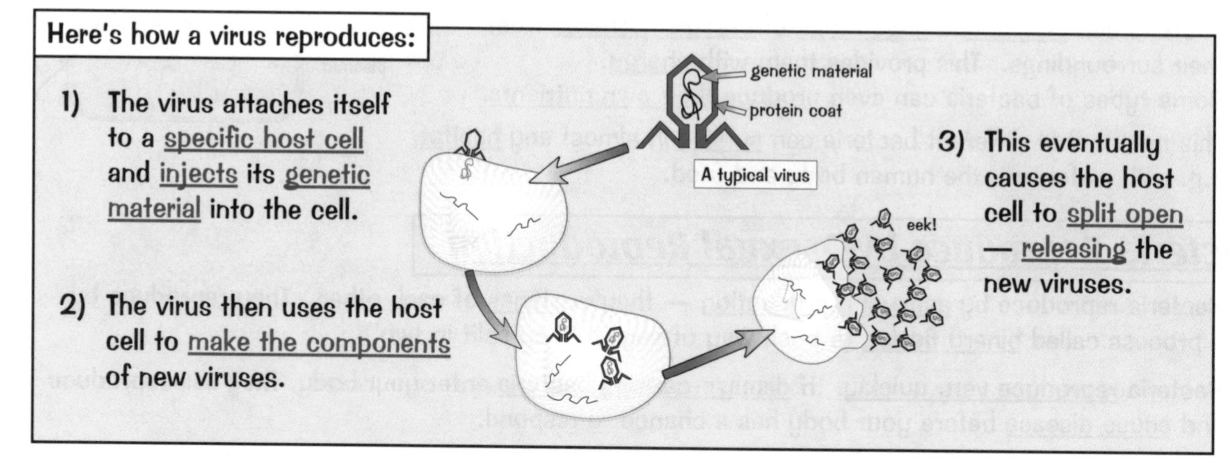

Different Diseases Can Be Transmitted in Different Ways

1) IN FOOD — e.g. food poisoning. You can get ill from eating food that's been contaminated with bacteria. It can be prevented by good hygiene and by making sure food is properly cooked before it's eaten.
2) IN WATER — e.g. cholera. You can get infected with cholera by drinking water that's been contaminated with sewage (nice). It isn't a big problem in the developed world, but it kills many people in developing countries where sanitation is poor. Good sanitation can prevent cholera and other waterborne diseases.
3) BY AIRBORNE DROPLETS — e.g. influenza (flu). Flu and other viruses can be spread via the tiny airborne droplets released when you cough or sneeze. Sneezing into a tissue, washing your hands properly and disinfecting contaminated surfaces can all help to prevent the spread of flu.
4) THROUGH CONTACT — e.g. athlete's foot. The fungus which causes athlete's foot can be spread by people walking in bare feet on damp floors in places like showers and bathrooms. You can prevent it by washing your feet regularly and by not walking around bare foot. Disinfecting surfaces also helps.

Poor Sanitation is Linked to a High Incidence of Disease

1) The incidence of a disease is the number of new cases that occurs in a population in a certain time.
2) Good sanitation and public health measures are linked to a low incidence of disease. A clean water supply, good sewage works, public health education and clean hospitals prevent the spread of disease. E.g. government campaigns to educate people about how influenza is spread are designed to help lower the incidence of flu.
3) Poor sanitation is linked with a high incidence of disease. E.g. a high incidence of food poisoning and cholera might be caused by a lack of clean water or a rubbish sewage system.
4) Developing countries are less likely to be able to afford good sanitation and public health measures.

Incidence of revision is increasing due to exams...

You could be asked to interpret data on the incidence of disease in the exam. Don't panic — just remember that poor sanitation and a lack of public health measures often contribute to a high incidence of disease.

Treating Infectious Diseases

You probably don't need telling that this page is important — some of the ideas here can literally save lives.

There Are Four Stages in an Infectious Disease

1. Firstly the microorganism enters the body — e.g. through the nose or mouth.
2. Once the microorganism is in the body, it reproduces rapidly, producing many more microorganisms.
3. The microorganisms then produce toxins (poisonous substances) which damage cells and tissues.
4. The toxins cause symptoms of infection, e.g. pain, diarrhoea and stomach cramps. Your immune system's reaction to the infection can also cause symptoms, e.g. fever. The time between exposure to the microorganism and the development of symptoms is called the incubation period.

Antiseptics and Antibiotics Help Control Diseases

1) Antiseptics and antibiotics are chemicals that destroy bacteria or stop them growing.
2) Antiseptics are used outside the body to help to clean wounds and surfaces. They're used to prevent infection rather than treat it. Plenty of household products contain antiseptics, e.g. bathroom cleaners. Antiseptics are also used in hospitals and surgeries to try to prevent infections like MRSA.
3) Antibiotics are drugs used inside the body, usually taken as a pill or injected. They're used to treat patients who are already infected. They only kill bacteria though — viruses aren't affected by them.

Bacteria Can Evolve and Become Resistant to Antibiotics...

1) Random mutations in bacterial DNA can lead to changes in the bacteria's characteristics. Sometimes, they mean that the bacteria are less affected by a particular antibiotic.
2) Bacteria with these genes are better able to survive and reproduce in a host who's being treated to get rid of the infection.
3) This leads to the gene for antibiotic resistance being passed on to lots of offspring — it's just natural selection (see page 36). The gene spreads and becomes more common in a population of bacteria over a period of time.
4) Bacteria that are resistant to antibiotics (e.g. MRSA) are definitely bad news as they cause infections that are very hard to treat.

...So Do Everyone a Favour and Always Finish Your Antibiotics

1) The more often antibiotics are used, the bigger the problem of antibiotic-resistance becomes.
2) It's important that doctors only prescribe antibiotics when it's really necessary:

> It's not that antibiotics actually cause resistance, but they do create a situation where naturally resistant bacteria have an advantage and so increase in numbers. If they won't do you any good, it's pointless to take antibiotics — and it could be harmful for everyone else.

3) It's also important that you take all the antibiotics a doctor prescribes for you:

> Lots of people stop bothering to take their antibiotics as soon as they feel better, but this can increase the risk of antibiotic resistant bacteria emerging — so you must complete the dose.

Coughs and sneezes spread diseases but antibiotic resistance is scarier...

Worrying stuff, but hold your horses — there's a whole other page on infectious diseases coming right up...

More on Infectious Diseases

Bacteria and viruses are always waiting to pounce as soon as you let your guard down... Bloomin' microbes.

Diseases Often Spread Rapidly After Natural Disasters

Natural disasters like earthquakes and hurricanes can damage the infrastructure of an area, and completely disrupt health services. In these conditions disease can spread rapidly among the population.

1) Some natural disasters damage sewage systems and water supplies. This can result in contaminated drinking water containing the microorganisms that cause diseases like cholera.
2) People can become displaced when their homes are destroyed. They might move into temporary camps, with large numbers of other people and poor sanitation. In these conditions, diseases could spread easily.
3) Health services can be disrupted by damaged transport links — allowing infections to spread rapidly.
4) Electricity supplies are also often damaged by natural disasters. This means that food goes off quickly because refrigerators can't work — this can lead to an increase in food poisoning.

Pasteur, Lister and Fleming All Improved Disease Treatment

Louis Pasteur (1822-1895) came up with the germ theory of disease

Until the 19th century people didn't understand how diseases were caused or spread. People used to think that diseases spontaneously appeared from nowhere. The scientist Louis Pasteur argued that there are microbes (also called 'germs' or 'microorganisms') in the air which cause disease and decomposition.

Pasteur carried out experiments to prove this theory, e.g.

1) He heated broth in two flasks, both of which were left open to the air. However, one of the flasks had a curved neck so that bacteria in the air would settle in the loop, and not get through to the broth.
2) The broth in the flask with the curved neck stayed fresh, proving that it was the microbes and not the air causing it to go off.

Flask 1: Air and microbes get in

Flask 2: Air gets in, but microbes can't

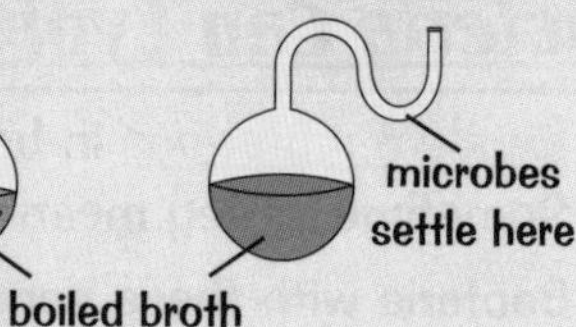

Joseph Lister (1827-1912) was the first doctor to use antiseptics in surgery

1) When Lister first started working as a surgeon, hospital conditions were pretty unhygienic. Nearly half of patients undergoing surgery died from infections of their wounds, known as 'hospital gangrene' or 'sepsis'.
2) Lister's observations of wounds led him to think sepsis was a type of decomposition. He knew about Pasteur's work on microbes in the air. He realised he needed to kill microbes that were getting into wounds from the air.
3) Lister began to treat and dress wounds using the antiseptic carbolic acid. This killed the bacteria in the wounds and prevented sepsis. Gradually, Lister's techniques were taken up by the rest of the medical profession.

Alexander Fleming (1881-1955) discovered the antibiotic penicillin in 1928 — by accident

1) Fleming was clearing out some plates containing bacteria. He noticed that one of the plates of bacteria also had mould on it and the area around the mould was free of the bacteria.
2) He found that the mould (called *Penicillium notatum*) on the plate was producing a substance that killed the bacteria — this substance was penicillin.

plate
bacteria
mould
area where bacteria have been killed

After Fleming there was no more phlegm-ing...

Fleming used to paint pictures using highly pigmented (coloured) bacteria. At first you wouldn't be able to see the picture. But as the bacteria grew, the picture would gradually appear... What a guy.

Yeast

This page is all about yeast — a type of fungus and a pretty useful microorganism.

Yeast Can Respire Anaerobically or Aerobically

1) When yeast respires anaerobically (without oxygen) it produces ethanol, carbon dioxide and energy. This process is called fermentation. Here is the equation for fermentation:

glucose → ethanol + carbon dioxide (+ energy)

$$C_6H_{12}O_6 \rightarrow 2C_2H_5OH + 2CO_2 \ (+ \text{energy})$$

Ethanol is a type of alcohol.

The fermentation process is used to make beer and wine (see next page).

2) Yeast can also respire aerobically (with oxygen). This releases more energy than anaerobic respiration. Aerobic respiration is the same for yeast as it is for plants and animals:

glucose + oxygen → carbon dioxide + water (+ energy)

3) Whether the yeast respire aerobically or anaerobically depends on whether there is oxygen present. If oxygen is present it respires aerobically. If oxygen runs out it switches to anaerobic respiration
4) Yeast prefer to respire aerobically (because it releases more energy),so fermentation only takes place in the absence of oxygen.

Yeast's Growth Rate Varies Depending on the Conditions

1) The faster yeast respires, the faster it's able to reproduce.
2) The speed that yeast respires and reproduces (its growth rate) varies. It's growth rate is controlled by temperature, availability of food, pH and how quickly waste products can be removed.

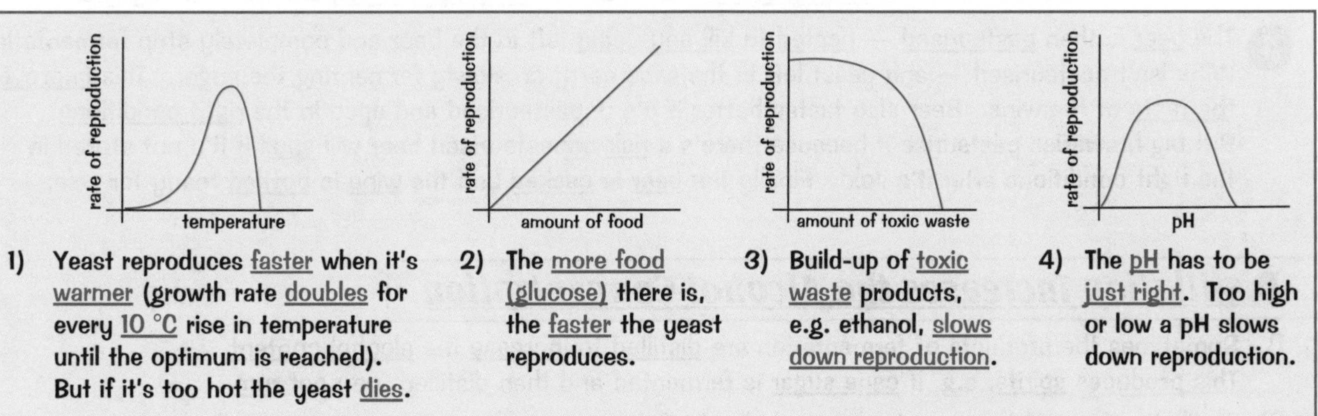

1) Yeast reproduces faster when it's warmer (growth rate doubles for every 10 °C rise in temperature until the optimum is reached). But if it's too hot the yeast dies.
2) The more food (glucose) there is, the faster the yeast reproduces.
3) Build-up of toxic waste products, e.g. ethanol, slows down reproduction.
4) The pH has to be just right. Too high or low a pH slows down reproduction.

3) Yeast also reproduces faster in the presence of oxygen. This is because it's able to respire aerobically, giving it more energy for reproduction.
4) One way of measuring how fast the yeast is reproducing is to measure how much glucose (sugar) it breaks down. The faster the yeast reproduces, the more glucose will be broken down.

Wastewater Can be Cleaned Up with Yeast

1) Food-processing factories need to get rid of sugary water. They can't just release it into waterways because it would cause pollution. Bacteria in the water would feed on the sugar and reproduce quickly, using up all the oxygen in the water. Other organisms in the water that need oxygen (like fish) die.
2) Yeast can be used to treat the contaminated water before it's released — it uses up the sugar in respiration.

At yeast it's an easy page...

You might get asked to interpret data on the breakdown of sugar by yeast in different conditions, e.g. changing the temperature, the absence of O_2. Just remember — the faster it reproduces, the more sugar it breaks down.

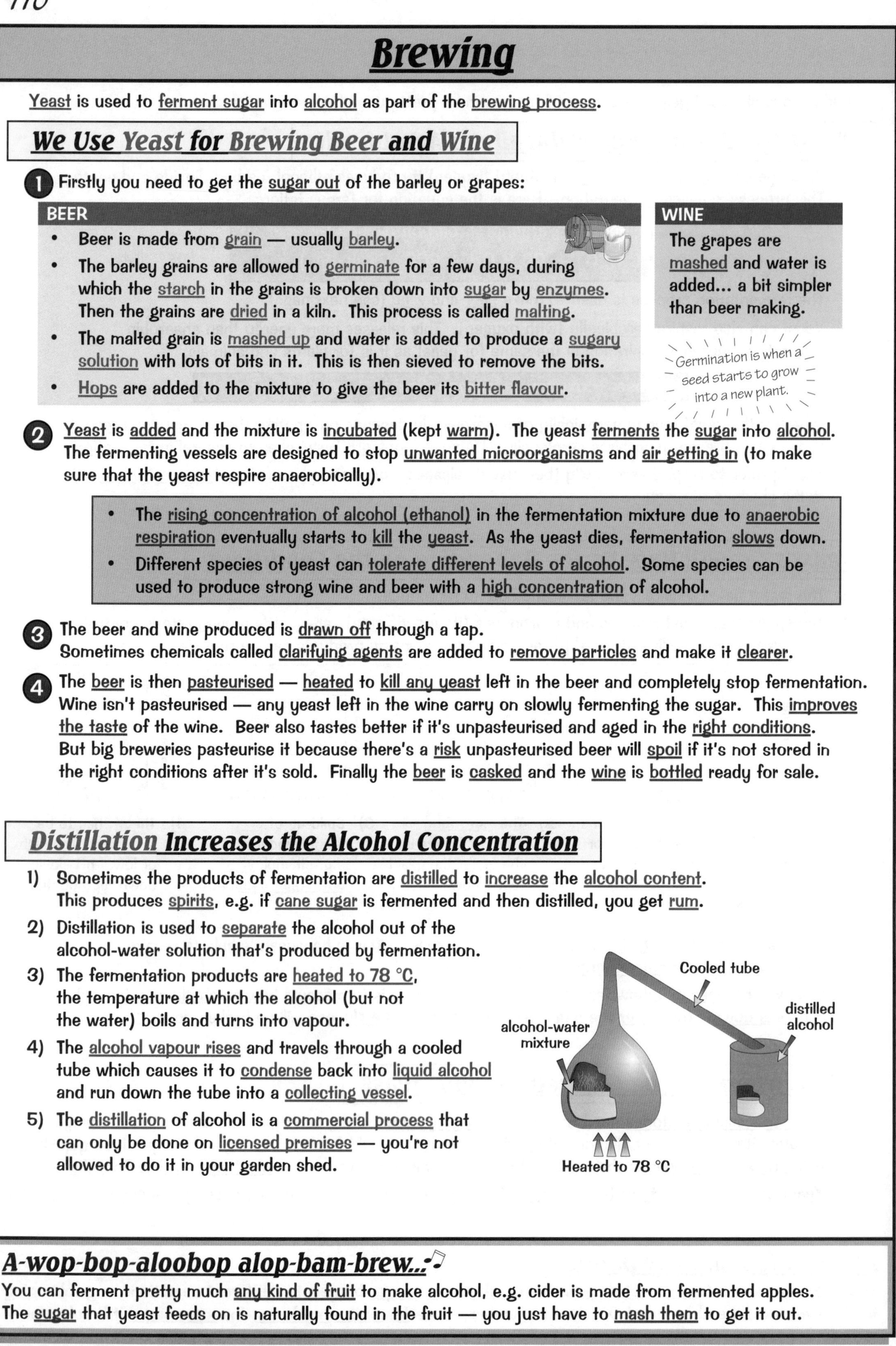

Brewing

Yeast is used to ferment sugar into alcohol as part of the brewing process.

We Use Yeast for Brewing Beer and Wine

1. Firstly you need to get the sugar out of the barley or grapes:

BEER

- Beer is made from grain — usually barley.
- The barley grains are allowed to germinate for a few days, during which the starch in the grains is broken down into sugar by enzymes. Then the grains are dried in a kiln. This process is called malting.
- The malted grain is mashed up and water is added to produce a sugary solution with lots of bits in it. This is then sieved to remove the bits.
- Hops are added to the mixture to give the beer its bitter flavour.

WINE

The grapes are mashed and water is added... a bit simpler than beer making.

Germination is when a seed starts to grow into a new plant.

2. Yeast is added and the mixture is incubated (kept warm). The yeast ferments the sugar into alcohol. The fermenting vessels are designed to stop unwanted microorganisms and air getting in (to make sure that the yeast respire anaerobically).

- The rising concentration of alcohol (ethanol) in the fermentation mixture due to anaerobic respiration eventually starts to kill the yeast. As the yeast dies, fermentation slows down.
- Different species of yeast can tolerate different levels of alcohol. Some species can be used to produce strong wine and beer with a high concentration of alcohol.

3. The beer and wine produced is drawn off through a tap. Sometimes chemicals called clarifying agents are added to remove particles and make it clearer.

4. The beer is then pasteurised — heated to kill any yeast left in the beer and completely stop fermentation. Wine isn't pasteurised — any yeast left in the wine carry on slowly fermenting the sugar. This improves the taste of the wine. Beer also tastes better if it's unpasteurised and aged in the right conditions. But big breweries pasteurise it because there's a risk unpasteurised beer will spoil if it's not stored in the right conditions after it's sold. Finally the beer is casked and the wine is bottled ready for sale.

Distillation Increases the Alcohol Concentration

1) Sometimes the products of fermentation are distilled to increase the alcohol content. This produces spirits, e.g. if cane sugar is fermented and then distilled, you get rum.
2) Distillation is used to separate the alcohol out of the alcohol-water solution that's produced by fermentation.
3) The fermentation products are heated to 78 °C, the temperature at which the alcohol (but not the water) boils and turns into vapour.
4) The alcohol vapour rises and travels through a cooled tube which causes it to condense back into liquid alcohol and run down the tube into a collecting vessel.
5) The distillation of alcohol is a commercial process that can only be done on licensed premises — you're not allowed to do it in your garden shed.

A-wop-bop-aloobop alop-bam-brew...

You can ferment pretty much any kind of fruit to make alcohol, e.g. cider is made from fermented apples. The sugar that yeast feeds on is naturally found in the fruit — you just have to mash them to get it out.

Biofuels

Biofuels could be hugely important in the future, as fossil fuel supplies run out. You need to know about them.

Energy Can be Transferred from Biomass

Biomass is living or recently-dead organic material, e.g. plant matter. It's also a store of energy.
The energy stored in biomass can be transferred into more useful forms, e.g.

- Fast growing trees can be burnt, releasing heat.
- Biomass can be fermented by yeast and bacteria to create products such as biogas, which can be used as fuel (see below).

It's better to burn fast growing trees than slow growing ones because they can be replaced quickly and easily.

Biogas is Made Mainly of Methane

1) Biogas is usually about 70% methane (CH_4) and 30% carbon dioxide (CO_2). It also contains traces of hydrogen, nitrogen and hydrogen sulfide.
2) Biogas containing more than 50% methane burns easily, but if it contains around 10% methane it can be explosive.
3) Biogas is made by bacteria in a digester (see below). The bacteria's respiration produces methane.

Biogas Can be Used as Fuel

1) Biogas can be burned to power a turbine, which can be used to generate electricity. This is especially useful for producing electricity in remote areas with no mains supply.
2) Biogas can be burned to heat water and produce steam to heat central heating systems.
3) It can also be used as a fuel for cars and buses.

Biogas is Made by Anaerobic Fermentation of Waste Material

1) Biogas can be made from plant waste and animal poo in a simple fermenter called a digester. Sludge waste, e.g. from sewage works or sugar factories, is used to make biogas on a large scale.
2) Several different types of bacteria are used to produce biogas. Some decompose the organic matter and produce waste, then another type decompose that waste, and so on, until you get biogas. This process is a type of fermentation — it involves the breakdown of substances without oxygen.
3) Biogas digesters need to be kept at a constant warm temperature (30-40 °C). This is the optimum temperature for the bacteria's respiration. Any cooler and the bacteria don't produce biogas as fast. Any hotter and the bacteria will be killed. The conditions in the digester also need to be anaerobic.
4) The diagram on the right shows a simple biogas generator. It needs to have the following:
   - An inlet for waste material to be put in.
   - An outlet for the digested material to be removed through.
   - An outlet so that the biogas can be piped to where it's needed.

Biogas outlet
Inlet for waste material
Gas
Waste material
Outlet for digested material (to be used as fertiliser)

Large-scale biogas production uses a continuous flow method — organic waste is continuously fed into the digester, and the biogas and solid digested material are continuously removed at a steady rate.

You can make biogas too — just eat some lentils...

Biogas isn't always a good thing — if it's released somewhere it shouldn't be it can cause problems. Methane is sometimes released from landfill sites and it can set alight and burn, or even explode. This can make a site unusable for many years, so a new site for dumping rubbish has to be found.

More on Biofuels

Biogas is better for the environment than burning fossil fuels. It's sustainable (unlike fossil fuels) and it's a relatively clean fuel — releasing fewer pollutants when burnt than oil and coal.

Biofuels Have Their Advantages...

1) One big advantage of biofuels over fossil fuels is that they can be produced in a sustainable way. The crops which are decomposed to make biogas can be replaced quickly with new plants. In contrast, there is a finite supply of fossil fuels like coal and crude oil — they will run out eventually.
2) Another advantage is that the plants grown to make biogas photosynthesise (see page 69). This removes CO_2 (a greenhouse gas) from the atmosphere and can balance out the release of CO_2 from burning the biogas. However this is only true if:
   - The biofuels are burnt at the same rate that the new biomass is produced.
   - Areas of land are cleared to grow biomass without burning other vegetation. When the vegetation is burnt it releases more CO_2 into the atmosphere.

   This is good because increasing greenhouse gas levels are causing global warming (see page 40).
3) Biogas is a cleaner fuel than diesel or petrol. Burning these fossil fuels produces particulates, which can cause lung disease. Burning biogas doesn't produce particulates.

...And Their Disadvantages

1) Biogas doesn't contain as much energy as the same volume of natural gas (from underground supplies) because it's more dilute.
2) Large areas of land are sometimes cleared of vegetation to create space to produce biofuels. As well as increasing greenhouse gas levels, this can create huge problems for ecosystems:
   - Habitat loss — as plants are cleared, the habitats of many plant and animal species are destroyed.
   - Extinction of species — the loss of habitats and a change in food availability might mean that some species are die out in the area. This is bad news.

Ethanol Can be Used as a Biofuel

1) Ethanol can be burnt as fuel. It's a cleaner fuel than petrol or diesel, producing fewer pollutants.
2) Ethanol is a renewable resource. It is produced by using yeast to ferment glucose (see page 109). Materials like sugar cane, corn and barley can be used as a source of glucose in ethanol production.
3) Cars can be adapted to run on a mixture of ethanol and petrol — known as 'gasohol'. Gasohol is a mixture of about 10% ethanol and 90% petrol.

4) Using gasohol instead of pure petrol means that less crude oil is being used up (petrol is refined from crude oil, which is a non-renewable energy source).
5) Another advantage is that the growth of crops for ethanol production means that CO_2 is being absorbed from the atmosphere in photosynthesis. This goes some way towards balancing out the release of CO_2 when the gasohol is burnt.
6) Some countries, such as Brazil, have made extensive use of gasohol. It's most economically viable in areas where there is plenty of sugar cane (e.g. tropical countries) and not a lot of oil.

You'd be a bio-fool not to learn this page...

Biogas probably isn't, sadly, the solution to all the world's energy needs. Some countries consume more energy than they could possibly get from biogas (because they don't have the land to grow enough crops).

Soils

I expect that you were hoping to discover that soil is just wet dirt. Unfortunately that's not quite correct. There's actually quite a bit you need to know — so knuckle down and get this page learnt, pronto.

Different Soils Contain Different Particles

1) Sandy soils are made up of large mineral particles. Because the particles are so large, they leave large pores (gaps) in the soil — this means that sandy soils often have a high air content and are very permeable (water can pass through them easily).
2) Clay soils are mostly made up of tiny particles. The small particles can pack tightly together and leave very small pores in the soil — so clay soils usually have a low air content and low permeability. They tend to retain more water than sandy soils because the water molecules cling to the small particles.
3) Loam soils contain a mixture of sand and clay particles. Their properties depend on the relative amounts of the different types of particles.
4) Most soils also contain humus — decomposed, dead organic matter. Humus helps to support soil life (see next page).

large sand particles
large pores
small clay particles
small pores
large sand particles
small clay particles

You Can Do Experiments to Work Out the Structure of a Soil Sample

You Can Measure The Water and Humus Content...

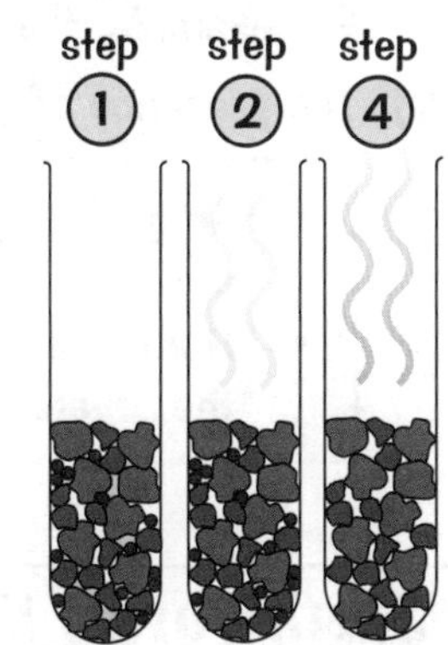

1) Take the mass of a small sample of soil.
2) Heat the sample to 105 °C until it reaches a constant mass — this will boil off all the water in the soil.
3) Take the mass of the soil sample again — The difference between the first and second reading is equal to the mass of water from the original soil sample.
4) Heat the soil sample to 550 °C for two hours — this will burn all the humus from the soil sample.
5) Take the mass of the soil sample for a third time. The difference between the second and third reading is equal to the mass of humus in the original soil sample.

step 1
step 2
step 3
A

... As Well As The Air Content

1) Loosely pack a sample of soil into a beaker or test tube and measure the volume of soil.
2) Fill up a pipette (or measuring cylinder) with a known volume of water and gradually add it to the beaker, letting it seep down into the soil sample.
3) Continue doing this until the water comes up to the top of the soil sample.
4) To find out how much water you added, subtract the volume of water left in the pipette from the volume you started with.
5) As the water has replaced the air in the soil, the volume of water added is the same as the volume of air that was in the sample to begin with. This is shown as 'A' on the diagram.

My friend eats humus and pitta bread for lunch every day — gross...

You might get asked to explain the results of experiments like these in the exam. Don't panic though — just apply what you've learnt on this page and you'll be fine. The important thing to remember is that particle size will affect both the permeability and air content of a soil. Humus content also affects air content (see next page).

Life in the Soil

As well as bits of rock, water and air, soil is teeming with life — which is what this page is all about.

Soil is Full of Living Things

1) Soil may not look all that exciting, but it's pretty important to us. Plants need it for anchorage (to stop them falling over) and for a supply of minerals and water. And animals need plants for food and oxygen.
2) Soil is an ecosystem in itself, containing complex food webs. Herbivores (plant-eaters), carnivores (meat-eaters) and detritivores (which feed on dead organisms) are all found in the soil.
3) There are several other types of organism that live in the soil — microscopic protozoans, fungi, nematode worms and bacteria.

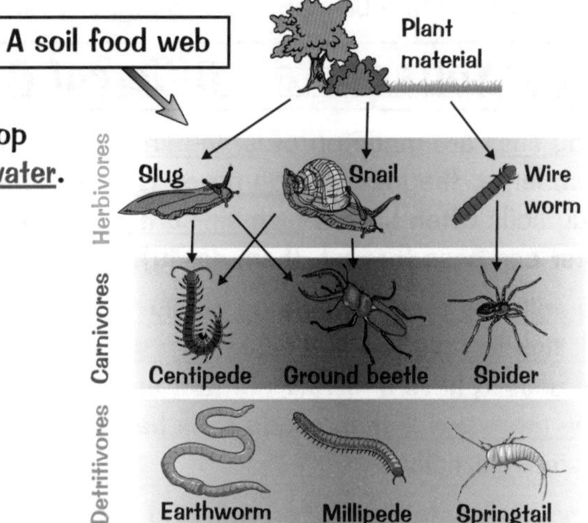

Soil Can Only Support Life If The Conditions Are Spot On

1) In order for a soil to support life, it must contain water and oxygen. All living things need water to carry out reactions in their cells, and cannot survive without it. Almost everything needs oxygen too, for respiration (see page 55). For example, the roots of plants need to get oxygen from the soil so they can respire.
2) The presence of humus (see previous page) also helps to support life in the soil:

- As organic material is slowly broken down by decomposers, minerals and nutrients are released into the soil. These compounds can then be used by other organisms.
- Humus also increases the air content of the soil, making more oxygen available to the organisms that live there.

Earthworms Help Keep Soil Healthy and Fertile

Charles Darwin, more famous for his theory of natural selection, spent an awful lot of his time studying worms. He observed them closely and experimented on them to see what sort of food they ate and how they behaved.
He discovered these reasons why worms are good for soil structure and fertility:

What's worse than biting into an apple and finding a worm?
... studying soil.

1) Earthworms bury leaves and other organic material in the soil, where bacteria and fungi can decompose them.
2) Their burrows allow air to enter the soil (aeration) and water to drain through it. Aeration provides the soil organisms with oxygen, but drainage is important, too — if the soil is waterlogged, there's less oxygen available.
3) They mix up the soil layers, distributing the nutrients more equally.
4) Soil in earthworm poo is less acidic than the soil they eat. This can help to neutralise soil acidity (although worms tend to avoid very acidic soils). Acidic soils are less fertile than neutral or alkaline soils.

Farmers and gardeners can buy earthworms (from worm farms) and add them to their soil to improve it.

Reading this page opens up a whole can of — well... worms...

Well, that page was a bit livelier. You might be one of those people that loves bugs and creepy crawlies, but all this worm business gives me the heebie jeebies. Those little rascals might be great for the soil but they freak me out. I'm not as bad as my friend though — he's afraid of butterflies — now that's just plain weird.

Life in Water

Life in water is very different from life on land...

Living in Water Has Its Advantages...

1) One advantage of living in water is that there's a plentiful supply of water... unsurprisingly. There shouldn't be any danger of water shortage or dehydration (unless a drought makes streams dry up).
2) In water, there's less variation in temperature. Water doesn't heat up or cool down as quickly as air, so you don't normally get sudden temperature changes — which water life can find difficult to withstand.
3) Water provides support for plants and for animals that have no skeletal system. E.g. jellyfish are umbrella-shaped in water (so they can swim) but if they get washed up on a beach they end up as quivering blobs, because there's not enough support... and then you stand on them. Ouch.
4) Waste disposal is easier. Poo and wee are easily dispersed. The loss of water in wee doesn't matter because there's plenty of water about to make up for it.

...and Its Disadvantages

1) Water is more resistant to movement than air, so animals living in water have to use more energy to move about. Think how much effort it takes to walk in the sea compared to walking on the beach.
2) Aquatic animals have to be able to control the amount of water in their body (water regulation). This is because the water an animal lives in has a different concentration of solutes from the animal's cells. If the animal couldn't regulate water, water molecules would enter or leave the animal's cells by osmosis to even up the solute concentrations. This would cause damage to the cells. E.g.

- If the animal lived in salt-water its cells would probably contain a lower solute concentration than the surrounding water. If the animal wasn't able to regulate water, then water molecules would leave its cells by osmosis, causing them to shrivel and die.
- If the animal lived in freshwater, its cells would probably contain a higher solute concentration than the surrounding water. If the animal wasn't able to regulate water, then water molecules would enter its cells by osmosis, causing them to swell and burst.

Amoebas Regulate Water Content Using Contractile Vacuoles

Most single-celled organisms, like amoebas, only have a cell membrane between them and the surrounding water. So they regulate their water content like this:

Amoebas regulate water with a contractile vacuole which collects the water that diffuses in by osmosis. The vacuole then moves to the cell membrane and contracts to empty the water outside the cell.

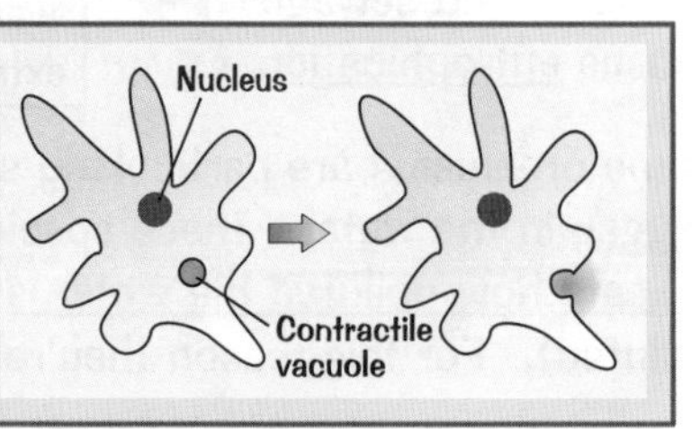

Plankton are Microscopic Organisms That Live in Water

1) Plankton are microscopic organisms that live in fresh and salt water. There are two types:
    - Phytoplankton are microscopic plants.
    - Zooplankton are microscopic animals. Zooplankton feed on phytoplankton.
2) Phytoplankton photosynthesise and are the main producers in aquatic food webs, so they're very important in both freshwater and salt-water ecosystems.

"Waiter, do you have frog's legs?" — "No, I always walk like this"...

Some organisms (mainly insects and amphibians) spend part of their life cycle in water and part on land to exploit both habitats. The two environments provide different challenges, so the different parts of the life cycle often have different body forms (e.g. tadpole and frog).

More on Life in Water

There are monsters in the water. Millions of them. They're only tiny, mind...

Plankton Populations Vary According to the Season

1) Photosynthesis is affected by temperature, light intensity and the availability of minerals like nitrates. These factors vary at different depths and in different seasons, causing the rate of photosynthesis to vary too.
   - During the winter months and in deep water, light intensity and temperature are low. Mineral concentration on the other hand is relatively high. In these conditions, light intensity and temperature limit the rate of photosynthesis.
   - During the summer and near the water's surface, light intensity and temperature are higher but mineral concentration is much lower. Mineral concentration limits the amount of photosynthesis.
2) Phytoplankton populations usually increase between late spring and late summer. This is called an algal bloom (phytoplankton are a type of algae). An algal bloom makes the water go all green and murky. The increase is due to longer, sunnier days in summer:
   - More light is available for photosynthesis and the energy is used for growth.
   - Temperatures increase, causing both photosynthesis and growth rates to increase.
   - The population of zooplankton also increases because there is more phytoplankton to feed on.

There are Different Types of Food Web in the Oceans

1) Most ocean food webs are 'grazing food webs' — this means that they begin with a living producer. (A producer is any organism which can produce its own food.)
2) Producers in ocean food webs are often phytoplankton. But in deep water where light can't penetrate, photosynthesis can't take place. In these places some grazing food webs are supported by bacterial producers that rely on sulfur from deep sea vents (instead of sunlight).
3) In other deep-sea food webs, animals often feed on dead, decomposing material that has slowly fallen from nearer the surface. This 'marine snow' is the major source of nutrients for these food webs.

There are Several Causes of Water Pollution

1) Fertilisers and Sewage

Pollution of water by fertilisers and sewage causes eutrophication. → Fertilisers and sewage enter water, adding extra nutrients → Algae grow rapidly → Algae die and decay → Bacteria feed on dead algae, using up oxygen in the water → Animals are unable to respire and die

Some organisms are particularly sensitive to the level of oxygen in the water. These species are used by scientists to indicate how polluted the water is (the less oxygen, the more polluted). For this reason they're called indicator species.

Pollution level	Indicator species
Clean	Stonefly nymph, Mayfly nymph
Low	Freshwater shrimp, Caddis fly larva
High	Bloodworm, Waterlouse
Very high	Rat-tailed maggot, sludgeworm

Species that are sensitive to different pHs can also be used as indicator species. By seeing which species live in a particular area, scientists can make a pretty good estimate of the pH.

2) Industrial Chemicals and Pesticides

Chemicals which have caused water pollution include pesticides like DDT (used to kill lice and mosquitoes) and industrial chemicals like PCBs (used as coolants and electrical insulators). If water is polluted by these, they are taken up by organisms at the bottom of the food chain. They aren't broken down by the organisms, so when they're eaten the chemical is passed on. The concentration of the chemical increases as it is transferred up the food chain — because each organism eats many of the organisms below it. Organisms at the top of the food chain, e.g. whales, accumulate a huge dose and may die.

Mouldy pizza — indicator species for dirty bedrooms...

You might be asked to interpret marine food webs in the exam. Think about how organisms in the food chain will be affected by an increase/decrease of plankton. If their food source decreases, so will their population.

Enzymes in Action

Enzymes are molecules made of protein, which speed up (catalyse) chemical reactions in living organisms.

Enzymes are Used in Biological Washing Powder...

1) Some stains are caused by soluble chemicals and so they wash out easily in water. Stubborn stains contain insoluble chemicals like starch, proteins and fats. They don't wash out with just water.
2) Non-biological washing powders (detergents) contain chemicals that break up stains on your clothes.
3) Biological washing powders contain the same chemicals as non-biological ones, but also contain a mixture of enzymes which break down the stubborn stains.

Stain	Sources of stain	Enzymes	Product
Carbohydrate	Jam, chocolate	Amylases	Simple sugars
Lipid (fats)	Butter, oil	Lipases	Fatty acids and glycerol
Protein	Blood, grass	Proteases	Amino acids

The products of these enzyme-controlled reactions are soluble in water and so can be easily washed out of clothes.

4) Biological washing powders usually work best at moderate wash temperatures because the enzymes are denatured (destroyed) by high temperatures (see page 49). However, some newer powders contain enzymes that are more resistant to heat and so can be used with a hotter water temperature.
5) Biological washing powders might not work very well in acidic or alkaline tap water. This is because the enzymes can be denatured by extremes of pH.
6) You can buy special stain removers (e.g. for wine, blood or oil). Some of these are just special solvents, but some contain specific enzymes that will break down the stain.

...and in Medical Products...

1) Diabetes (see page 20) is diagnosed by the presence of sugar in the urine. Many years ago, doctors actually used to taste patients' urine to test for sugar... yuk. Later they tested the urine for sugar using Benedict's solution. When it's heated, the solution changes colour from blue to orange if sugar is present. This test relies on chemical properties (not enzymes).
2) Nowadays, reagent strips (strips of paper with enzymes and chemicals in them) are used. They're dipped in urine and change colour if sugar is present.
3) This test is based on a sequence of enzyme reactions. The product of the enzyme-controlled reactions causes a chemical embedded in the strip to change colour.
4) There are similar strips which can be used to test blood sugar levels (see next page).

...and in the Food Industry

Low-Calorie Food

1) Table sugar (sucrose) is what you normally sweeten food with at home.
2) In the food industry an enzyme called sucrase (or invertase) is used to break down sucrose into glucose and fructose. Glucose and fructose are much sweeter than sucrose.
3) This means you can get the same level of sweetness using less sugar. This helps to make low-calorie food sweeter without adding calories.

Cheese

The enzyme rennet is used to clot milk in the first stages of cheese production.

Juice Extraction

The enzyme pectinase is used in fruit juice extraction. It breaks down pectin (a part of the cell wall in apples and oranges), causing the cell to release its juice.

Stubborn stains — not just dirty, but grumpy...

Not everyone can use biological washing powders. Some of the enzymes remain on the clothes and can irritate sensitive skin, making it sore and itchy. People with sensitive skin have to use non-biological powders.

More Enzymes in Action

When enzymes are used to speed up reactions, they end up dissolved in the mixture with the substrates and products — and can be difficult to remove. One way to avoid this is to immobilise the enzymes...

Immobilising Enzymes Makes Them Easier to Remove

1) Many industrial processes use immobilised enzymes, which don't need to be separated out from the mixture after the reaction has taken place.
2) Enzymes can be immobilised in different ways. One way is to encapsulate them in alginate beads (alginate is a gel-like substance). The beads are formed by mixing the enzyme with alginate, then dropping the mixture into a calcium chloride solution.
3) The immobilised enzymes are still active and still help speed up reactions.

enzyme molecule encapsulated within a bead of alginate

Advantages of Immobilising Enzymes

1) The enzymes don't contaminate the product.
2) Immobilised enzymes in alginate beads can be used in continuous flow processing (see below).

Immobilised Enzymes Can be Used to Make Lactose-Free Milk

1) The sugar lactose is naturally found in milk (and yoghurt). It's broken down in your digestive system by the enzyme lactase. This produces glucose and galactose, which are then absorbed into the blood.
2) Some people lack the enzyme lactase. If they drink milk the lactose isn't broken down and gut bacteria ferment it, causing abdominal pain, wind and diarrhoea. These people are said to be lactose intolerant.
3) Lactose-free milk can be produced using immobilised lactase. The lactase breaks down lactose into glucose and galactose. These simple sugars can be absorbed by someone who's lactose intolerant.
4) A method called continuous flow processing is often used for this:

Milk

Column of immobilised lactase

Lactose free milk

MILK MILK MILK MILK

- The substrate solution (milk) is run through a column of immobilised lactase.
- The enzymes convert the substrate (lactose) into the products (glucose and galactose), but only the products emerge from the column. The enzymes stay fixed in the column.

Immobilised Enzymes are Also Used in Reagent Strips

1) Diabetics use reagent strips to measure their blood glucose concentration on a daily basis. They're quick and convenient to use. Before reagent strips diabetics had to 'guess' when they needed to inject insulin (e.g. before meals), because there was no quick way of knowing what their glucose level was.
2) There are immobilised enzymes on the reagent strips.
3) A drop of blood from a finger prick is added to the strip. The enzymes in the strip cause it to change different colours depending on the glucose concentration. The colour is then compared to a chart to find out the level of blood sugar.

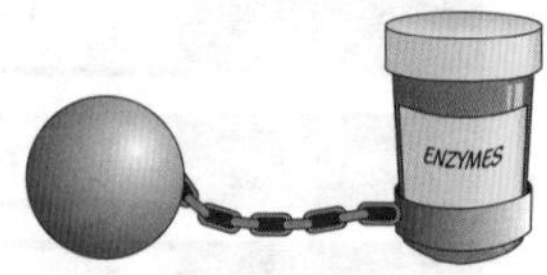

Abdominal pain, wind and diarrhoea — that fudge sundae was worth it...

Lactose intolerance affects millions of people. There's a pretty big industry out there providing them with lactose-free milk, lactose-free ice cream, lactose-free chocolates... You get the idea. Making these things is a whole lot easier thanks to immobilised enzymes. There you have it — proof that science is actually useful.

More on Genetic Engineering

You've already learnt about genetic engineering in Module B3, but there's more detail in this Module.

Genes Can be Transferred Between Different Organisms

1) Genetic engineering alters the genetic code of an organism. A gene giving a desirable characteristic is removed from one organism and inserted into another organism.
2) We're able to transfer genes from one organism to another because the genetic code is universal (i.e. the same four bases are used in the DNA of all organisms).
3) A genetically modified organism is called a transgenic organism.

There Are Five Main Steps to Genetic Engineering

Whatever gene you're transferring, and whatever organisms you're transferring it from or to, you need to do the same five things:

These steps are basically the same for any gene that you might want to transfer into another species.

1) Identify the gene that you're after in an organism.
2) Remove the gene from the organism's DNA.
3) Cut open the DNA of the organism that you want to put the gene into.
4) Insert the gene into the DNA of the second organism — where the gene should now work.
5) The host is now a transgenic organism. You can clone it to produce more copies.

The cutting and inserting of DNA is done using enzymes.

Example: Bacteria Can be Engineered to Produce Human Insulin

The idea is to put the human insulin gene into bacteria so that the bacteria can make human insulin. The modified bacteria reproduce, and you end up with millions of insulin-producing bacteria.

1) Scientists identify the gene which controls the production of human insulin.
2) They remove it from the DNA of a human cell by 'cutting it out' with restriction enzymes. This leaves the DNA with so-called 'sticky ends'.
3) A loop of bacterial DNA called a plasmid (see page 105) is then prepared for the insulin gene to be inserted. Restriction enzymes are used to cut open the plasmid, leaving it with sticky ends too.
4) The insulin gene is inserted in the plasmid. The sticky ends allow another enzyme called ligase to join DNA strands together. The plasmid is then taken up by bacteria.

The plasmid is known as a vector — something that carries a gene into another organism.

5) The bacteria are now transgenic organisms. They're checked to make sure they contain the new gene using assaying techniques and are then cultured by cloning. Millions of bacteria can be produced in this way, allowing large quantities of insulin to be harvested.

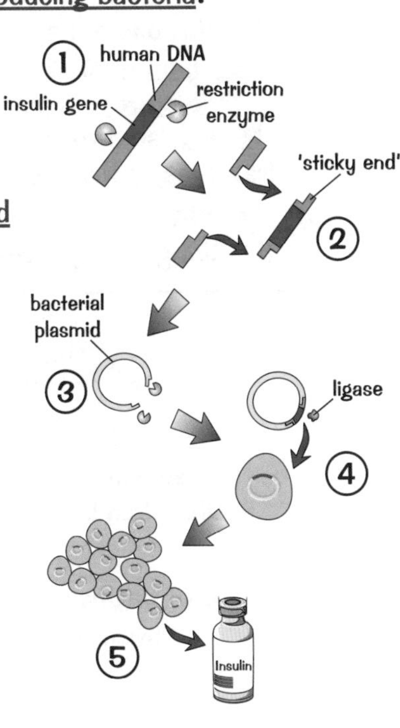

What would a genetic engine wear if it had its ears pierced?...

...A genetic engine earring, of course. More importantly though — what's a genetic engine? And why on earth would it need ears? You need to make sure you know the human insulin example inside out, but remember that this is just one example — the process is pretty much the same, whatever gene or organisms you're dealing with.

DNA Fingerprinting

Now this is more interesting — forensic science being used to catch murderers, just like on the telly.

DNA Fingerprinting Pinpoints Individuals

1) Your DNA is unique (unless you're an identical twin — then the two of you have identical DNA).
2) DNA fingerprinting (or genetic fingerprinting) is a way of comparing DNA samples to see if they come from the same person or from two different people.
3) DNA fingerprinting is used in forensic science. DNA (from hair, skin flakes, blood, semen etc.) taken from a crime scene is compared with a DNA sample taken from a suspect.
4) It can also be used in paternity tests — to check if a man is the father of a particular child.
5) Some people would like everyone's genetic fingerprints to be stored on a national genetic database. That way, DNA from a crime scene could be checked against everyone in the country to see whose it was — which would make solving some crimes much easier. But others think this is a big invasion of privacy, and they worry about how safe the data would be and what else it might be used for. There are also scientific problems — false positives can occur if errors are made in the procedure or if the data is misinterpreted.

The 'Fingerprint' is Made in a Special Gel

HOW IT WORKS

1) First you have to extract the DNA from the cells in your sample.
2) Restriction enzymes are then used to cut the DNA into fragments. They cut it at every place where they recognise a particular order of bases. Where these sections are in the DNA will be different for everyone.
3) If the DNA sample contains that little section of bases lots of times, it'll be cut into lots of little bits. If it only contains it a few times, it'll be left in bigger bits.
4) The DNA bits are separated out using a process called electrophoresis. The fragments are suspended in a gel, and an electric current is passed through the gel. DNA is negatively charged, so it moves towards the positive anode. Small bits travel faster than big bits, so they get further through the gel.

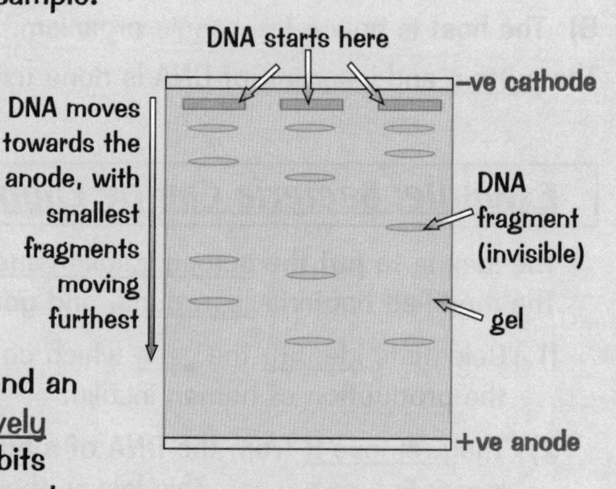

5) The DNA is "tagged" with a radioactive probe. Then it's placed onto photographic film. The film goes dark where the radioactivity is, revealing the positions of the DNA fragments.

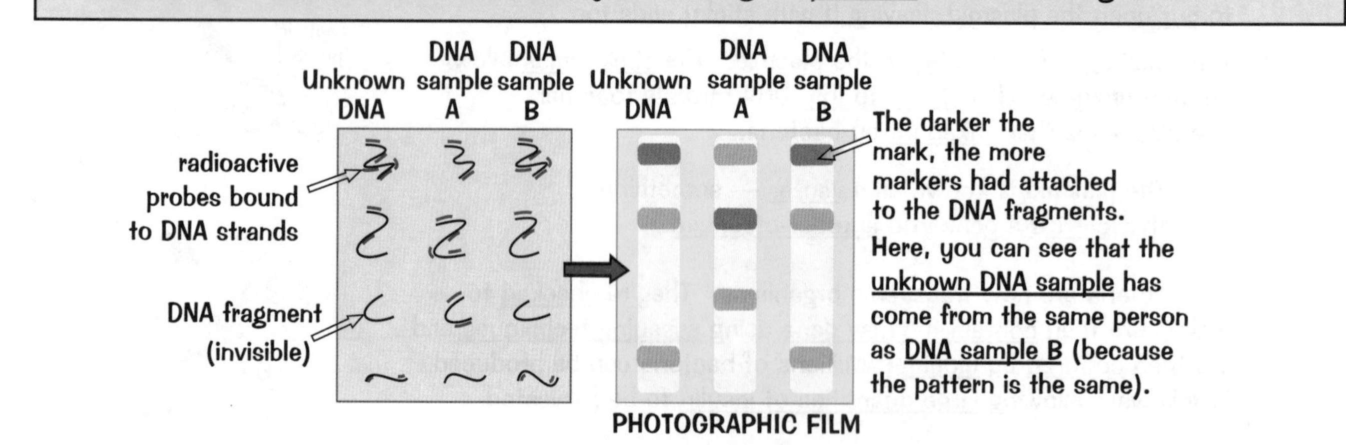

So the trick is — frame your twin and they'll never get you...

In the exam you might have to interpret data on DNA fingerprinting for identification. They'd probably give you a diagram similar to the one at the bottom of this page, and you'd have to say which of the known samples (if any) matched the unknown sample. Pretty easy — it's the two that look the same.

Revision Summary for Module B6

I bet you thought you'd never get to the end of this book... well, here you are and there's just one more revision summary to go. I never knew how interesting microorganisms could be, they do so many things — making yoghurt, causing disease, clearing up sugar spills, making booze, biogas and insulin. And as for those useful enzymes... they're a barrel of laughs.

1) State the function of the following parts of a bacterial cell: a) flagellum, b) cell wall, c) bacterial DNA.
2) Describe the main stages in making yoghurt.
3) Describe how viruses reproduce.
4) Describe four ways in which diseases can be transmitted.
5) Describe the four stages in an infectious disease.
6) How are antiseptics and antibiotics used to control disease?
7) Explain why natural disasters often cause rapid spread of disease.
8) Describe how Alexander Fleming discovered penicillin.
9) State the word equations for anaerobic respiration and aerobic respiration in yeast.
10) How is the rate of breakdown of sugar by yeast affected by temperature?
    Sketch a graph to illustrate your answer.
11) Describe the main stages in brewing beer.
12) How could you increase the alcohol concentration of a fermented product?
13) Give two ways in which energy can be transferred from biomass.
14) Which gas is the main component of biogas?
15) List three advantages of biogas compared to fossil fuels.
16) Explain what gasohol is and how it's made.
17) What are loam soils?
18) Describe an experiment to measure the air content in a soil sample.
19) Give two reasons why humus is important to soil life.
20) Describe four ways in which earthworms improve soil fertility.
21) Name two advantages and two disadvantages of living in water.
22) How do amoebas regulate their water content?
23) Explain why phytoplankton populations usually increase in summer.
24) Explain the process of eutrophication. Name two things that can cause it.
25) Why do biological washing powders need a moderate wash temperature and neutral pH?
26) Name an enzyme that breaks down sucrose. What is this enzyme used for in the food industry?
27) Give two advantages of immobilising enzymes.
28) What is lactose intolerance?
29) What is a transgenic organism?
30) How are bacteria genetically engineered to produce human insulin?
31) What is DNA fingerprinting?
32) Describe how a DNA fingerprint is produced.

Index

Index

Index and Answers

Answers

Revision Summary for Module B1 (page 27)

2) a) Non-smokers. Group B have higher blood pressures so they are likely to be the smokers because smoking increases your blood pressure.
   b) 2
   c) E.g. quit smoking, cut alcohol intake, do more exercise, reduce stress levels, lose any excess weight, have a more balanced diet.

30)

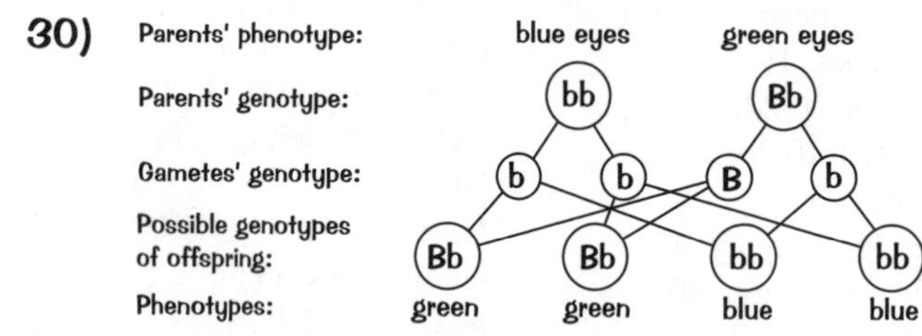

Revision Summary for Module B4 (page 84)

2) 80 ants × 4000 m² = 320 000 ants in the whole car park.

3) (23 × 28) ÷ 4 = 161 woodlice.